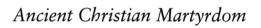

Ancient Christian Martyrdom

The Anchor Yale Bible Reference Library is a project of international and interfaith scope in which Protestant, Catholic, and Jewish scholars from many countries contribute individual volumes. The project is not sponsored by any ecclesiastical organization and is not intended to reflect any particular theological doctrine.

The series is committed to producing volumes in the tradition established half a century ago by the founders of the Anchor Bible, William Foxwell Albright and David Noel Freedman. It aims to present the best contemporary scholarship in a way that is accessible not only to scholars but also to the educated nonspecialist. It is committed to work of sound philological and historical scholarship, supplemented by insight from modern methods, such as sociological and literary criticism.

John J. Collins
General Editor

THE ANCHOR YALE BIBLE REFERENCE LIBRARY

CANDIDA R. MOSS

Ancient Christian Martyrdom

DIVERSE PRACTICES,

THEOLOGIES, AND

TRADITIONS

Yale UNIVERSITY PRESS
New Haven &
London

Published with assistance from the foundation established in memory of
William McKean Brown.

"Anchor Yale Bible" and the Anchor Yale logo are registered trademarks of
Yale University.

Yale University Press books may be purchased in quantity for educational,
business, or promotional use. For information, please e-mail sales.press@yale
.edu (U.S. office) or sales@yaleup.co.uk (U.K. office).

Set in Sabon type by Westchester Book Group.
Printed in the United States of America.

Library of Congress Cataloging-in-Publication Data

Moss, Candida R.
   Ancient Christian martyrdom : diverse practices, theologies, and traditions /
Candida R. Moss.
       p. cm.—(The Anchor Yale Bible reference library)
   Includes bibliographical references (p.   ) and index.
   ISBN 978-0-300-15465-8 (alk. paper)
   1. Martyrdom—Christianity—History.   2. Persecution—History—Early
church, ca. 30–600.   3. Church history—Primitive and early church, ca.
30-600.   I. Title.
   BR1604.23.M67 2012
   272'.1—dc23
                                                                2011044938

A catalogue record for this book is available from the British Library.

This paper meets the requirements of ANSI/NISO NISO Z39.48-1992
(Permanence of Paper).

10 9 8 7 6 5 4 3 2 1

For Adela

Contents

Acknowledgments

I owe many debts—both great and small—to institutions, friends, family, and colleagues who supported this project. John J. Collins, the editor of the Anchor Yale Bible series, invited me to write this book, and I am thankful to him for the opportunity to sharpen my ideas. I am similarly indebted to Jennifer Banks, of Yale University Press, who worked with me over the course of several years and saw the project to completion. The research for this book was supported by grants from the Institute for Scholarship in the Liberal Arts in the College of Arts and Letters at the University of Notre Dame and by the generosity of the National Endowment for the Humanities.

My editor, Bert Harrill, has gone above and beyond what could reasonably be expected of him. I am grateful for his careful and dedicated work, humbled by his vast knowledge, and inspired by his excellent scholarship. His careful eye has saved me from many mistakes, and I know that this book is greatly improved for his involvement in it. The two anonymous readers for Yale University Press made numerous suggestions for improvement that have proved most useful. Rona Johnston Gordon was a tower of strength when it came to editing the manuscript. My research assistant Mary Young checked numerous references with good humor and great efficiency, and the whole process would have fallen to pieces without Jessie Dolch, my copyeditor for Yale University Press.

Various sections of this book have been presented at conferences or in lecture form at the Humboldt University of Berlin, Chicago Divinity School, Duke University, University of Heidelberg, Kalamazoo College, the London Society for the Study of Religion, University of Kentucky, University of Manchester, Oxford Patristics Conference, University of Regensburg, Yale Divinity School, and various colloquia at the University of Notre Dame. I am grateful to the organizers, participants, and attendees of these events for their helpful suggestions and criticisms. Special thanks must go to Hans Dieter Betz, Elizabeth Clark, Kate Cooper, David Hunter, Hans-Josef Klauck, Margaret Mitchell, Tobias Nicklas, and Clare Woods. I am grateful to Jan Bremmer, Kate Cooper, David Eastman, Tom Heffernan, James Kelhoffer, Jennifer Wright Knust, Mikeal Haxby, Pamela Mullins Reaves, and Glenn Snyder for generously allowing me to read prepublication versions of their work.

The chapter on Carthaginian Christianity was forged during an exhausting, exhilarating, and eye-widening summer in Tunisia. I am indebted to my colleagues—Charlotte Allen, Sarah Byers, Cindy Cho, Jennifer Ebbeler, Stephanie Cobb, Kate Cooper, Kevin Gustafson, David Hunter, George Heffernan, Amalia Jiva, Katie Peters, Jo Shaya, Ken Steinhauser, and John Whitmire—for sharing their ideas and excitement and, above all, to Tom Heffernan for his tireless work organizing an unforgettable summer.

Martyrs and martyrdom literature encourage their audiences to form close, personal ties with the objects of their adoration. It is therefore with great generosity that my colleagues have shared their ideas and allowed me to trespass on their relationships with the saints. In particular, I am grateful to Jan Bremmer, Kate Cooper, Brad Gregory, Jan Willem van Henten, Blake Leyerle, and Michael Holmes, who have read drafts, answered questions, pressed me on my ideas, challenged me, and improved my work. In an act of great kindness Brad Gregory proofread the final copy of the manuscript. Jan Bremmer carefully read and corrected the entire final draft in a single whirlwind week. His helpful criticism, encouragement, and friendship have meant a great deal to me.

Since I arrived at the University of Notre Dame, my colleagues there have provided wise counsel, friendly advice, and an atmosphere of great collegiality. Steve Fallon, John Cavadini, and Matt Ashley have been exemplary chairs; and my colleagues in the Christianity and Judaism in Antiquity division of the theology department have been scholarly paradigms. I owe special debts to Mary Rose D'Angelo, David Aune, Kathy Cummings, Blake Leyerle, and Greg Sterling. Outside of Notre Dame I remain grateful to a number of other colleagues and friends whose examples and friendships spur me to better things on a daily basis: Charlie Camosy, Lennard Davis, David Eastman, Meghan Henning, Luke Timothy Johnson, Christine Luckritz Marquis, Timothy Luckritz Marquis, Taylor Petrey, Clare Rothschild, Kristi Upson-Saia, Jeffrey Stackert, Jeremy Schipper, and Kenneth Wolfe.

Particular thanks must go to Joel Baden, my coauthor, comrade in arms, and amicable competitor, who diligently and supportively reads everything I write with less than his usual dose of sarcasm.

My husband, Kevin, read drafts of the manuscript and endured many months of academic widower-hood. I am thankful to him for his patience, his support, and the many unspoken things that he quietly does to improve my life.

This book is dedicated to Adela Yarbro Collins, my doctoral adviser, my mentor, and my friend. I am grateful to her for her instruction, her scholarship, and her kindness, for all of which she is well known. She both taught me a craft and graciously enabled me to develop my own scholarly identity. It is with great affection, and in the knowledge that it is the very least that I can do, that I dedicate this book to her now.

Abbreviations

Ancient Sources

1 Apoc. Jas.	*First Apocalypse of James*
Ac. Justin	*Acts of Justin and His Companions*
Ac. Scilli.	*Acts of the Scillitan Martyrs*
Cicero, *Tusc.*	*Tusculan Disputations*
Clement, *Strom.*	*Miscellanies*
Cyprian, *Ep.*	*Letters*
Diogenes Laertius, *Lives*	*Lives of the Philosophers*
Eusebius, *Hist. eccl.*	*Ecclesiastical History*
Ign. *Eph.*	Ignatius, *To the Ephesians*
Ign. *Magn.*	Ignatius, *To the Magnesians*
Ign. *Rom.*	Ignatius, *To the Romans*
Irenaeus, *Haer.*	*Against the Heresies*
Justin Martyr, *1 Apol.*	*First Apology*
Justin Martyr, *2 Apol.*	*Second Apology*
Justin Martyr, *Dial.*	*Dialogue with Trypho*
Livy	Livy, *The History of Rome*
Lyons	*Letter of the Churches of Vienne and Lyons*
Marcus Aurelius, *Med.*	*Meditations*
Mart. Carp.	*Martyrdom of Carpus, Papylus, and Agathonike*

Mart. Paul	*Martyrdom of Paul*
Mart. Pionius	*Martyrdom of Pionius*
Mart. Pol.	*Martyrdom of Polycarp*
P. Oxy.	Oxyrhynchus papyri
Passio	*Passion of Perpetua and Felicitas*
Plato, *Phaed.*	*Phaedo*
Pliny, *Ep.*	Pliny the Younger, *Letters*
Plutarch, *Inim. util.*	*De capienda ex inimicis utilitate*
Tacitus, *Ann.*	*Annals*
Tertullian, *Apol.*	*Apology*
Tertullian, *De anim.*	*On the Soul*
Tertullian, *Fug.*	*On Flight in Persecution*
Val. Max.	Valerius Maximus, *Memorable Doings and Sayings*

Scholarly Literature

ANRW	*Aufstieg und Niedergang der römischen Welt*
CIL	*Corpus inscriptionum latinarum*
HTR	*Harvard Theological Review*
JBL	*Journal of Biblical Literature*
JECS	*Journal of Early Christian Studies*
JRS	*Journal of Roman Studies*
JSOT	*Journal for the Study of the Old Testament*
JTS	*Journal of Theological Studies*
NHC	Nag Hammadi codices
P&P	*Past and Present*
PG	Patrologia Graeca
PLS	Patrologia Latina supplementum
SP	*Studia patristica*
SPAW	Sitzungsberichte der preussischen Akademie der Wissenschaften
TC	Codex Tchacos
VC	*Vigiliae Christianae*
VCSup	Supplements to Vigiliae Christianae
WUNT	Wissenschaftliche Untersuchungen zum Neuen Testament
ZNW	*Zeitschrift für die Neutestamentliche Wissenschaft*
ZWT	*Zeitschrift für wissenschaftliche Theologie*

Introduction

In the study of ancient Christianity, no figure polarizes the scholarly world as effectively as the martyr. Study of the martyrs is as often a disdainful preoccupation as it is a preoccupying delight.[1] The martyr commands attention, fascinates the skeptic, and confounds the rationalist. How and why people would immolate themselves for Christ are questions that consume scholar and layperson alike. Even when viewed in light of modern terrorism, martyrdom is extreme and removed, either necessitated by dire historical circumstances that arise in far-flung places and at distant times or instigated by aliens and outsiders.[2] The exceptionality and otherness of martyrdom prompt the question "Where does martyrdom come from?" This search for the legal, intellectual, historical, and psychological sources of martyrdom has a broad-based appeal both inside and outside the academy, particularly in the post-9/11 era. Given that the term *martyr* emerged out of Christianity and that early Christians were the first to develop a full-fledged ideology of martyrdom, the origins of martyrdom in Christianity have taken on a particular significance. Identifying and describing the cradle of martyrdom has been a consuming task both for those exploring ancient Christianity and for those interested in martyrdom in general.

The question "where does martyrdom come from?" presupposes, however, that there is a single notion of martyrdom that can be pinned down and placed under the historian's magnifying glass. Is martyrdom an event, or even a practice and performance, in which an individual is executed? If an event, then we might ask what legal and historical circumstances led to its occurrence. Alternatively, is martyrdom an idea or set of values that a community holds dear? If an idea, then we might locate its generation in other ideas, in literature, and in culture. In comparing these ideas, we would look for the moment of conception when not-martyrdom became martyrdom. The idea of martyrdom, however, does not spring forth from intellectual curiosity but instead is attached, however tenuously, to a series of events and a constellation of practices, and to the possibility of actual death. If martyrdom is a historical event— let's say, for now, a historical *death*—then how is it to be distinguished from other kinds of death, such as murder or suicide? To answer this question, and to engage the broader question of the history of martyrdom, we need a definition of the martyr.

Difficult Definitions

Why someone would become a martyr and where martyrdom "comes from" are questions related to the more ambiguous issue of what, precisely, makes an individual a martyr and qualifies his or her death as a martyrdom. According to the *Oxford English Dictionary*, a martyr is, in the Christian church, "A person who chooses to suffer death rather than renounce faith in Christ or obedience to his teachings, a Christian way of life, or adherence to a law or tenet of the Church; (also) a person who chooses to suffer death rather than renounce the beliefs or tenets of a particular Christian denomination, sect, etc." The citation of a modern dictionary entry may appear trite, but this definition exposes something important about the act of writing a history of martyrs. To indulge in a little meta-history: traditionally, martyrdom is seen to begin at the moment when ancient Christians started using the Greek term *martys* in a way that corresponds to the modern definition of the martyr. In other words, the origins of martyrdom are found by identifying the point in time at which the modern definition of the martyr, as cited here, can be directly mapped onto the definition inferred from ancient literature.

This approach is evident in Norbert Brox's classic study *Zeuge und Märtyrer* on the linguistic development of the term *martys,* a work that has had a pronounced effect on the history of martyrdom.[3] Brox traces the evolution of the term from its pre-Christian use in courtrooms to its titular use in Christianity. Originally, *martys* referred to the testimony or witness presented by an individual in a trial setting or to the individual who affirms or attests. The term was used, therefore, primarily within a legal context. Over time and with use, the connotations of the term gradually changed so that *martys* came to mean an individual who, as the *Oxford English Dictionary* would have it, "chooses to suffer death rather than renounce faith in Christ or obedience to his teachings." In his study, Brox locates the first unequivocal usage of the term and, thus, the birth of martyrdom in the *Martyrdom of Polycarp*. For Brox, the particular linguistic usage of a term (*martys*) was indicative of the existence of a concept (martyrdom), which in turn identified the text as a member of a specific genre (the martyrdom account or martyr act).

It is the modern definition of "martyr" and the linguistic debt that modern language owes to classical Greek that has led to this scholarly focus on the use of the term *martys* among ancient Christians—and with good reason. Within a matter of two centuries of the death of Jesus, the meaning of this term had been transformed from a material witness to an executed Christian. Yet some caution should be exercised here. Even if there was a general shift, we must be wary of accepting that the linguistic transformation was a fait accompli in the second century.[4] The production of language is a far more complex and nuanced matter than Brox allows us to see. Language is constantly changing and evolving, adapted and discarded as people see fit. To propose that the meaning of the term was irrevocably fixed by the *Martyrdom of Polycarp* is to obscure both the way that language works and the heterogeneity of the Greek language across the expansive Roman empire. In short, even if Asia Minor in 157 CE—the location and traditional dating for the composition of the *Martyrdom of Polycarp*—marked the turning point for Christian usage of the term, this need not mean anything for the use of *martys* in Rome and Ostia, in Gaul or even in Galatia.[5]

The problem with Brox's argument is that it makes the *idea* of martyrdom synonymous with a specific linguistic term. Brox takes the modern concept of martyrdom, which values the act of dying for a religious commitment, and marries it to *martys*. Evolution holds at its core the idea of multiple forms of mutation, but he traces only this single linguistic path. Moreover, a group or culture might value death for a particular religious commitment without having a linguistically related title for the person who dies. Much has been made, for instance, of the ancient Greeks who valued the good or noble death (*euthanasia*). The term for someone who achieved such a death was not "good death–arian," but "hero" or "man."[6] For Brox, martyrdom begins at the point where ideological rubber meets linguistic road; yet if we extract martyr from martyrdom we can imagine groups, texts, and people valuing the idea of "martyrdom" without identifying the concept using this word group. This recognition opens up the possibility that the set of values or the concept we call martyrdom existed before the advent of Christianity and independently of the *martys* word group.

On the obverse, *martys* was not frozen in time post-*Polycarp* and does not necessarily reflect our modern emphases. The term, like all elements of language, retained a certain fluidity and flexibility. The early Christian heroine Thecla, whose legend spawned a vibrant cult in Syria and Egypt, is hailed by some as a martyr despite the fact that in the earliest version of the *Acts of Paul and Thecla* she is never successfully executed.[7] In a similar manner, the element of choice, so critical for adjudicating in modern times between murder and martyrdom, is not a perpetual crux in all ancient martyr acts. The second-century heresiologist Irenaeus of Lyons calls the infants executed by Herod in the Matthean infancy narratives martyrs because they died for Christ, even though choice and verbal testimony clearly played no part in their deaths (*Haer.* 3.16.4). The existence of such examples suggests that elements we see as structural to the practice of martyrdom were not a prerequisite for the application of the title martyr.

The meaning of the term *martys* was discursively reshaped by early Christian communities long after its first application to an executed person. In some cases the use of the label "martyr" was an attempt to harness the status and authority that the title conferred on the deceased and on the community preserving his or her memory. For instance, designating Thecla a "proto-martyr" in the fourth century assimilated the person and cult of Thecla to the person and cult of Stephen. That Hagia Thekla, the martyr shrine of Thecla, stood on the pilgrimage route to the site of Stephen's martyrdom in Jerusalem made the association a matter of economic pragmatism as well as theological significance. Whether or not Thecla is "really" a martyr may loom large in our minds today, but does not appear to have been a question in antiquity. While the later editions of the *Acts of Paul and Thecla* accentuate the martyrological elements in the story of Thecla's disappearance, the work does not describe her death. The definition of a martyr, implicit in the use of the title "protomartyr," was not exclusively framed using categories of death and choice. Usage, rather than lexical entries, should dictate the meaning of the term. The title signified authority as much as death and self-abasement and, as such, was mechanistically powerful in asserting the legitimacy of one's position.

Examinations of the language of martyrdom after the middle of the second century have tended to focus on internal debate and discussion, on how and why Christians adapted and deployed the term and for what rhetorical purposes. It is often assumed that the terminology has an intra-ecclesial focus, that Christians used it for the purposes of forging identities and defining boundaries. Yet *martys,* which has been hermetically sealed by linguistic historiography as a *terminus technicus,* continued to derive its meaning from extra-Christian ancient discourse long after the second century. The intersection of Roman legal terminology and Christian usage remains relevant even after the titular turn. Moreover, in using a modern definition of martyr to gauge important linguistic and ideological shifts, we write a history of linguistic victors. Admittedly, *martys* was an important word both for ancient Christians and, by means of its descendent *martyr,* for ourselves, but we should not permit linguistic nepotism to narrow the purview of this study. In the early churches, other categories such as confessor, imitator, God-bearer, and sufferer were used as part of the language of martyrdom. Like *martys,* this language was constantly reshaped and reproduced as part of early Christian discourse. These other terms add texture and depth to early understandings of martyrdom.

If terminology is divorced from theme, the search for the beginnings of martyrdom takes us into the expanses of Greco-Roman and ancient Jewish literature, to the tales of the Maccabees, the epic poems of Homer, and the paradigmatic death of Socrates. A number of formidable scholars have probed the intellectual ancestry of martyrdom, shedding light from Athens, Jerusalem, and everywhere in between. Looking to ancient Judaism, Jan Willem van Henten's study of the Maccabean martyrs posits that the deaths of Jewish heroes for the "salvation" of their people formed the notion of martyrdom in the early church.[8] A number of the classic pre-Christian martyrs—Daniel, Socrates, and the Maccabees and their mother—make allusive cameos in the martyr acts, demonstrating the potent shadows these figures cast over later history making. In seeking to solidify the origins of martyrdom, some scholars have looked to the literary ancestry of the martyrdom story, variously labeled the *acta, passio,* and martyr act.[9] The relationship of the genre to official court records (*commentarii*), lives of Greek philosophers such as those presented by Diogenes Laertius, and the "martyrdom accounts" of contemporary Greeks (*Acta Alexandrinorum*), and even to the passion narrative of Jesus, has become a locus for this discussion. Yet as Christian martyrs are connected to a lineage of pre-Christian heroes, the similarities become increasingly blurred. A history of martyrdom becomes a history of ideas, and the definition of martyrdom starts to lack definition.[10]

As a history of ideologies of martyrdom, this book will utilize a functional definition of martyrdom that incorporates texts whose protagonists are memorialized as martyrs, even if the texts do not use *martys* in a technical sense.[11] This methodology purposefully leaves the edges of the definition ragged, allowing us to incorporate accounts, such as the stories of lion tamers in Daniel and the *Acts of Thecla,* that are not traditionally categorized as martyrdom narratives. This raggedness is productive as it reflects the extent to which ideologies of martyrdom were interwoven with other culturally loaded concepts of sacrifice, suffering, and heroism. We will, however, continue to note the use of the terminology of *martys,* for if we discard philology entirely, then we risk losing sight of something important. Even if the shift in the term's meaning does not mark the beginning of martyrdom per se, the refinement of language and the application of titles as identity markers are important historical developments. These moments of transition expose changes in the structures of ancient social and conceptual hierarchies. The task, then, is to describe a web woven with threads of linguistic, literary, ideological, intellectual, and cultural history. These histories of martyrdom are closely enough intertwined to be at times indistinguishable, but they are not synonymous. Martyrdom does not begin where language, practice, and ideology coalesce in a way that approximates our own definition of martyrdom. The idea of martyrdom may predate the formulation of specific terminology and may be attached to linguistic terms that do not present themselves to us in modern parlance as martyrological. Perhaps most importantly, the ideologies and language of martyrdom are never stagnant and fixed. This book ends its chronological survey of martyrdom with the turn of the third century, but ideologies of martyrdom continued to be augmented, fashioned, and adapted long after the period of our study. Indeed, ideologies of martyrdom continue to be reshaped today.[12]

Pathologies of Passio

The difficulties of defining martyrdom aside, beneath the surface of histories of martyrdom lies a commitment to a particular characterization of martyrdom itself. There is an assumption that martyrdom is a singular ideology whose genealogy can be traced in a linear fashion. Early-twentieth-century martyrdom scholars had a penchant for diagnosing or pathologizing the martyr's task, a tendency particularly evident in the writings of Donald W. Riddle, who sees martyrdom as both brainwashing and a form of insanity.[13] Ignatius of Antioch, in particular, has borne the brunt of the amateur psychoanalyst's ire: for his longing for death Ignatius is called "abnormal" and "pathological" by G. E. M. De Ste. Croix[14] and described as "bordering on mania" by W. H. C. Frend.[15] The diagnosis of the martyr's desire as dementia is more than an inappropriately pejorative judgment that breaches the historian's self-professed code of impartiality. This response betrays a commitment to the assumption that it is natural to want to live and that to desire otherwise is a sign of mental dysfunction. The desire to diagnose and alienate "the other" is part of an assumption of self-normalcy. This normalizing impulse extends even to language itself; Edward Gibbon, in his classic *History of the Decline and Fall of the Roman Empire,* calls the transformation of the term *martys* in the early church a "strange distortion" of its original sense.[16] According to this view of martyrdom, even language is susceptible to the distortive effects of martyrdom: the ideological disease.[17]

Nineteenth- and early-twentieth-century discourse about martyrdom as unnatural and the pathological model of martyrdom it produces explain a number of assumptions in scholarly descriptions of the "spread" of martyrdom in the early church. That martyrdom has an origin—intellectual, geographical, and social—from which it spread to the rest of the Roman empire is an idea common to studies of martyrdom.[18] This approach presupposes that martyrdom is a homogenous entity, whose origins can be identified and pathways tracked. Martyrdom operates much like a disease spreading pathologically across the empire.[19]

This idea that Christian martyrdom spread is not without ancient support. In his correspondence with the emperor Trajan, the governor Pliny describes Christianity as a "depraved, immoderate superstition" (*Ep.* 10.96–97). Similarly, the Roman historian Tacitus describes Christianity using language of contagion. It is a "recurrent superstition" that had invaded Rome from Judea (*Ann.* 15.44). Scholarly classification of martyrdom as a disease is an effective topos drawn from ancient invective, and the use of the term *superstitio* invokes classical philosophical critiques of barbarian religion.[20] A disease is not only abnormal and abhorrent, but it is incumbent on society to attempt to root it out. Even today, the designation of certain practices as diseases serves a valuable rhetorical purpose in proposing that they be suppressed and eradicated.[21] The move is powerful, because one does not deal seriously or on an intellectual footing with that which is pathologized. Ancient Christians were also accustomed to designating ideas that they opposed as diseased: Eusebius calls superstition an ancient disease and compares the followers of Simon Magus to a "pestilent and leprous disease" (*Hist. eccl.* 2.3.2; 2.1.12). It must be noted, however, that the use of pathological language for the spread of martyrdom does not come from Christians, but rather from their opponents. Such usage is a classical rhetorical trope, and when scholars choose to use a pathological model to describe the spread of martyrdom, they implicitly align themselves with the Roman opponents of Christianity and unwittingly adopt a polemical stance.

The influential work of Judith Perkins has shifted the search for the origins of martyrdom from psychological to cultural pathology. Her book *The*

Suffering Self demonstrates the pervasive ancient interest in the self as sufferer. She writes, "Since this epithet ["pathological"] has now been heard so often, one may suspect that if there is pathology, it belongs to the culture rather than to the psychology of any individual."[22] Even cultural pathology implies abnormality and deviance from an implicit sense of the "natural" (although it is precisely this sense of the natural that Perkins correctly seeks to redescribe in her chapter titled "Ideology, Not Pathology").[23] The assumption persists that martyrdom, like disease, is a singular phenomenon; this notion is not only present in the work of scholars such as Riddle and De Ste. Croix, who are markedly anti-martyrdom; it lingers in the scholarly concatenation of the martyrs Polycarp, Justin, and Perpetua, whose invocation in an academic litany implies a smooth chronological development of the idea of martyrdom across time and terrain.

The Nature of the Evidence

Ancient ideas are mediated through the artifacts of ancient culture—through texts, art, rituals, and architecture—an assortment of relics preserved by accident as well as by affection. The eccentricities of historical preservation aside, texts are not produced in order to explain themselves; they are embedded in a complex of ancient ideas and practices, the significance of which was constantly changing. In order to understand the particular nuance of a word, idea, or text, these entities must be considered within their own philological, literary, and cultural milieux. Ideas cannot be studied as abstract things. Even the most erudite, ascetic intellectuals construct their arguments within the context of their embodied experiences of the world. So it is with the idea of martyrdom, suffused within a broader Christian discourse that, in turn, is intelligible only as part of the larger social institutions and conceptual structures of the ancient world.

The task of writing a history of martyrdom is further complicated by the nature of the extant evidence. In addition to scanty Roman legal information that is used to narrate the history of martyrdom from "the Roman perspective" and the martyr acts that are variously used to reconstruct historical events and ancient ideology, there are references to suffering and death in the literature of the Jesus movement, descriptions of the deaths of the apostles in the apocryphal acts of the apostles, and discussions of persecution in the writings of contemporary Christian thinkers.

Whereas discussions of the legal basis for the prosecution of Christians may offer an unproblematic (if partial) picture of the historical realities of persecution, Christian literature does not have the same focus. Traditionally, scholars have placed the Christian evidence on a sliding scale of historicity. For many years, the writings of the apologists were viewed as unproblematic historical records of Christian responses to Roman persecution. The apocryphal acts of the apostles, by contrast, were considered more romantic and fictional and have often been marginalized in favor of the "more historical" apologetic texts. The martyr acts themselves, with their interest in subjects other than martyrdom, thus occupied the middle space between the apologists and the apocryphal acts.

A notional principle of "historicity" has served as a guide for the assembly of evidence for early Christian martyrdom. For those scholars especially interested in the historical reality (that is, how many people died, when, and where), the evidence provided by Roman legal documents, papyri, and the more "historical" apologetic literature and courtroom-styled martyrdom texts has weighed heavily. For those scholars more concerned with representation and ideology, the more detailed and "literary" apocryphal acts and *passiones* have been preferred for the ethical norms that they legislate and power structures that they reinforce.[24] The extent to which a historical/literary binary has underwritten what counts as evidence for the history of martyrdom and what counts as better evidence should not be underestimated.

ROMAN EVIDENCE

Popular opinion, following Melito of Sardis, maintains that early Christians were a beleaguered group sought out and persecuted by oppressive Roman emperors.[25] In the late nineteenth century, Roman legal historians began to reappraise the extent to which the Christians were really the targets of systematic and sustained persecution.[26] These scholars incorporated Roman historical, epistolary, and legal evidence into the study of ecclesiastical history. The intent was twofold: to redress the view that Christians were actively persecuted by imperial decree and to examine the legal grounds for the arrest and trial of Christians.

Although the fourth-century church historian Eusebius describes the persecutions of manifold Roman emperors, there is almost no evidence to suggest that Roman emperors were in the habit of targeting Christians for special treatment. As De Ste. Croix notes, "We know of no persecution by the Roman government until 64, and there was no general persecution by the Roman government until that of Decius. Between 64 and 250 there were only isolated, local persecutions; and even if the total number of victims was quite considerable . . . most individual outbreaks must usually have been quite brief."[27] There were, however, flurries of arrests before the persecution of Decius, particularly outside of Rome. In these situations the judicial process followed was that used for the majority of criminal trials under the Principate: the *cognitio extra ordinem*. As a result, capital trials in the provinces took place only before the provincial governor and then only as the situation arose, that is to say, if individuals were denounced before the governor. The authority of provincial governors in such cases was almost unlimited, and they acted very much under their own guidance. Writing around the turn of the third century, the Christian author Tertullian notes that while the Roman governor Saturninus did condemn Christians to death, his successors were far more lenient (*Ad Scapulam* 3–5). The only official line, conveyed via imperial instructions (*mandata*), was that the provincial governors should take pains to rid their provinces of bad men (*mali homines*). While the pressure to ensure that the area remain settled and orderly (*pacata atque quieta*) may have involved the execution of troublemakers, there was no official decree that forced the hands of the Roman governors. The process under which Christians were executed was idiosyncratic. Given this legal situation, it is difficult to gauge the importance of the extant evidence for Roman prosecutions. The evidence here includes papyrological data for the Roman trials and legislation in general and specific references to the prosecution of Christians in extant Roman correspondence and historiography.

The correspondence between Pliny, the governor of Bithynia and Pontus (modern-day Turkey), and the Roman emperor Trajan around 110 CE has weighed heavily in scholarly discussions of why Christians were persecuted.[28] In book 10 of his correspondence, Pliny writes to Trajan complaining about the Christians and enquiring about the best manner in which to proceed. He describes the religio-economic effects of Christian conversion on local religious practices before the measures he has taken. The temples, he records, had been deserted, and no one had been purchasing sacrificial meat. Christianity had won admirers from every quarter; its participants included "persons of every age and every class, both genders . . . not only [in] the town but villages and countryside as well." Pliny writes that he has examined the Christians and found them innocent of any real crime. All the same, he is exasperated by their "stubbornness and inflexible obstinacy," which he feels deserve punishment (*Ep.* 10.96). As a result, he has devised a system to deal with them. He asks the accused individuals three times whether they are Christian, with a warning about the punishment that awaits them: if they continue to confess that they are Christian, he will have them executed or, if they are citizens, sent to Rome for trial. For those who deny being Christians he has devised what has become known as the sacrifice test, in which an accused person is instructed to offer wine and incense to an image of the emperor and to curse Christ. Pliny's letter asks Trajan for advice; he is unsure whether the punishment should be the same for all and whether confessing to having been Christian in the past is sufficient for a guilty verdict. In his response, Trajan (if it is truly Trajan responding) commends Pliny for his work and insists that Christians should be neither hunted down nor accused anonymously.[29] Trajan confirms that for an accused person to offer sacrifice is sufficient proof of innocence (*Ep.* 10.97).

In the letter, Pliny's frustration with Christian obstinacy is almost palpable. Against De Ste. Croix, A. N. Sherwin-White argues that it was for their defiance (*contumacia*) that Christians were arrested and executed.[30] Certainly, they attracted the derision and scorn of Roman writers and administrators, and the martyr acts present their protagonists as evasive and difficult in the courtroom. At the same time, however, as De Ste. Croix notes in his rejoinder to Sherwin-White, obstinacy (*obstinatio*) and defiance (*contumacia*) were separate charges, and the latter is not mentioned in the Pliny-Trajan correspondence. Only once they were in the courtroom did Christians have the opportunity to display their obstinacy, and therefore it is unlikely that they were arrested for *being* defiant.[31]

The Pliny-Trajan correspondence and Pliny's uncertainty about how to proceed have been cited by many as examples of the ad hoc nature of Roman persecution of Christians.[32] Yet we would do well to view this correspondence with the same dose of skepticism that we do early Christian literature.[33] In the first place, Pliny's correspondence was conserved not by accident but by his own determination to preserve his literary prowess for posterity. The collection was intended to draw comparisons with the libri of Catullus.[34] In the second place, letter writing, like other compositional forms, was subject to the dictates of etiquette and to codes of genre.[35] These considerations were at play even for book 10, which Pliny apparently never intended for publication. When addressing the emperor, Pliny was bound by certain modes of self-presentation. As Carlos Noreña has proposed, "These official and utilitarian letters could also serve as vehicles for Pliny's epistolary self-representation, in a manner analogous to the literary letters of Books 1–9."[36] When considering Pliny's tentative approach to the prosecution of Christians, we would do well to recall the warning of Raymond Van Dam that "authors were concerned more about protocol than candor, more about form than substance and emotion."[37]

As noted, provincial governors exercised a great deal of personal power. While the publication of the Pliny-Trajan correspondence after the death of the emperor may have lent the text a degree of gravitas, its contents would not have been legally binding. Roman governors were amateurs in Roman law.[38] "Roman law" did not have standardized procedures in the provinces, against which we can compare and so assess the "reality" of the martyrdom accounts. Consequently, we should not treat the Pliny-Trajan correspondence as prototypical for the trials of those Christians who were executed before the persecutions of the emperor Decius in the mid-third century.[39] Agreement between the events described in the Pliny-Trajan correspondence and the portrayal of trials of Christians in the martyr acts should not automatically be taken as indicative of historical authenticity. It is important to consider the possibility that the authors of the martyr acts tailored their narratives to accord with Pliny's account and to recognize that, more broadly, the relationship of the Christian discourse of martyrdom to Roman caricatures and criticisms of early Christians was complicated and nuanced.[40]

The paucity of evidence for the formal persecution of Christians during our period means that a historical narrative of legal persecution and prosecution cannot be re-created. Before the decree of Decius around 250 CE—which itself may have stemmed from a desire to unify the Roman empire rather than from a decision to root out Christians—the persecution of Christians was largely the product of the inclinations of individual Roman administrators.[41] Roman governors could exercise magnanimity as well as cruelty. While the sporadic nature of persecution is frequently cited as evidence of the early Christians' tendency to exaggerate the dangers that they experienced, the unpredictability of persecution was itself destabilizing. Isolated experiences of exceptional cruelty no doubt reverberated in the Christian unconscious long after the events themselves. In fact, one of the functions of early Christian martyrdom literature was to perpetuate this process and amplify the echoes of earlier struggles.[42] In the absence of detailed Roman evidence, the Christian's place in the Roman legal system is crafted by Christians themselves.

EARLY CHRISTIAN LITERATURE

Scholarly treatment of martyrdom has often focused exclusively on those writings that narrate the deaths of otherwise anonymous Christians. These texts, called "acts of the Christian martyrs" or "martyr acts," are partitioned off from other early Christian literature, both canonical and noncanonical, as generically distinct. This division posits a firm divide between the martyr acts and other early Christian literature, even works such as the apocryphal acts of the apostles and early Christian apologies that explicitly deal with suffering and death. If the object of our study is the development of ideologies of martyrdom, then all the early Christian literature that can be brought to bear on this subject must be incorporated, not just texts that have traditionally been viewed as exclusively concerned with martyrdom.[43] This task is even more important if martyrdom literature, as traditionally conceived, is about more than simply martyrdom. If, as many have argued, martyrdom literature serves to create a particular sense of Christian identity, then it is appropriate that such writings are considered within the broader context of early Christian culture making.

The relationship between the canonical texts of the New Testament and martyrdom literature is often conceived monodirectionally, as one of biblical text and its interpretation/reception. The literature of the Jesus movement is, as scripture, often treated as the source for later understandings of martyrdom and, as such, as part of the background to the emergence of early Christian martyrdom. As critical as scripture and portraits of Jesus were for the characterization of early Christian martyrs, the relationship between those texts composed in the first and second centuries and later designated as scripture and those texts composed in the first and second centuries and destined to be noncanonical is dialogical. Not only were martyrs framed using Pauline scaffolding or modeled on the (cruci)form of Jesus, but also scriptural accounts were read through the lens of later martyr traditions.[44] The recognition of this mutual intertextuality allows that the texts of the New Testament remained vital, living, impressionable elements of early Christian martyrdom traditions long after their composition. Thus the corpus of texts that now forms the canonical New Testament is a part of the discourse of martyrdom in the early church.

The literature of the Jesus movement, that is, the texts composed by followers of Jesus in the first century CE, often refers to the "tribulation," "suffering," and "persecution" of followers of Jesus. The pervasiveness of the theme may be neither accidental nor historical; Dennis Farkasfalvy and William Farmer have argued that martyrdom was an important cultural influence in the formation of the Christian canon.[45] There is, however, a general sense among scholars that early Christians such as the authors of 1 Peter and Revelation may in historical reality have suffered more from paranoia than from actual persecution.[46] Given that, with the exception of Revelation, these texts do not use the term *martys* to describe members of their communities, they are more readily deemed part of the background to early Christian martyrdom than part of the ideology of martyrdom itself, an attitude that reflects an enduring scholarly commitment to the linguistic definition of martyrdom. Texts are part of the history of martyrdom only if they employ the appropriate terminology and if they reflect actual, historical persecution. Whatever the historical circumstances of the composition of these texts, the early churches do not appear to have shared our skepticism. Scriptural accounts, both canonical and noncanonical, were treated by early Christian communities as evidence that the church was, from its beginning, in conflict with the world.

This narrative of early Christian history is picked up and augmented by the apocryphal acts of the apostles, a corpus of later second-century literature that, like other early Christian apocryphal literature, has suffered from a certain degree of scholarly neglect. These stories of the adventures, travels, and lives of the apostles after the death of Jesus have much in common with both Greek romance novels and the canonical Acts of the Apostles. In many of these texts, the narrative concludes with a detailed account of the trial and execution of the apostolic protagonist. Although traditionally the apocryphal acts have been treated in isolation from the more "historical" martyr acts, these sections of the apocryphal acts are as much martyrdom literature as they are apostolic biography or romance novel. Many of the literary and narrative elements of these apocryphal traditions resonate with nonapostolic martyrdom literature. Lipsius, the great nineteenth-century editor of the apocryphal acts, himself noted their martyrological elements, but traditional scholarship has tended to treat the apocryphal acts as a separate, nonhistorical genre.[47] This divorce, arranged by scholars largely on the basis of generic incompatibility, has rendered the picture of early Christian martyrdom woefully singular.[48]

The five accounts that can be most reliably dated to the years covered by this book are the *Acts of Paul, Acts of Peter, Acts of John, Acts of Andrew,* and *Acts of Thomas,* which together span the approximate period 150 to 220 CE.[49] The textual traditions of these accounts are difficult and fragmentary; only the *Acts of Thomas* survives in its entirety in Greek, and even then the text shows the heavy-handed brush of a later redactor. The literary relationship among the texts is similarly complicated. All five share literary topoi, thematic interests, and traditions, but at the same time the force of these mutual concerns is undercut by the acts' resemblance to other literary traditions. These works have much in common with the larger genre of the Greek romance novel, which together with the canonical Acts of the Apostles may serve as a kind of macro-genre for these texts.[50] The novelistic features of the apocryphal acts suggest that stories about apostles and martyrs were received as romances; once again, the edges of martyrdom are blurred.

Stories about the deaths of Christians, commonly referred to as martyr acts, provide a reservoir of information about the ways in which early Christian communities interpreted the experience of persecution and the deaths of their members. The acts of the martyrs were collected together in late antiquity for a variety of catechetical, pedagogical, and liturgical functions. More recently, the collection of martyr acts was motivated by a desire to identify and preserve the actual words of the martyrs. This study was inaugurated in 1607 by the publication of Heribert Rosweyde's *Fasti sanctorum,* in which the author announced his intent to use historical and philological criteria to identify the "authentic" lives of the saints.[51] The hagiographical baton was picked up by Jean Bollandus and his eponymously named Société des Bollandistes, whose work proved invaluable to subsequent generations of hagiographers and scholars. In collecting and analyzing the corpus of texts variously referred to as the acts of the martyrs, *acta Christianorum*, and *acta martyrum*, the hagiographer aimed to identify the *ipsissima verba* of the saint.

The prodigious methodologies of hagiography, further refined by Th. Ruinart, Oscar von Gebhardt, and Hippolyte Delehaye, are in tension with an obscure sentimental attachment to the saints themselves.[52] Adolf von Harnack, a herald of critical study of the early church, writes that the words of the martyrs were piously protected from distortion and redaction:

> Whoever would falsify here [the acts of the martyrs], set themselves up to the most serious reproach, because such a one would falsify the words of the Holy Spirit, i.e., of Christ. It was most certain, therefore, that persons themselves obtained records from the confessors in the prisons whenever possible; if that was not possible, one sent trustworthy brethren to them to hear their testimony. One sought to examine the trial records, since these were not completely adequate—because they did not completely contain the speeches of the defendants—one sent brethren to the trial, who must have faithfully recorded the words of the confessors.[53]

Von Harnack's argument, while attractive and romantic, cuts against the grain of a wealth of evidence about early Christian writing practices. In their composition of works in the name of apostles such as Peter (2 Pet; *Gospel of Peter*) and Paul (2 Thess, 1 Tim, 2 Tim, Titus, 3 Cor), scriptural characters such as Pilate (*Gospel of Pilate*), Mary (*Gospel of Mary*), and even Jesus himself (for example, the letters between Jesus and King Abgar contained in Eusebius's *Hist. eccl.*), Christians do not seem especially wary of the charge of blasphemy against the spirit of Christ.

The assumption underlying the work of all these scholars is that martyrdom literature has a historical nucleus, that is, the words and deeds of the martyrs can be distilled from the interpretation that surrounds them. With the goal of retrieving the historical martyr in view, many scholars focused more on the identification of authentic martyr acts than on the identification of early texts.[54] With this interest in mind the eminent hagiographer Hippolyte Delehaye classifies martyrdom accounts using a sliding scale of authenticity:[55]

1. Official court documents of the martyrs' trials (*acta proconsulari*)
2. Literary narratives based on the accounts of eyewitnesses or texts composed by the martyrs themselves

3. Edited documents relying upon eyewitness reports and/or texts composed by the martyrs themselves
4. *Passiones:* historical romances based on and containing historical information
5. Purely fictional compositions
6. "Deceptive forgeries"

The quest for the historical martyr has rested in part on the conviction that underlying the martyr acts are official court records detailing the martyr's words. These court documents were believed to have been obtained by early Christians and used as sources for the composition of martyr acts. Yet none of the martyr acts conforms to this genre precisely.[56] These stories are generic hybrids; the *acta* are broken up and interpolated. Such emendation is to be expected: why would an early Christian writer want to duplicate a *commentarius* without embellishment, expansion, or interpretation? The recognition that none of the martyr acts is a pristine historical account, however, demonstrates that the historicity of any of these accounts can never be taken for granted and is always a negotiation.

Just as the apocryphal acts of the apostles intersect and overlap with the interests and genre of martyrdom literature, so too apologetic literature forms a critical component of early Christian descriptions of persecution. Although a problematic generic category in its own right, apologetic literature also offers a different mode of engaging Roman authorities and interpreting the experience of persecution. The generic boundary between martyr acts and apologetics is at best permeable. Justin Martyr, the author of some of the most famous apologetic works (*1 Apology, 2 Apology,* and the *Dialogue with Trypho*), incorporated a martyrdom account into his work and himself died as a martyr in Rome around 165 CE. The home that martyrdom literature finds in apologetics demonstrates the rhetorical force that martyrdom lends to the apologetic rhetorical program. In the words of R. M. Grant, "martyrs make the best apologists."[57] The bleeding of apologetics into martyrdom literature and martyrdom literature into apologetics suggests that we should not artificially rend one from the other. During the first centuries of the Christian era many, indeed all, forms of literature contributed to the creation of Christian culture.

The Aim of the Present Study

For all the reasons just explored, writing a history of martyrdom is a perplexing and daunting task. Not only is the evidence complicated and opaque, but even the subject itself can be tackled from a variety of perspectives. What, exactly, is the thing that one seeks to describe? Illustrious early-twentieth-century histories of martyrdom attempted to pin down the historical facts, to isolate what really happened: who died, when, where, in what legal circumstances, and for what motivations. Philologists attempted to isolate the origins of the phenomenon of martyrdom in the evolution of the linguistic category of the martyr. Others still have tapped the intellectual reservoirs of the ancient world for stories and motifs that resonate with martyrdom. More recent studies have asked not "where does martyrdom come from?" but "what do ancient ideologies of martyrdom tell us about ancient Christianity more broadly?"

A number of scholars have looked at the extent to which martyr acts and discussions of martyrdom in the early church serve to create an ideal Christian self and distinguish Christians from others.[58] Describing martyrdom is about the production of identity categories and the creation of meaning. Yet martyrdom is not only about crafting boundaries and forging resistance in relation to other groups and external forces. In *Formations of the Secular,* anthropologist Talal Asad offers a brief appraisal of martyrdom in which he attempts to move the discussion of suffering from symbolic resistance to reconfigured economies of action.[59] Asad suggests a slightly different mode of analysis in which Christian experiences and narrations of persecution, execution, suffering, and death produced a new *"economy* of action."[60] In this economy, pain was a constitutive part of activities that maintain and sustain relationships. Early Christians used it "to create a space for moral action that articulates this-world-in-the-next."[61] Asad reinscribes a tendency within martyrdom scholarship to treat suffering and pain as synonyms, yet his critique rightly draws our attention to the fact that the Christian embrace of suffering is not only a means of resisting Roman values or even forging identity; it establishes suffering as part of the expected human experience.[62]

This book treats martyrdom as a set of discursive practices that shaped early Christian identities, mediated ecclesiastical and dogmatic claims, and provided meaning to the experience described by early Christians as persecution, and in doing so produced a new economy of action. This account, therefore, is less about what makes or does not make a martyr in some ontological sense than about how martyrs are created and for what purposes. As a history of martyrdom, it traces the contours of distinctive ideologies of martyrdom that arose in specific cultural settings. What intellectual and cultural influences shaped the expression of martyrdom in these locations? Given the ideological power that martyrs and exhortations to martyrdom wielded, how was power utilized, channeled, and controlled? In some ways this book is an attempt to nuance a question posed by Robin Lane Fox, "How had this powerful ideal of the martyr been constructed?"[63] In contrast to Lane Fox, however, it will argue that there was not one construction, but many interlocking, overlapping, and competing constructions of the martyr. And, going beyond Lane Fox, it will ask, "What kinds of rhetorical and theological work do these constructions do?"

Even as this book is a history of martyrdom, it does not have a singular trajectory in its sights. Although both ancient and modern commentators have sought to describe martyrdom as a singular practice, ideology, and concept, a glimpse behind the rhetoric of uniformity will reveal striking diversity. It might be proposed that these different ideologies are mere variations on a theme and that they hold in common the view that suffering and martyrdom are good, but even this statement will be shown to oversimplify the manifold ways in which suffering and martyrdom were viewed. At the same time as this book is interested in the diversity of ancient thought and practice, it is also committed to a reexamination of the historical evidence for these ideologies. In contemporary scholarship there is a lingering unspoken commitment to traditional dating of the acts of the martyrs. The majority of texts discussed in this work were adjudged authentic eyewitness accounts by nineteenth- and early-twentieth-century scholars and were dated on the basis of the events that they purported to record. If a text was deemed authentic, it was presumed to have been composed shortly after the death of the martyr it described. In recent decades, there has been a marked shift in scholarly attention from a focus on historical martyrs (what martyrs said and did) to an interest in what early Christians thought about martyrs. Academic skepticism about the ability to speak positively about historical martyrs has given way to an increased focus on what ideas about martyrs can tell us about early Christianity.[64] Yet despite this new set of interests, many scholars continue to use traditional dates for the acts of the martyrs in order to assess early Christian views of martyrdom. This methodology is somewhat problematic. The traditional dates for these accounts relied on the assumption that these were authentic, eyewitness reports. If this assumption is to be abandoned, then the dates of these key texts and the history of martyrdom that they form need to be reappraised. In describing the way in which martyrdom is expressed in various locations, therefore, this book also undertakes a reconsideration of the nature of our literary evidence.

Chapter 1 contains a survey of the intellectual, cultural, religious, and literary traditions that serve as analogs to the ideologies of martyrdom and whose influence is felt, directly or indirectly and to a greater or lesser extent, in writings about the martyrs. The concatenation of these traditions should not be taken to mean that they are determinative for the emergence of any particular martyrdom account or ideology, but rather that they provide us with a sense of the intellectual and cultural reservoir that sustained the early Christian imagination. Some of these cultural influences, most notably the memory of the trial of Socrates and the accounts of the deaths of the Maccabees, have been posited by scholars as the intellectual origins of Christian martyrdom. In ascertaining which cultural and intellectual forces flowed into Christian martyrdom, we do not have to appoint one specific text (for example, 2 and 4 Maccabees), idea (noble death), or figure (Socrates or Jesus) as regent over subsequent ideologies of martyrdom. As we will see in the following chapters, different ideologies utilized different values, concepts, and reading traditions to shape their presentation of the martyr.

Chapter 2 tackles the church in Asia Minor, the traditional birthplace of martyrdom. The discussion begins with an examination of the dating of the *Martyrdom of Polycarp* and the influence—or lack of influence—that this account exerted on second-century discussions of death. It argues that whatever the date of this tradition, the *Martyrdom of Polycarp* did not initiate "the era of Christian martyrdom." Fascinating, sophisticated, and informative though it is, the *Martyrdom of Polycarp* is neither typical nor prototypical. The narrative plays a disproportionate role in histories of martyrdom, for even if it is the earliest martyrdom account, no fewer than seven other martyrdom accounts have been dated between 157 and 205 CE.[65] Stylistically and ideologically these accounts differ widely from the *Martyrdom of Polycarp,* and yet they have failed to leave a comparable imprint on evolutionary accounts of martyrdom.

Chapter 3 follows the epistolary tracks of Paul and Ignatius to Rome and the heart of the imperial monster of Revelation. Yet second-century Roman martyr acts preserve not a church of apocalyptic warriors, but rather the discourses of Christian philosophers. The steady, Stoic, dogmatic martyrdom accounts of Justin and others contest contemporary philosophical notions of the good life and portray martyrdom as an integral part of the contemplative life. This philosophical martyrdom, we will see, relied heavily on the exemplar of the noble death of the philosopher and functioned as part of early Christian philosophical discourse.

Chapter 4 moves to Gaul, from the center to the margins of the Roman empire, and examines the famed *Letter of the Churches of Vienne and Lyons* in dialogue with the writings of (in)famous heresiologist Irenaeus of Lyons. While neither Irenaeus nor the *Letter of the Churches of Vienne and Lyons* can be as securely tied to Gaul as scholars have claimed, both reflect a distinctive theological perspective and view of martyrdom. The *Letter of the Churches of Vienne and Lyons* demonstrates how the charisma of the martyrs could be harnessed for the promotion of church unity and the denouncement of heresy and exemplifies the way in which martyrs could be used to form not only the Christian self, but the church writ large.

Chapter 5 travels south to Scillium and Carthage in proconsular North Africa, the home of the Scillitan martyrs, Tertullian, and the much-loved Perpetua. It argues that martyrdom in Carthage is distinct from the types of martyrdom found in Gaul, Asia Minor, and Rome. The high esteem in which Perpetua is held and the visionary flavor of her martyr act has led to a caricature of martyrdom as a subset of apocalyptic literature. This chapter argues that while Carthaginian martyrdom literature reflects an apocalyptic worldview, there is little evidence to suggest that this feature is a universal characteristic of martyrdom or that martyrdom literature was more or less apocalyptic than any other Christian genre.

Chapter 6 visits Alexandria and yet journeys away from geographical types to the larger discourse of martyrdom in the early church. It examines the ways in which both ancient Christians and modern scholars have distilled an essential form of martyrdom that is extracted from the cruder perspectives of heterodox anti-martyrdom and enthusiastic voluntary martyrdom. Traditionally, martyrdom has been seen as a tool of ancient orthodoxy and has been tied to the doctrinal belief in the resurrection of the body. A closer examination of the evidence reveals that martyrdom and the discourse of martyrdom were not exclusively the domain of ancient orthodoxy (if such a thing exists). This chapter uses the writings of Clement of Alexandria to deconstruct the scholarly binary between orthodox pro-martyrdom and Gnostic anti-martyrdom attitudes in the early church and suggest that the discourse of martyrdom was a valuable tool in ancient claims to authority. It further seeks to reset debates about "true martyrdom" within broader claims to authority, doctrinal discussions, and ecclesiastical scuffles in the early church.

The arrangement of this book into discrete geographically and sociohistorically grounded ideologies is an attempt to do justice to regional variations of Christianity and should not be taken too literally.[66] I do not intend to reproduce either a false sense of geographical isolation or the rigid provincial boundaries that this organization presumes. While the presence of constellations of texts, ideas, and individuals in various locations around the ancient Mediterranean prompts me to describe ancient martyrdom in this way, these martyrological types were not hermetically sealed from one another. The cartographer produces a two-dimensional representation of the world that does not always account for human interaction. These representations do not adequately reproduce the social networks that unfurled across the empire.[67] Nor do they reflect patterns of everyday life that relied on interactions between merchants from different cities and countries, the dissemination of imperial coinage, or just the simple act of walking across unmarked borders to fetch water.

Geographical units should not be taken to mean that these groups—and the ideologies that they produced—operated in isolation. Christian social networks, patterns of pilgrimage and missionary activity, and the art of letter writing united Christian communities and networks across the empire. Mercantile exchange yielded a similar effect as a flow of people and ideas washed in and out of major urban centers, trading ideas, anecdotes, and practices and trafficking in ideologies of martyrdom. Physical geography is webbed with social networks, navigated by correspondence, plotted by travel, and reimagined by ancient cartographers. The focus on geography and types of martyrdom does not suppose mutually exclusive models or concepts, but, rather, constellations of ideas that intersect and interact. Cultural exchange between these regions and—at the frontiers of the Roman empire—with the "barbarian" lands outside of the empire contributed to the shaping of the discourse of martyrdom.[68] The conceptual map that informs my study grounds itself in regional, largely urban, centers but is sketched with the social networks that connected these various micro-Christianities.[69]

Writing historiography almost invariably involves a commitment to chronology and the passage of time. We trace the development and movement of ideas over a framework of years, decades, and centuries. Although we can safely assume that ideas about martyrdom are always fluid and dynamic, constantly reshaped by thinkers, readers, and teachers, we should beware of assuming that time always forces intellectual progress. The temptation to overlay time, and especially its passage, with the development of ideas is beguiling. But ideas do not develop everywhere at a steady rate, plodding uniformly toward an unseen goal; they are not dreamed by some disembodied agent.[70] Personalities, readers, and communities engineer the development of ideas because, as Descartes taught us, people think ideas. *Chronos* is not *Zeitgeist;* ideas develop over time, but time itself does not necessitate progress. If time is implicitly equated with progress, we can be misled about the way that ideas about martyrdom were produced by different groups of early Christians. The ideology of martyrdom does not "progress" or "develop" merely because time marches on. To assume otherwise is to become an intellectual time traveler, forcing development in the absence of evidence.

Just as there were different types or ideologies of martyrdom, so also the identity of the martyr was shaped by and interacted with other identities and social statuses. Martyrs are not just martyrs; martyrs are women, priests, soldiers, philosophers, writers, and lectors. As early as von Harnack the characterization of the soldier martyr, the *miles Christi,* as a martyrological stereotype was well established. In a similar vein, since the 1970s scholars have noted the distinctive portrayal in the martyr acts of their female protagonists, most notably Perpetua, Felicitas, Blandina, and Thecla but also, if to a lesser extent, Agathonike, Agape, Irene, and Chione.[71] This approach exemplifies not only the ways in which identity is reshaped and gender redefined in the martyr acts, but also suggests that we can, and indeed should, push this kind of analysis further. The relative social statuses of slaves, bishops, philosophers, teachers, deacons, and lectors might also affect the presentation of the martyr. The philosophical debate between the Stoic Rusticus and the philosopher-martyr Justin in the *Acts of Justin and His Companions* is appropriate—in a manner appealing to Aristotle—to their rank and occupation (Aristotle, *Poetics* 1454a). The theater of the courtroom affords Justin the opportunity to provide a précis of his own work to his Roman accusers. Likewise, the bibliophilia of the Coptic martyr Timothy in the *Martyrdom of Timothy and Maura* is illuminated by his status as lector.

Yet even as some statuses are reinforced by the narratives, others are reversed or transgressed. The ugly slave girl Blandina of the *Letter of the Churches of Vienne and Lyons* becomes the leader and source of consolation for a whole group of martyrs, rising from her lowly position as a sexually undesirable slave to the head of this elite group. Early Christian narratives, and especially early Christian martyr acts, constructed a particular kind of identity vis-à-vis other groups.[72] This identity, however, was multifaceted. The manner in which a martyr was presented as an ideal Christian or ideal martyr was augmented by the manner in which that martyr was also portrayed as an ideal man, woman, member of the clergy, Roman, or soldier. Even if these other identities were sometimes subsumed by the portrait of the ideal Christian or martyr, their effect is subtly felt. In sum, martyrs are not incarnations of the ideology of martyrdom, and the details of their lives that shape the idiosyncrasies of their presentations affect the ideologies of martyrdom themselves.

I

Cultural Contexts:
The Good Death and
the Self-Conscious Sufferer

For much of the Christian era, martyrdom was viewed as particular to Christianity and as an indication of Christianity's unique possession of religious truth. If Christians alone were prepared to die for their beliefs, it was thought, then there must be something special about Christianity. The widespread literary caricature of early Christians as fodder for lions in the Colosseum contributed to the notion that Christianity invented martyrdom, an idea that was in part a product, as already discussed, of the philological debt that martyrdom owed to the Greek *martys*.[1] Whatever the reason, until relatively recently Christianity held both a patent on and monopoly over the concept of martyrdom. With the advent of higher criticism in the nineteenth century, however, Christianity's ingenuity began to be called into question. Within the study of martyrdom, antecedents for Christian martyrs have been posited in the figures of Socrates, the Maccabean martyrs, and the so-called pagan martyrs of Alexandria. In some respects, these attempts to locate the origins of the concept of martyrdom in pre-Christian traditions parallel and intersect with the efforts of members of the *religionsgeschichtliche Schule,* who trawled the writings of the ancient world tracing the history of religious thought from Mesopotamia to Constantinople. For some scholars, such pre-Christian examples serve as evidence that martyrdom is not an exclusively Christian practice and that there were others—most notably the Maccabees—

whose conduct should properly be called "martyrdom," even if the title "martyr" had not been conceived or applied to them at the time of their deaths.[2]

On the other side of this debate stand those scholars who posit a concrete divide between, on one hand, "pagan" and Jewish attitudes to death and, on the other, Christian martyrdom. These pre-Christian examples may have been influential, they argue, but only with Christianity do we find "real" martyrdom.[3] To take G. W. Bowersock as our example: "Martyrdom was not something that the ancient world had seen from the beginning. What we can observe in the second, third, and fourth centuries of our era is something entirely new. Of course, in earlier ages principled and courageous persons, such as Socrates at Athens or the three Jews in the fiery furnace of Nebuchadnezzar, had provided glorious examples of resistance to tyrannical authority and painful suffering before unjust judges. But never before had such courage been absorbed into a conceptual system of posthumous recognition and anticipated reward, nor had the very word martyrdom existed as the name for this system."[4] Bowersock appeals both to the notorious rewards of martyrdom and to the linguistic specificity of Christian use of the word *martyr*. He, like many others, focuses on the linguistic transformation of the term *martys*, illustrating the extent to which the debate over pre-Christian antecedents revolves around the axis of linguistic development. For those scholars who value linguistic origins more highly than conceptual or functional definitions, martyrdom begins with Christianity.

Judith Perkins's work radically alters the terms of the discussion. Rather than focusing on literary parallels, linguistic *Vorlagen,* or even instances of martyrdom, Perkins probes the cultural significance of suffering in the ancient world. Whereas Brox and Bowersock have posited a radical division between simply "yearning for death" and practicing martyrdom, Perkins refocuses the question on suffering itself. If, for Bowersock, "a happy ending . . . hardly constitutes anything like martyrdom," Perkins demonstrates that for many, death was the happy ending.[5] Perkins's work is instrumental because she reconfigures the scholarly understanding of suffering in the ancient world. She suggests that before we evaluate the novelty, ingenuity, or significance of martyrdom among ancient Christians, we should first consider the cultural construction of death in the ancient world.

The focus on and description of cultural constructions of death in the ancient world in the present chapter might suggest that these ideas served as the fertile intellectual soil from which Christian martyrdom sprang. The parable of the sower should not be taken, however, as the model for the emergence of the discourse and practice of martyrdom. Scholarly efforts to isolate martyrdom and describe its relationship to pre-Christian ideas and practices often employ language that envisions a particular kind of association between the two. The use of *tradition* implies that a later author has reused an earlier concept or text in a manner that is unreflected.[6] In a sense, the earlier part of the tradition has hoisted itself on the later. Similarly, the idea of *influence* presupposes a backward orientation that views the source of an idea as determinative for its meaning.[7] The term *reception* presupposes the existence of bounded religious and cultural entities.[8] Yet, as many have noted, "Jewish," "Greek," "Roman," and "Christian" were hardly distinct identity categories in the first two centuries of the Christian era; the use of *reception* therefore obscures the instability, fluidity, and complexity of ancient religious groups by producing a compartmentalized view of the ancient world. Moreover, even after their composition, texts were continually interpreted, edited, and reproduced. Thus, the death of Socrates in 399 BCE, narrated in the first place by Plato, had been repeatedly adapted and reinterpreted before its use by early Christians. The regard in which Socrates had been held by generations of Greeks and Romans contributed to the composite portrait of Socrates viewed by the early Christians.[9] These multiple attendant interpretations are often obscured by studies of textual reception and conceptual influence. The methodological paradigm for describing the relationship between Christian martyrdom and preexisting concepts should not be simply one of influence, tradition, or text and reception; attention must also be given to strategies of interpretation and to the ways in which these interpretations re-create the text.

In addition to the inherent difficulties of describing Christianity "in context," we face the question of how Christian authors constructed Christian martyrdom in relation to non-Christian examples. Early Christians did not necessarily see dying for Christ as unequivocally new and distinctive. Even if the arrival of Christ was deemed to have inaugurated a new age in human history, some writers self-consciously represented themselves as standing in continuity with those who had gone before them. The opening of the *Passion of Perpetua and Felicitas* compares its subjects to the "ancient examples," the biblical heroes who served as models of good conduct and sources of consolation and comfort (*Passio* 1). The text situates the martyrs and the Christian audience within a history of dying exempla. The effect of such invocations is not only to reconfigure the audience's understanding of Perpetua, but also to reshape their notions of the heroes of the past invoked under the rubric "ancient examples." The comparison draws these figures into a group, binds them together, and reinterprets them in light of Perpetua's narrative. Just as the interpretation of Perpetua is altered by her association with ancient examples, the ancient examples are reframed by the Perpetua narrative. Each group is reinterpreted in light of the other.

At the same time, however, authors such as Justin Martyr use martyrdom as a way of positing a disconnect between Christians and others. Justin's proposition that heretical groups (*haeresis*) do not have martyrs as the Christians do is a rhetorically powerful move that forces a wedge between Christianity and its opponents.[10] For both the editor of the *Passion of Perpetua* and Justin Martyr, martyrdom is a mark of orthodoxy that distinguishes Christianity. The task of isolating martyrdom as distinctively Christian is for Justin as much about reifying Christian identity and dislocating "Christians" from "heretics" as it is about the nature of martyrdom. For the scholar, the task is both to locate the textual contexts for the reformation of ancient valuations of death and to trace the intertextual strategies at work in the use of these earlier texts. The art of connecting or disconnecting Christian martyrdom from non-Christian examples is a rhetorical strategy. The scholarly task of assessing the relationship between Christian martyrdom and everything else is distinct from this ancient Christian agenda. The uncritical reproduction of ancient taxonomies often obscures their rhetorical function.

What follows is a brief survey of the variety of ways in which violent death was constructed in non-Christian texts in the period of our study. The constraints of this book do not afford the opportunity to examine at length the intricacies of the texts and practices that are merely sketched here. The distinctions drawn between Greek, Roman, and Jewish are not intended to signify cultural separation; they are merely heuristic devices that provide various points of entry into the tapestry of ancient thought. There is something artificial and misleading about dividing Jewish ideas from Greek and Roman ideas. Subject groupings and side-headings reinforce traditional divisions where cross-pollination and permeability should exist. The influence of Greek thought on Jewish art, literature, architecture, and life is well documented, even in first-century Palestine. Moreover, the composition of Jewish literature during the Hellenistic period owes much to the ideals, language, and stylistic forms of Greek literature. The similarities between these Jewish and Greek texts and their mutual influence will be readily apparent. Links between non-Christian and early-Christian literature will be intimated here; subsequent chapters will provide further opportunities to explore these resonances in more detail.

Greek and Roman Ideas about Death

The ancient Greek and Roman love of death is well documented in classical literature and modern historiography. This "noble death tradition," as it is frequently called, is often associated with philosophy.[11] Certainly, the question "what makes a death good?" produced stimulating dinner party conversation among the intellectual elite where it permeated discussions about honor, masculinity, and patriotism.[12] Ideas about and examples of good death were not confined, however, to the academy: they are implicit in the rituals surrounding sacrifice, in which a compliant sacrificial animal was a good omen; in the dramatic deaths of the heroes and heroines of Greek theater and epic poetry; and in the anecdotes of the historians. Rather than providing a survey of Greek and Roman understandings of noble death, we here tease out some of the ways in which these views can illuminate our study of early Christian ideologies of martyrdom.

DEATH MAKES THE MAN

In an ambiguously apocryphal story from Herodotus's *Histories* (ca. 425 BCE), Solon, the beloved founder of the Athenian laws, tells the hubristic Croesus that "no man can be called happy until he is dead."[13] The prophetic warning is as much a statement about the role of death as it is a foreshadowing of Croesus's unhappy demise. Solon speaks of both the fragility of humankind on the unforgiving wheel of fortune and also the instrumental role that death plays in the evaluation of a person's life. Neither Herodotus nor Solon can be credited with the sentiment that lies under this pithy turn of phrase. The pages of recorded Greek history are marked with the idea that a good death brings glory, memorialization, and immortality. The Homeric heroes of the Trojan War fight for honor and everlasting fame. As he slaughters the Trojan princes, Achilles schools them, and the captivated Homeric audience, that to die well they must not "be piteous about it"; they must stand courageously, greeting the death that waits for every man.[14] Even though the *Odyssey*'s Achilles bemoans his fate in the underworld, it was his initial decision to choose a brief, fiery, glorious death that enthralled ancient audiences (*Odyssey* 11.489–91).

Even Pericles's famed funeral oration in Thucydides's *History of the Peloponnesian War* plays on contemporary notions of death as the measure of a man. As he exhorts the mourning Athenians to return to war with renewed vigor, Pericles commends their dearly departed, saying that by the "offering of their lives . . . they each of them individually received that renown which never grows old" (2.43),[15] and he contrasts the random accidents of birth with the "glorious death" of the Athenian soldiers (2.44). In death, writes Thucydides, the heroes have "the whole world for their tomb," their epitaph enshrined unwritten in the heart of every breast (2.43). The deaths of the heroic dead are memorialized in the hearts of their compatriots. The relationship between death and memory underscored by Thucydides is typical of the period. The anxiety that surrounds slipping from life into obscure death is here soothed; dying well secures one's memorialization.

The good death also provided an opportunity to prove, decisively, one's worth and manliness. Dying well with dignified self-control was long considered the mark of a good soldier. As Achilles says to Lykaon, when the Trojan prince clasps his knees and begs for mercy: "Come, friend, face your death, you too. And why are you so piteous about it?" (*Iliad* 21.122–23). Courage in the face of death is expected of heroes. The notion of manliness implicit in Homer's formulation of the good death is one of self-control and courage, in contrast to cowardly displays on the battlefield that are associated with womanly tears and girlish displays of emotion. We might note Menelaus's rebuke to the Achaean troops who had greeted his encouragement to embrace their destiny and honor won in death with a shameful, cowardly silence. Menelaus responds by calling the soldiers "women, not men" (*Iliad* 7.95). Apuleius's Fotis also emphasizes the importance of masculinity in battle and death when she instructs Lucius to "fight vigorously, for I will not retreat before you or turn my back on you. Stiffen up and close in for a vigorous frontal assault—if you are a man! Slay, for you are about to die" (*Metamorphoses* 2.17). Seneca's Achilles, likewise, elects to assume the mantle of manhood; he "chose the sword and professed himself a man" (*Troades* 214).

The idea that dying a courageous death is both a sign of virtue and a mark of manliness is related to the wider discussion of virtue in antiquity. The content of virtue is theorized by Greek and Roman philosophers and moralists, who articulate taxonomies of virtue in which the association of masculinity and self-mastery is everywhere implied. The relationship is explicit in Plato, who lists prudence, justice, manliness, and self-control as the four principal virtues (*Phaed.* 69C), and is implicit in condemnations of excessive mourning as "womanly" behavior (see Seneca, *Letters* 63.13; the Plutarchian *Consolation of the Passions* 102E; Marcus Aurelius, *Med.* 1.1–2). Plutarch labels anger unmanly and connects it to women (*On Controlling Anger* 475B), and Seneca agrees that anger is a womanish and childish weakness (*On Anger* 1.20). In the writings of Seneca's younger contemporary Musonius Rufus, a philosophical moratorium on anger appears complete; only condemnable slaves, women, and barbarians, he writes, express themselves in such a way.[16] For Plutarch, effeminacy and a lack of discipline go hand in hand with other forms of conduct that he counterposes with the self-control of the virtuous man (*Inim. util.* 88C). Certainly, for some authors not emotion itself, but excessive emotion is the larger problem. The salient point is, however, that *virtus* and manliness are inextricably linked. The association is ingrained on a philological level, as Craig Williams notes, for etymologically *virtus* is "nothing more than 'manliness.' "[17] This association of courage, virtue, death, and masculinity meant that the notion of dying well was itself gendered. To die a good death, in or out of battle, entailed dying with self-control. In other words, it meant taking it like a man.[18]

The gendering of self-control provided a standard for the evaluation of the heroism of one's subjects. In Roman culture men were not born, they were made. It was the exercise of masculinity that distinguished the born male (*mas*) and the human (*homo*) from the man (*vir*). For the Roman Stoic orator Cicero the distinction is apparent in the tendency of the natural man (*homo*) to reject unnecessary pain that the heroic man (*vir*) is able and proud to withstand (*Tusc.* 2.22.53). Cicero relates, by way of example, the story of one Gaius Marius, "a rustic man, but a man indeed" (*rusticanus vir, sed plane vir*), who refused to be placed in restraints while an operation was carried out on his leg for varicose veins. After this display of valor, Gaius insisted on an operation on his second, unaffected leg. Gaius Marius's display of fortitude embodies the philosophical division between the natural mere man (*homo*) and the heroic man (*vir*) whose conduct surpasses his natural state.[19] Cicero's example resonates strongly with the account of the death of the Christian bishop Polycarp, whose refusal of restraints and easy embrace of suffering mark him as a hero. The heavenly voice that urges Polycarp to "play the man" (*Mart. Pol.* 9.1) is greeted with a muscular display of Christianity. Dying nobly became the prime location for the display of *virtus* and, thus, of masculinity. In the Roman period, as Catharine Edwards has demonstrated, as an opportunity to demonstrate self-restraint, courage, and clear-headedness, the noble death came to supplant military victory as the finest articulation of virtue.[20]

DEATH AND THE MAIDEN

That dying well was a masculine art did not mean that women were excluded from noble death. Even among women—their powers normally limited to the bedroom and the household—dying well can transform oneself into a model of patriotism or heroism. Perkins argues that early Christians constructed death as a kind of "happy ending" and that by adapting and subverting the conventions of the romance novel, they wedded Christians to death. Yet the use of marital and romantic imagery to describe a longing for death and to subvert traditional marriage is not unprecedented in Greek literature. Antigone, the much-loved heroine of Sophocles's Theban play, eschews her fiancé, Haemon, in order to become a bride of death: "Not mine the hyemenal chant, not mine the bridal song / For I, a bride, to Acheron belong" (*Antigone* 758–59). At the conclusion of the play the messenger describes the chamber in which Antigone is sealed as "the cavern of Death's bride" (1134) in which she is found with her (bridal) veil wrapped around her neck as a noose (1152); her relationship with death is consummated in the raising of the bridal veil. While the use of marital language continues throughout the play, Antigone's affair with death remains ambiguous. Her early speeches invoke the language of romance, but as events unfold her tone grows embittered. As she approaches death and thinks on how she has cast aside marriage and motherhood, she grieves over the "bridal-chamber" of her death and the marriage joys lost (821–60). Her initial passion for death, betrayed by the brashness of her conduct, gives way, in the final analysis, to sorrow and mourning. The romantic imagery is resurrected and reversed at the conclusion of the play in the words of the messenger, whose tale re-dresses Antigone in bridal attire, joined this time to her self-immolating fiancé, Haemon, to whom she is wedded in the house of death. Their final embrace is as much *petit mort* as *mort*. Yet Antigone is no Juliet; she remains, to some extent, wedded to death. Death, in this case, makes the maiden a bride.

The notion of death as romantic partner resurfaces in the plays of Euripides, whose delicate heroines willingly go to their deaths in order to secure safe and effective passage for their countrymen.[21] In *Iphigeneia at Aulis* the hapless protagonist, at last resigned to dying, embraces death as her partner, saying: "Take me, kill me, and bring down Troy. That will be my wedding, my children, the meaning of my life. Mother, it is the Greeks who must rule Barbarians" (1390–95). Iphigeneia's understanding of her death reproduces and subverts the conventions of matrimony: in her own death she will become a bride and her offspring will, naturally, be the death and destruction that the Greeks bring to the Trojans. The virgin princess Polyxena (Euripides, *Hecuba* 568–70) modestly arranges her dress to cover herself as Achilles's son Neoptolemus slits her throat.[22] The topos of the sacrifice of the heroic virgin had a dramatic draw.

In ancient Rome, stories of the deaths of notable women also drew a crowd, but for different reasons. Histories of Rome's founding build their narratives on the heroic suicide of Lucretia.[23] According to Livy (1.57–60), Collatinus, Lucretia's husband, and Sextus Tarquinus, the son of the Etruscan king of Rome, make a wager as to which of their wives is the more virtuous. Upon returning to Rome they find Tarquin's wife drinking and Lucretia overseeing loom work, a particularly virtuous womanly pastime.[24] Tarquin, having lost his wager, is seized by desire for Lucretia on account of both her appearance and her virtue. He returns and threatens her with death and shame if she does not comply with his sexual demands. After being raped, Lucretia summons her father and her husband and tells them what has happened. She holds herself (her *animus*) to be innocent, even if her body has been violated, but nonetheless elects to kill herself using the traditional Roman method—a dagger plunged into the heart. Her family drive Tarquin from the city and place Lucretia's body on display in the forum at Collatia as a symbol of the brutality of Tarquinian rule. The event is intertwined with a political narrative: Lucretia's rape is an embodiment of Tarquin's tyranny, and her "sacrifice" precipitates the founding of the Roman republic.[25]

To modern readers, Lucretia's suicide may seem befuddling. Although she would rather die than suffer the ignominy of rape, her good name is not at risk: her family believes her story and view her as innocent. Her death, though, functions as the ultimate proof of her innocence. Utilizing the language of legal testimony, Lucretia pronounces "death shall be my witness" (*mors testis erit*) and says that she dies so that impure women will be unable to use her as an excuse (*nec ulla inpudica Lucretiae exemplo vivet*). Livy's account was composed shortly before female adultery became a crime under Julian law in 18 BCE. The story of Lucretia's rape therefore functions as a warning to other women and as a *bonum exemplum* of female chastity.[26] In his account of her rape, Ovid calls Lucretia a lady of manly spirit (*animi matrone virilis*) (*Festivals* 2.847) and holds her up as a model of chastity (*pudicitia*). Martial language is employed by Valerius Maximus to describe Lucretia's virtue; she is a military leader on behalf of Roman virtue (*dux Romanae pudicitiae*), a term used almost exclusively of men.

In a similar way, masculine valor in the face of pain is displayed by the Roman heroines Porcia and Arria. In 43 BCE, Porcia, the wife of Caesar-slayer Brutus and daughter of Cato, consumed live coals upon hearing of her husband's death. According to Valerius Maximus, Porcia imitated the manly death of her father with a woman's courage (Val. Max. 4.6.5). Following his involvement in a political conspiracy, Arria's husband was condemned to death and purportedly hesitated to take his own life; his wife boldly took the dagger and plunged it into her abdomen, protesting that it did not hurt her. Arria's bravery and her claim that she felt no pain, reported by both Pliny and Martial, turn her into an exemplum of masculine noble death. The physiological site of death blows for men is usually the abdomen, accentuating Arria's masculine courage and implicitly condemning her husband for his inability to act.[27] In the cases of both Porcia and Arria, female bravery is used to indict further the conduct of male family members: Arria's masculine pose with the dagger invokes the traditional way to execute men; Porcia's ability to swallow live coals creates a new form of execution, outdoes her father's courage in death, and overshadows her husband. The female figure's ability to exercise *virtus* diminishes and feminizes the accomplishments of her conspiratorial male relatives. In these cases the courage of the women serves as a shaming device to condemn and emasculate the men.

The valorization of the self-sacrifice and the *virtus* of women does not necessarily imply, even in these examples, that women transcended the social structures that constrained them. Deaths of women in literature, and suicidal deaths in particular, often are less examples of heroism than they are of victimization. The focus on the corpse and the casting of death as spectacle meant that the bodies of these women were on narrative display. Similarly, the author of the *Passion of Perpetua and Felicitas* repeatedly lingers on the bodies of the young women (Felicitas's breasts dripping with milk, Perpetua's hair and thighs being covered to protect her modesty) and highlights the crowd's desire to watch the execution of the martyrs, who are brought back into the arena to be viewed as they die (*Passio* 21.7). The audience is invited to drink in the spectacle of these delicate, attractive bodies. Analysis by Elisabeth Bronfen has demonstrated that for the ancient male reader, the description of dead female bodies may have served to "other" death itself, by presenting a reassuring image of death set at a distance.[28] The voyeuristic appreciation of the female corpse may speak more about objectification than masculinization.

The influence of Iphigeneia, Polyxena, and Antigone is discernible in the depiction of female martyrs in early Christianity. Female martyrs composed a significant proportion of early Christian martyrs and generated some of the most thought-provoking and dearly beloved narratives. Few can forget the moving "diary" of Perpetua and her account of her relationship with her family members, Felicitas's labor pains, or the slave girl Blandina's triumphant leadership of the martyrs of Lyons. The presentation of the female martyr and the manner in which her actions undermine, transgress, and reinscribe Roman family values and gender norms have rightly occupied a generation of scholars.[29] The gendering of biologically female martyrs in their trials, contests, and visions has been variously interpreted as instances of masculinization,[30] glorification of the feminine,[31] and a movement from one pole to another.[32] Placed within the context of Greek drama, the actions of the female martyr conform in many important ways to Greek dramatic topoi of female resistance. Thus, if the portrayal of female martyrs functions as resistance to Roman familial and social structures, it is stylized using Greco-Roman dramatic and literary conventions. Perpetua's conduct in the tribunal and arena reproduces the iconic image of the tragic heroine at odds with family and culture. Just as Antigone eloped with Acheron, so too Perpetua seeks union with Christ as wife of Christ (*matrona Christi*). At the same time, the masculine suicide of the Roman heroine was well established: Arria and

Porcia are level-headed and stout, and Porcia's ability to withstand the blade is a gesture to ancient medical theories that viewed men as more capable of dealing with pain. Lucretia presents a more complicated example as her depiction vacillates between the masculine and the feminine. As demure, chaste weaver, she is the embodiment of feminine virtue; as emboldened, rational self-killer, she exemplifies masculine courage. Yet Lucretia is only temporarily masculinized for, in the end, her manly suicide by plunging a concealed dagger into her own heart reads—in a text voyeuristically preoccupied by the form of her body—as penetration. Ambiguous gendering is an element in non-Christian illustrations of the deaths of women. If the art of dying well is masculine, death remains in many respects feminine.[33]

SOCRATES

Many philosophers met with sticky ends, but the death of Socrates carried a cultural weight unmatched by those of his peers and successors. Socrates has been called "the world's first recorded martyr,"[34] his legend was shaped by a succession of disciples and imitators, and his image was transformed by his biographers into a multifaceted figure molded by hearsay, slander, and adoration. As with all martyrs, Socrates's malleability makes it difficult to divorce man from myth.[35] Jacques Derrida's *Post Card,* a meditation on a medieval depiction of Plato standing behind Socrates and directing his actions, illustrates the extent to which Socrates was his students' shadow puppet.[36] Various aspects of the trial and death of Socrates are recorded in multiple Platonic dialogues. The *Apology* narrates the details of the trial; the *Crito* relays a conversation about whether or not it is ethical for Socrates to escape prison and go into exile; and the *Phaedo* records the final day of Socrates's life, his conversations and his consumption of hemlock. Additionally, Xenophon's *Apology*—his own version of Socrates's trial—covers some of the same ground, albeit with a somewhat more triumphalist perspective. The multiplicity of views even in antiquity is hard to sort. To these portraits of Socrates can be added the less appreciative satire *The Clouds* by the playwright Aristophanes and the now-lost pamphlet *Prosecution of Socrates* by Polycrates (ca. 393 BCE), which purportedly contained a speech delivered during Socrates's trial and denounced him as an enemy of democracy. The third-century CE biography by Diogenes Laertius provides evidence of the growth of Socrates's legend in its collection of traditions from Damon of Alexander, Favorinus, Demetrius of Byzantium, and Antisthenes (*Lives* 2.18–47).

The accounts of Socrates's death articulate not only the legal basis for his execution and the events leading up to his death, but also his approach to death and dying. A plethora of scholars have asserted or attempted to discern the historical cause of Socrates's death, which they attribute variously to political unrest, social subversion, and personal animosity.[37] Socrates's apologia during his trial can hardly be said to be a valiant effort to escape execution. On the contrary, in his portrayal by Xenophon, Socrates appears to be deliberately seeking his conviction by a display of arrogance (*Apology* 1–2). In Plato's account, Socrates takes a similarly antagonistic, almost belligerent approach to his accusers, even suggesting that for his punishment he be fed at public expense for the rest of his life. Whatever the causes of the execution of Socrates, however, the important point for our purposes is the example he sets for subsequent generations and the manner of his death.

In the course of the trial and in those dialogues set in the period before his death, Socrates makes a number of statements about death, dying well, and the world to come. He insists that death is not to be feared but rather welcomed with some degree of joy as "a man who has really devoted his life to philosophy should be cheerful in the face of death" (*Phaed.* 64A). According to Plato, Socrates was a noble person (*Phaed.* 58D) unfairly charged with atheism (*Euth.* 3B), who refused to flee death in order to go into exile (*Phaed.* 98E–99A). He embraced death calmly, even insisting on silence (*Phaed.* 117E), and became, in death, a model for other followers. In the moments immediately preceding his death, Socrates performed a quasi-religious ritual: in an echo of sacrifice, he suggested pouring out some of the poison as a libation to the gods and offered a prayer as he drank the liquid (*Phaed.* 117B–C); his final, possibly ironic, statement was that his disciples should offer a sacrifice to Asclepius, the god of healing (*Phaed.* 118).

In his manner of dying, Socrates exhibited many of the qualities respected in men. During his trial and the days leading up to his execution, he displayed an intellectual detachment from his fate, berating his wife and friends for their emotional and irrational conduct (*Phaed.* 60A, 117E). In the *Apology* the focus of his attention is not on death itself but on virtue: he states, "a man who is doing good for anything ought not to calculate the chance of living or dying; he ought only to consider whether in doing anything he is doing right or wrong" (*Apology* 28B). In the *Phaedo,* as his mind turns to death, Socrates reveals that dying well is the *habitus* of the philosopher: "the true philosophers practice dying, and death is less fearful to them than to any other man" (*Phaed.* 67E). In his final, methodically planned moments, Socrates converses cheerfully with his tearful jailor and allows adequate time to bathe before taking the poison. Socrates's composure has struck some commentators as sterile.[38] This assessment is grounded in modern constructions of masculinity; Socrates's passive countenance, as we have seen, casts him as the classical embodiment of masculine self-control. While his friends weep tears like women,

Socrates is composed, arguably joyful. Even this joy, however, is predica[ted on]
rationality, as it is grounded in a well-reasoned argument about death a[nd free]-
dom from the body. Other commentators have cynically argued that Soc[rates's]
death was a necessary part of his mission, for only by dying with full control
of his faculties could he guarantee that he would be both "sorely missed" and
remembered.[39]

One interesting aspect of Socrates's final conversations with his friends is
their discussion of the fate of the soul after death (*Phaed.* 107B–115C). Socrates
offers an extended treatment of the topography of the world, expounding on
the hollows in which humans presently dwell, the true earth above them to
which the souls purified by philosophy ascend, and the lakes of Tartarus and
Acheron in which punishment is exacted. His confidence that a certain kind of
conduct in the face of death will bring him a glorious reward in the afterlife
invokes the tried and tested notion of just recompense in the hereafter. In fact,
this "complex of science, pseudo-science and mythology of which the myth (in
the wider sense) consists, is designed with marvelous skill to support the eschatological doctrine of rewards and punishments."[40] By the exercise of "self-
restraint, justice, courage, freedom, and truth" (*Phaed.* 114E), Socrates hopes
to win a better afterlife. In the *Phaedo*, dying well, that is, displaying those
masculine virtues prized by soldiers and philosophers, secures a postmortem
ascent to the "real earth." The taut association of noble death, merit, and postmortem reward resonates powerfully with early Christian depictions of the
afterlife.

Socrates's death won him many more admirers than he had had in life. The
Stoic philosopher Epictetus describes him as an ideal philosopher, a witness
to truth, and one who refused to make concessions that would ultimately
lead him to betray his ideals.[41] Socrates's dying on principle in many ways
stands as guarantor of the truth of his message. His nonchalant and at times
joyful approach to death earned him admiration from many quarters, not
least from the early Christians.[42]

The ethics of choosing death in preference to life were debated by a number
of prominent ancient philosophers and philosophical schools.[43] The Roman
period presents an array of famous examples of self-killing philosophers, no
doubt influenced by the model of Socrates, most of whom seem to have been
Stoics.[44] The writings of Seneca, for instance, famously extol the merits of
self-killing as the ultimate triumph of an individual over death (*On Providence* 2.9 and *Letter* 71.16). A number of these philosophical examples are
particularly striking in their depiction of the deaths of philosophers at the
hands of oppressive tyrants. According to one tradition, Zeno of Elea died
after becoming involved in a plot against Nearchus, the ruler of Elea. Rather

than reveal the name of any of his accomplices, Zeno first implicated Ne-archus himself and then bit off his own tongue and spat it out at the tyrant in protest. Zeno's actions resisted and subverted Nearchus's attempts to con-trol him (*Lives* 9.25–29). Self-mutilation as strategic resistance was an ele-ment of the philosopher's protest. The contortion of the philosopher's body circumvented the attempts of the tyrant to bend the philosopher's will.

DEATH BEFORE DISHONOR

If death brought glory to the heroes of ancient Greece, it could also serve as an alternative to shame and dishonor. To return briefly to the heroes of Troy, a classic example of such a death is found in the suicide of the Greek hero and warrior Ajax. According to the myths, after the death of Achilles, Ajax and Odysseus fought over who would be awarded Achilles's legendary armor. The decision was eventually made in favor of the articulate Odysseus; at this point the specifics in the various versions of the story diverge. In the permutation known to the poet Pindar, Ajax immediately killed himself out of anger (*Nemean Odes*, 7.26; 8.25 [ca. 467 BCE] and *Isthmian Ode* 4.35 [ca. 473/474 BCE]).[45] Sophocles's slightly later version (ca. 450–430 BCE) is more elaborate: the slighted Ajax attempted to take vengeance on the Greeks by killing them. His plan was foiled, however, by Odysseus and Athena. The goddess drove Ajax mad and prompted him to slaughter a herd of animals that he mistook for his compatriots. When Ajax came, literally, to his senses and realized what he had attempted to do, he killed himself because he was incapable of bearing the shame. Any second thoughts are dispelled by his realization that continuing to live would be cowardice: "It is a shameful thing [*aischron*] to want to live for-ever" (Sophocles, *Ajax* 473).

The notion of death before dishonor and especially the act of choosing death over dishonor persisted into the Roman period. We have already seen the ways in which the suicides of Lucretia, Arria, and Porcia transformed women in danger of being shamed into heroines of Rome. The Romans devel-oped other traditions that articulated self-sacrifice for the nation. The practice of *devotio* (dedication) acted out this value on the battlefield.[46] Livy describes how the Roman commander would dress in his official toga, cover his head, stand on a spear, and hold his hand against his chin as the priest pronounced a formula of *devotio* in which the general dedicated himself and the enemy troops to the gods of the underworld and the goddess of the earth for the ben-efit of Rome and its military forces (Livy, 8.9.4–9). The general would then seek death in battle; that death, in these circumstances, would guarantee mili-tary victory. One important caveat to the ritual was that the commander was able to elect a substitute. Should the substitute fail to be killed, the Romans were obligated to displace the ritual one more time and bury a seven-foot-tall statue and offer a sacrifice in the place of the general (Livy, 8.10.11–14). Altruistic self-offering was a way of winning honor but served also as a test of loyalty and means of avoiding shame. In 68 CE, following the death of Nero, Otho committed suicide both as a means of avoiding public humiliation and as a way of protecting his troops. In his rendition of the story, Dio Cassius construes Otho's suicide as a noble conclusion to an otherwise shameful life and states that it was better for one to perish on behalf of many than for many to perish for one (*Roman History* 63.13.10–15). The self-offering of the leader for the greater good of the many echoes in the literature of the Jesus movement (John 11:50). It fostered not just an economy of self-sacrifice, but also a notion of embodied leadership that held strategic self-destruction at its core.

Jewish Ideas About Death

After the death of Alexander the Great in 323 BCE, Palestine came under the control of the Ptolemies and Seleucids, who held the region until 198 BCE. Escalating tension between the rulers of Egypt and the Jewish people culminated in a series of conflicts. The texts that prove most important for our discussions of martyrdom were produced in the context of resistance to reforms attempted by Antiochus Epiphanes in the second century. These accounts of persecution involved the formation of a particular, distinct, and coherent Jewish identity in which Jewish history was reframed as a history of loyal and obedient suffering. The closely debated question of whether or not these accounts are the earliest martyrdom accounts is not relevant for our purposes. That these accounts shaped the development of Jewish and Christian identity makes them a vital part of the cultural context of martyrdom. Although we focus here on the narratives relayed in the biblical book of Daniel and the Maccabean literature, numerous narratives of suffering, death, sacrifice, and near-sacrifice were heralded by ancient Jews as examples of noble death. Josephus's *Jewish Antiquities* (ca. 93 CE), which renarrates Jewish history for a Roman audience, highlights the nobility of his subjects. His account of the near-sacrifice of Isaac, for instance, adds that Isaac was joyful to be sacrificed to God (1.223–36).

The portrayal of the Jews as a people ready to suffer in obedience to God and to the laws reified what it meant to be Jewish during the Hellenistic period and beyond. Defense of this ideal intersected with non-Jewish value systems and ideologies of nationhood. Writing in the first century CE, Josephus proposes in *Against Apion* that the Jewish attitude to death and suffering was comparable to that of the Spartans. The Spartans were highly regarded for their military reputation, their contempt of death, and their obedience to the laws. Josephus claims that Jews surpass the loyalty of the Spartans in being obedient to their laws even when a conquered people, whereas the Spartans exhibited fidelity only when independent (2.226–28). The presentation of the Jewish people as a historically grounded independent group utilized and relied on a system of values that prized the loyalty, nobility, and social structures of the Spartans.[47] The notion that Judaism was set apart from and superior to the heroes of Greek culture was expressed using the system of values embedded in contemporary culture. By adapting these literary tropes and cultural values Josephus may well transgress the hierarchies ingrained in Roman society, but he does not stand apart from them.[48]

INTO THE LIONS' DEN

The stories of the three young men in the fiery furnace (Dan 3:1–30) and of Daniel in the lions' den (Dan 6:1–27) relayed in the apocalyptic Old Testament book of Daniel became important narratives for early Christian art and literature. In Daniel 3, Shadrach, Meshach, and Abednego refuse to worship a golden statue set up by King Nebuchadnezzar. As a result they are bound and thrown—clothes and all—into a furnace of fire. The flames are so intense that those men responsible for tossing the young Jews into the furnace are themselves killed by the heat, yet Shadrach, Meshach, and Abednego remain unharmed. The king sees the three men unscathed and joined by a fourth figure who has the appearance of a god (Dan 3:25). The young men emerge from the flames unharmed and are promoted in Babylon.

In a similar manner, political opponents of Daniel scheme to remove him from favor at court by creating a situation in which he will be discredited. Having found no actual fault in Daniel, they encourage King Darius to institute an edict by which "whoever prays to anyone, divine or human, for thirty days, except to [the King] shall be thrown into a den of lions" (Dan 6:7). The pious Daniel continues to pray to Yahweh three times a day despite the edict and the protests of the distraught King Darius, who attempts to save him. Eventually, Daniel is thrown into the den of lions overnight, where an angel of the Lord intercedes and closes the lions' mouths so that they will not hurt him (Dan 6:21). Daniel is delivered, we are told, because he trusts in his God; by contrast his enemies, and their wives and children, are torn to pieces by the lions even before they hit the bottom of the den into which they have been tossed (Dan 6:23–24).

These court tales captured the imagination of early Christians who identified with the morally righteous protagonists unfairly betrayed to their deaths by political opponents.[49] The stories of deliverance from death and trust in the providence of God were particularly instrumental in the development of Christian ideas about the afterlife and resurrection. Nowhere is this influence more apparent than in early Christian funerary art in which the young men in the fiery furnace and Daniel in the lions' den became icons of God's promise to deliver Christians from death.

With respect to martyrdom, the domesticated lions became a literary topos in the apocryphal acts of the apostles and the martyr acts themselves. The taming of wild animals, most particularly lions, was part of the martyrological script. The biblical example of Daniel in the lions' den left a deep imprint on the iconographic and literary self-expression of early Christians. Thecla is first paraded through the city's center bound to a female lion and then stripped naked and thrown to the beasts that Alexander, her scorned suitor, has helpfully supplied for the occasion. Once in the arena, Thecla is protected by a series of miraculous events, most notable of which is that the female lioness fights off the other animals that attempt to approach Thecla. Finally, the women of the city and Queen Tryphaena intervene, and Thecla is safely returned to Paul. The image of Thecla protected by her docile lioness was the most popular way in which she was depicted in her cult. She was consistently shown using a single image: a female *orans* with arms outstretched and accompanied by at least one docile lioness, though usually flanked by two.[50] The centrality of this image in the cult of Thecla was such that it adorned not only the central mosaics and frescoes of churches, but also found its way onto devotional items that formed an integral part of the dissemination and practice of the martyr's cult.[51]

The representation of Thecla recalls the stock iconography of the biblical Daniel, which appeared in Christian catacombs, most notably those of Priscilla and Callistus in Rome.[52] The visual pairing of Daniel and Thecla replicates the formal similarities between the accounts of their near-executions: both characters are saintly individuals threatened by dominant powers and rescued by supernatural intervention from perilous situations involving wild animals.[53] Later artists incorporated martyrological motifs such as palm trees to invoke the Christian idea that Daniel should be regarded as a martyr.[54] Daniel as the prototypical tamer of lions became a stock image in later Christian articulations of the power of the martyr.

THE MACCABEES

The deaths of the "Maccabean martyrs" have served as a perpetual crux in scholarly accounts of the history of martyrdom. Their presentation fits in many ways the traditional scholarly (and *Oxford English Dictionary*) definition of what makes a martyr. The classic treatment of Wilhelm Bousset and Hugo Gressmann describes the Jewish religion characterized by these texts as a religion of martyrdom (*Religion des Martyriums*).[55] Even the skeptical Bowersock, who is loath to view martyrdom as a pre-Christian phenomenon, remarks that the accounts of the Maccabees are altogether another matter.[56] Many scholars dub the mother with her seven sons and elderly Eleazar as the first martyrs. W. H C. Frend's classic history of martyrdom, for instance, begins with a chapter on the Maccabees before moving to the Jesus movement and early church, and Jan Willem van Henten's influential study of 2 and 4 Maccabees similarly traces martyrdom to the distinguished deaths of the Maccabees, the saviors of the Jewish people.[57]

The first notable death in the Maccabean accounts is recorded in 1 Maccabees when Eleazar Avaran attempts to kill the Seleucid king Antiochus V Eupator during the battle of Beth-Zechariah by attacking the king's elephant (1 Macc 6:43–46).[58] The incident has much in common with Roman *devotio* practices of seeking death in the ranks of the enemies. Scholarly focus, however, has rested on the deaths of the Maccabees that are relayed in 2 and 4 Maccabees, widely thought to be dated to circa 125 BCE and 100 CE, respectively.[59] The narratives situate the deaths of Eleazar, the Maccabean mother and her seven sons, and Razis during the rule of Antiochus and his suppression of many Jewish religious practices. These events form part of a history of the Jewish people between the reign of Seleucus IV (187–175 BCE) and the defeat of the Seleucid general Nicanor in 161 BCE. Within this history of political liberation the martyrs play pivotal roles. Following a betrayal by Jewish leaders (2 Macc 4:7–5:10; 14:1–11), the Jewish people suffer military and ideological attack (2 Macc 5:11–6:11; 14:11–36), which ends with the martyrs' display of absolute loyalty and execution (2 Macc 6:18–7:42). The temple, city, and state are delivered (2 Macc 8:1–36; 15:1–28), vengeance is visited upon the enemies of the Jews (2 Macc 9:1–18; 15:28–35), and a feast is instituted to commemorate the victories (2 Macc 10:5–8; 15:36).[60] Within the individual episodes of persecution, the deaths of the martyrs are turning points in the struggle for emancipation: they restore the ruptured relationship with God and initiate periods of renewed military success and eventual triumph for the Jewish people. These triumphs are incorporated into sacred history as decisive moments that, in turn, punctuate the liturgical calendar. Moments of political resistance help create a particular sense of Jewish identity, an identity forged, tested, and proved in struggles with Greek administrators and embodied in the actions of the martyrs.[61]

The first account that includes a dialogue with a martyr is that of Eleazar, an important scribe advanced in age and looks (2 Macc 6:18). Even though he is ninety years old, Eleazar cannot be forced to consume pork, refusing even to pretend to eat the meat (2 Macc 6:25). Before walking toward the instrument of death, he says, "I will show myself worthy of my old age and leave to the young a noble example of how to die a good death willingly and nobly for the revered and holy laws" (2 Macc 6:27–28). Eleazar's description of himself as a paradigm recalls Greek stories of exemplary deaths, especially Socrates's self-construction as an example for others.[62] The similarities between Eleazar and Socrates are noteworthy: they are both aging, influential figures who will not take the opportunity to escape death through ruse or pretense but rather insist on casting their deaths as instruction. As he dies, however, Eleazar's rhetoric recalls that of Jewish wisdom traditions in which noted characters remain faithful despite suffering. He proclaims, "It is clear to the Lord in his holy knowledge that, though I might have been saved from death, I am enduring terrible sufferings in my body under this beating, but in my soul I am glad to suffer these things because I fear him" (2 Macc 6:30). Eleazar's death weaves together a medley of cultural tropes: the exemplary death of the revered figure and the fidelity of the righteous person with the concept of adherence to the laws.

Immediately after the Eleazar story there follows another account of cross-examination and execution. In 2 Maccabees 7:1–42 seven brothers and their mother are also brought before the king to be coerced into eating pork. Immediately, one of the brothers proclaims that they are ready to die and will not transgress ancestral laws (2 Macc 7:2). This brother is summarily punished for his speech: the young man is scalped, his tongue is removed, his hands and feet are cut off, and he is placed in a skillet and fried. There is a certain irony to the scene: the apparent idiosyncrasy of the Jewish unwillingness to eat pork is rendered banal by the barbaric way in which the body of the young man is prepared, as if for consumption. The language invokes the topos of cannibalism, a taboo practice used in invective to charge one's opponents with tyranny and factionalism (see Cicero, *Philippics* 2.71).[63] One by one, each of the young men is tortured and executed. The political and social dimensions of their adherence to ancestral custom and laws are implied in the manner of their refusals to eat. One brother answers the king in his ancestral language (2 Macc 7:8), and their mother incites them to courage using the same tongue (2 Macc 7:21, 27). The final brother, having been spurred on by his mother's encouragement, declares that he too will not obey the "king's decree" but only "the law given to our ancestors by Moses" (2 Macc 7:30). Finally, the mother also surrenders her body and life for the laws of the ancestors, calling upon God to show mercy to the people.

Throughout their examination and torture the young men and their mother display confidence that their bodies will be restored to them at the resurrection

(2 Macc 7:11, 14, 23, 29, 36). This posthumous vindication and restoration is in turn linked to the notion of divine creation. One brother proclaims that he received his hands from heaven and can expect them back again (2 Macc 7:11). Another refers to God as the "creator of the world" (2 Macc 7:23). Rhetorically, the brothers' confidence in resurrection resists the king's efforts to threaten and constrain them. The victorious resurrection of the brothers is not threatened by dismemberment or disfigurement. In many respects, not just the exercise of power but also mythological accounts of the afterlife are being subverted. Whereas Greek religion maintained that proper burial was a prerequisite for safe passage to Hades and that disfigurement in death imprinted itself on the shade of a warrior, the Maccabean martyrs are confident that their God will be able to restore their bodies to wholeness. Greek might is thwarted by Jewish eschatology.

Torture and death are, for the Maccabees, the consequences of sin. The final brother states that they suffer because of their own sins and that their executions function to "punish and discipline" them (2 Macc 7:33). Many scholars have remarked upon the sacrificial language here and analyzed the passage in terms of Jewish and Greek sacrificial schema.[64] Certainly, within the historical program of 2 Maccabees the deaths of the martyrs in 2 Macc 6–7 precipitate a period of military success for the Jews. The pedagogical language here should not be overlooked. The detailed descriptions of punishment and torture meted out to the brothers on account of their sins are arresting. As examples of God's punishment, this treatment can be compared, functionally, to the tortures visited upon the sinful dead in mythological accounts of Hades. These accounts utilize the rhetorical form of *ekphrasis* to dissuade their audiences from transgressing laws and customs. Implicit in 2 Maccabees is the understanding that the traitors of the Jewish people will meet similarly gruesome fates at the hands of God. In the same way the purpose of the martyrdom stories may be multilayered, offering examples of how to die nobly and in defense of the laws and customs of old, constructing a sense of identity that is tied to these customs and reinforces both their practice and the identity itself, and functioning pedagogically as *ekphrasis* schooling the audience in ethical conduct.

During the persecutions of Nicanor and immediately before the final victory of Judas Maccabeus, more than five hundred soldiers are dispatched in an attempt to arrest Razis, an elder of Jerusalem who had "most zealously risked body and life for Judaism" (2 Macc 14:38). Finding himself surrounded, Razis attempts to fall on his own sword, "preferring to die nobly rather than to fall into the hands of sinners and suffer outrages unworthy of his noble birth" (2 Macc 14:42). In the heat of the moment, Razis succeeds only in self-disembowelment and attempts to throw himself off a tower. Still breathing after the fall and with a final burst of energy, he climbs to a high rock. Here, drained of blood, he hurls his entrails at the crowd, "calling upon the Lord of life and spirit to give them back to him again" and casts himself off.[65] The death of Razis has been something of a sensitive subject; he is rarely even called a martyr and is described as having either suffered a "heroic death" or committed suicide.[66] While the modern interpreter may distinguish between the deaths of Eleazar and the Maccabean mother and her sons on one hand and Razis on the other, it is clear that the same cannot be said for the author of 2 Maccabees, for whom the death of Razis serves the same purpose in the cycle of liberation as the deaths of the other martyrs. Just as the deaths of the martyrs in 2 Macc 6:18–7:42 inaugurate a period of military success for the Jewish people, so too the death of Razis is the beginning of something new, the final triumph of Judas Maccabeus in 2 Macc 15:1–28. Furthermore, the death of Razis works to resist coercion in the same way as the deaths of the Maccabees. Antiochus's efforts to make the Jews eat pork and Nicanor's desire to kill Razis are endeavors to control the populace through fear and exemplary punishment. By preempting Nicanor's attempt to utilize his body for this purpose, Razis, like the other Maccabean martyrs, resists Greek efforts to assert power.[67] The death of Razis is functionally identical to that of the other martyrs.

The stories of the Maccabean martyrs intersect with the cultural fabric of the Hellenistic world. Van Henten has persuasively compared Razis's flight from life to that of Menoeceus, the little-known hero of Euripides's *Phoenissae*.[68] As has been noted, the death of Eleazar has more than a passing similarity to that of Socrates. Both are elderly men who reject the opportunity to escape death and who regard their manner of dying as a model for imitation. In the philosophically bent 4 Maccabees (ca. 100 CE), the politically submissive Jews display in their firm resistance to death the kind of masculinity prized by ancient Greeks. As Stephen Moore and Janice Capel Anderson have recognized, 4 Maccabees concerns "what it means to be a true man."[69] The self-control of the martyrs and their mother is culturally rendered as manliness. In 4 Maccabees, as in Christian martyr acts, the masculinization of the martyrs is balanced by the effeminacy of the antagonist, in this case Antiochus. As narrative foils, the martyrs' opponents drown in passionate outbursts and displays of anger, their effeminate, barbarian conduct only amplifying the self-control of the burly protagonists. Both 2 and 4 Maccabees therefore resonate with the cultural values of Greek society. The cultural exchange is not monodirectional. The Maccabean reexpression of Greek paradigms of the noble death serves multiple purposes: demonstrating the piety and courage of the martyrs' protagonists, claiming the rhetorical power of Socrates, aligning Seleucid rule with the antitypes of the *Apologies,* and trumping all of these traditions by presenting the Jewish heroes as supreme examples of valor.

A great deal of scholarship has parsed the influence of the Maccabees on early articulations of what it meant to die for Christ.[70] Both the *Martyrdom of Marian and James* and the *Martyrdom of Montanus and Lucius* refer to the mother of the Maccabees as the prototype for Christian mothers, and, as Kate Cooper has decisively shown, the *passiones* of Symphorosa and Felicitas were deeply influenced by the story of the Maccabean mother.[71] At the same time, however, the stories of the Maccabees were reinterpreted during the Jewish war with Rome in the first century. Josephus's description of the execution of young men who had dared to remove the Roman golden eagle from the roof of the temple evokes comparisons with the Maccabean martyrs. The extended dialogue between the young men and King Herod presents the latter as behaving like a foreign king. The young men protest that they acted in accordance with ancestral law (*patrios nomos*), which ordered them to remove the symbol of Roman authority (Josephus, *Jewish War* 1.653). The version in *Antiquities* 7.159 contrasts the king's decrees and Mosaic law, layering the allusion to the Maccabees with an echo of Daniel 3 and 6.[72] It is important to note the continued identification of the Jews as a people who die for the laws, as the idea of dying for the law or laws is present in the Christian discourse of martyrdom. Recognizing this identity marker for Jews after the fall of Jerusalem illuminates our understanding of the ways in which claims to ancestral tradition and legal codes function for early Christians.[73] This congruence directs us more broadly, as Daniel Boyarin has noted, to the intersection of Jewish and Christian martyrologies in the second century CE, when Judaism and Christianity were not socially or culturally discrete communities divorced by differing self-conceptions and phenomenologies.[74]

Writing Death: Genus and Genre

Even if one should never judge a codex by its cover, expectations for a text are framed by its packaging.[75] One of the distinctive elements of the martyr act is its literary presentation—the narration of a Christian's death apart from the details of his or her life. The origins of the genre of the martyr act are as contested and frustrating as the origins of the concept of martyrdom. Scholarly investigations into the relationship of the martyr act to other forms of literature are a microcosm of the relationship of martyrdom to pre-Christian ideas in general. One posited but much-debated literary background to the martyr act is the *bios,* or life. The origins and form of this ancient precursor to the modern biography have been the source of much scholarly debate on account of the influence of the *bios* on the development of the gospel genre. During the Hellenistic period death narratives for prominent individuals were collected together as part of a protobiographical tradition called the *exitus illustrium virorum.*[76] The Peripatetic Hermippus of Smyrna's third-century BCE collection of lives focuses especially on the deaths of his subjects, always interesting, if not always noble. From fragments of Hermippus preserved by the biographer Diogenes Laertius, we learn that both Chrysippus and Epicurus died as a result of drinking unmixed wine (*Lives* 7.184–85; 10.15–16). It is noteworthy that in Diogenes Laertius's collection of essays, the philosophers are immortalized by their deaths, their teachings, and their pithy humorous sayings. The axioms of the philosophers appear to have influenced the satirical parting shots of Christian martyrs. The martyr Lawrence, for instance, executed by placement on a fired grill, plays *chef de cuisine* for his executioners, reputedly instructing them, "This side is done, turn me over and have a bite" (Ambrose, *On the Duties of the Clergy* 1.41.207). Such wry comments recall the famous last words of the philosophers. The interest in these death-focused vitae together with the production of formal apologies for prominent deceased individuals may have played into the development of martyrdom genres.

The closest literary analogues for the martyrdom account's close relation, the apocryphal acts of the apostles, lie elsewhere, in the popular romances of Greek society.[77] These narratives of love lost and retrieved tend to follow a narrative formula: typically the story begins with two attractive young people from good families falling in love and being cruelly separated by fate. While apart, they suffer many misfortunes, both on account of their love for one another and because of the dangerous situations into which they have wandered. Slavery, imprisonment, pirate attacks, human sacrifice, and the omnipresent shipwreck are just some of the narrative elements that season the Greek romance, their function being to delay the happy ending that will be found in the reunion and marriage of the couple. Scholars have identified such narrative devices in the canonical Acts of the Apostles as well as in the more dramatic apocryphal acts of the apostles. In the Christian accounts of the *Acts of John, Peter, Paul, Andrew,* and *Thomas,* parallel plot lines are at work as each story follows the adventures, preaching, and martyrdom of an individual apostle.[78]

The influence of both romantic and apostolic narratives extends beyond literary clichés and special effects, for these texts were responding to the needs of certain communities. The romances functioned as celebrations of elite social hierarchies and practices in the Greek East. In the words of Judith Perkins, "The society that the devotion and fidelity of the principal couple imaged in microcosm in the romance was the traditional elite patriarchal society passing, essentially unchanged, from one generation to another."[79] These were, in other words, narratives that reinforced the structures of society, encapsulated social values in a pair of individuals, and subjugated personal attachment to these social structures (namely, marriage). The same function can be ascribed to the apocryphal acts. Averil Cameron's work discusses the manner in which the apocryphal acts served to create and maintain social structures.[80] Perkins has pressed further still, demonstrating the extent to which the narrative expectations of the readers of the Greek romance are subtly challenged and altered by the reading of the apocryphal acts. Where the romance concludes with a joyful marriage or reunion, the happy ending of the apocryphal acts is found in the execution of the protagonist. Death has replaced marriage as the narrative resolution and optimistic climax of the story. As texts, the apocryphal acts and the martyr acts defined new sources and avenues of power, thereby undermining the social structures of their audiences' worlds. The influence of the Greek romance on Christian narratives of suffering was structural and antithetical. Christian authors adapted, subverted, and rearticulated the popular genres of fictive romance.

To the romances can be added the more prosaic, legally styled accounts of the trials of "pagan martyrs." Since their discovery in the nineteenth century, the collection of fragmentary papyri called the *Acta Alexandrinorum* or *Acts of the Pagan Martyrs* have aroused great scholarly interest both for their possible connections with the genre of the Christian martyr act and for the intriguing question of their purpose.[81] These accounts of conversations, trials, and executions of various Alexandrians in Rome are in many cases contemporary with the composition of early Christian martyr acts. One of the most famous and most complete of the texts, the *Acts of Appianus*, records the trial of an Alexandrian *gymnasiarch* in front of the emperor Commodus at the end of the second century.[82] The circumstances of Appianus's arrest are unclear, but from the lively, clever dialogue it emerges that he had accused the emperor of making a profit at the expense of Alexandrians. The text, while entertaining, is fragmentary. Heliodorus says: "Go to your death quickly son. The glory of dying for your dearest native city will be yours. Be not distressed" (col i. 40).[83] The combination of composure in the face of death and glory in dying for one's city places this text in line with earlier notions of noble death. Although the *Acta Alexandrinorum* present themselves as court records, they do not follow the generic conventions of *acta proconsularia,* official court documents. The dialogues between the condemned and the emperor are reminiscent of the dialogues between philosophers and tyrants, and some motifs of the accounts resonate with elements of the Greek romance tradition. The *Acts of Isiodous* has an anti-Jewish bias that may tie the texts to the historical clashes between Jews and non-Jews in Alexandria in 38 CE, as recorded by Philo in *Embassy to Gaius* and *Against Flaccus*.

The intersection of elements of court documents, philosophical *bioi,* and Greek novels is instructive for our reading of early Christian martyrdom literature. The medley of generic forms and interests suggests that it is misguided to attempt to divide martyr acts and apocryphal acts into separate categories and to dissect further these accounts into microgenres that can be connected to Greek literary traditions. We should rather examine the ways in which these accounts utilize certain forms of rhetorical power and literary tropes and should consider, moreover, how this utilization might subvert, appropriate, or transgress the commitments of the traditions with which they intersect.

Conclusion

Death comes to all, but the art of dying was a test of character. In the act of dying, identities were exposed, values and virtues revealed, and claims to truth laid bare. A willingness to die proved the purity of one's intentions and served as a guarantor of the veracity of one's claims. At the same time, death could function as a means to subvert the attempts of others to exercise control. Dying nobly in these circumstances frustrated efforts to constrain the individual, destabilized political structures, and reclaimed power in the face of aggression.

The place of death in life—at its end or its beginning, as its antithesis or climax, as peripheral or essential—is a subject as enduring as any. The value placed on death, the hierarchies of good and bad deaths, and the characterization and even personification of death speak volumes about the worlds we create and inhabit. In the same way, the characterizations of suffering as meaningful or pointless, good or evil, frame the ways in which people understand certain bodily experiences. This chapter has explored the construction of death in pre-Christian ancient Mediterranean societies and has painted the cultural backdrop of Christianity in broad strokes; the intended goal, however, is not to homogenize but to provide context. These literary, cultural, and ritual motifs contribute to a broader conception of death, but this conception is multifaceted and ambiguous. When interpreting their own experiences and crafting their own concept of martyrdom, early Christians adapted, transformed, shaped, and subverted existing cultural tropes. Things changed; things stayed the same. It is important to note, however, that we should not assume that a particular notion of death must be at work in a particular author; rather, we must acknowledge that other complex and overlapping cultural motifs—sacrifice, suffering, national identity, gender, and social status, among others—were also at play and that the rhetorical function of placing these accounts within these cultural frameworks remains a critical component of their use.

2

Asia Minor:
Imitating Christ

Many consider Asia Minor to be the cradle of Christian martyrdom. The area of the Roman empire that stretched from Bithynia in the north to Lycia in the south, and from the coast of the Mediterranean in the west to Cappadocia in the east, was one of the first regions of the empire to be evangelized by the followers of Jesus. The earliest Christian literature from the region refers, explicitly and obliquely, to the important role of suffering in the life of Jesus's followers. In the potentially pseudonymous letter to the city of Colossae, Paul joyfully delights in and even touts the merits of his suffering, depicting it as "completing what was lacking in Christ's afflictions" (Col 1:24). It was to the churches of Asia Minor that the author of Revelation addressed his letters, exhorting them to "conquer" like Christ through suffering and promising them heavenly rewards for their obedience (for example, Rev 2:11; 2:17; 2:26–28; 3:12; 3:17). And it appears to have been to the inhabitants of Asia Minor that the author of 1 Peter addressed his epistle of suffering, warning them of the "fiery ordeal" that was to come (1 Pet 4:12).

At the same time, our earliest evidence for a formal Roman legal stance toward Christians comes from Asia Minor, from the correspondence between the governor Pliny and the emperor Trajan around the turn of the second century. While taking a firmly negative position on the status of Christians, the

Pliny-Trajan correspondence demonstrates that rather than being actively persecuted, early Christians were subject to specific legal processes only in the
event that they were publicly denounced and formally tried. The roaming bands
of local police rounding up the Jesus followers in the night appear to have been
the stuff of nightmares. The scant evidence for active targeting of Christians
contrasts greatly with the shrill rhetoric of early Christian claims of being persecuted, prompting the question "Were early Christians really persecuted in Asia
Minor?"

Scholarly assessments of the situation have tended to side with the Romans.
It is often said that if Christians were singled out by other groups, then the
persecution was "sporadic and local." Although there may have been limited
prosecution of Christians, they were not actively persecuted. Scholarly estima-
tions of the severity of the situation often hang on an implicit sense of what
counts as "persecution." It is the dearth of executions that has led to the conclusion that Christians were not persecuted. In instances where Christians
were excluded (or self-excluded) from social practices, the experience is often
termed "social marginalization." The language of exclusion and marginalization finds its ancient partner in the deuteropauline and Petrine claims that
Christians are aliens and sojourners in the world (Eph 2:19; 1 Pet 1:1; 2:11).

The reality, of course, lies beyond our grasp. The extant ancient literature
is interested in theological readings of the circumstances of Christians, not in
outlining these circumstances. Revelation refers to the execution of a man
called Antipas, Ephesians offers a sacrificial interpretation of Paul's death,
and 1 Peter seems to envision the likelihood that Christians would be persecuted. It is revealing that in quantifying the extent of discrimination, only
death counts as persecution. As a way out of this bind, scholars have utilized
the distinction between "perceived" and "real" persecution or local and imperial persecution as a means of articulating the difference between what
happened in second-century Antioch and the conditions under the emperors
Decius and Diocletian. The implication is that only imperially organized active discrimination that ends in death can be properly termed persecution.
The problem is not with an ahistorical rubric that measures the degree of
persecution according to geographical dispersion or number of affected
people, nor is it even with deeming persecution local and sporadic.[1] The
definition and application of the term *persecution* are bounded by modern
technologies of violence. Just as certain physical ailments seem mild by contrast to life-threatening illness, so too social marginalization becomes incon-
sequential when measured against genocide. The grand scale of comparatively
recent technologically sophisticated persecutions renders ancient examples
relatively meek.

It is difficult to find appropriate language to describe the situation that these texts envisage. On one hand, we must be wary of being seduced by an ancient discourse of persecution that casts the smallest of slights as a direct attack and claims that Christians were always and everywhere persecuted. With respect to martyrdom, the experience of Christians in the fourth century has been masked by the *Ecclesiastical History*, Eusebius's narrative of a persecuted church. The kinds of rhetorical work that persecution does for communities and groups should not be overlooked. On the other hand, the assessment that Christian rhetoric outstrips historical reality seems to be grounded in an unspoken modern hierarchy of social evils. The historians' assessment of the second-century situation is that Christians endured a rather tame form of social marginalization, which originated with local groups (rather than imperial mandate) and only occasionally led to execution. This depiction contrasts strikingly with Christian portraits of a barbaric world, drunk on the blood of saints and propelled by demonic forces running amok. The contrast has led some to treat early Christian rhetoric as hysterical. While the situation in Asia Minor may not have been as grave as it could have been, it is anachronistic to judge Christian rhetoric as hysterical or disproportionate based on some preexisting modern notion of what counts as persecution. There is no objective transhistorical spectrum of mistreatment against which to measure various instances of persecution. In the third and fourth centuries, more serious imperial legal measures against Christians will develop that will seem to eclipse the situation in the second century. In retrospect, the fevered pitch of 1 Peter and Revelation may seem hysterical, but the discourse of persecution should not be evaluated against the course of human history.

By the end of the first century, a number of different early Christian groups had begun to describe themselves as afflicted or suffering. Often, these descriptions were explicitly tied to the figure of Christ. The exhortations and promises to those who conquer in the letters to the churches in Revelation use Christ as their reference point; the congregants are encouraged to conquer like Christ, the victor. The use of identical terminology of witness/martyrdom binds the Christians to the example of Christ. In the same way, Paul's references to imitating Christ and the deuteropauline claim that Paul's suffering completed what was lacking in the sufferings of Christ tied the apostle to the Savior (Col 1:24). The instrumental role that suffering plays in Paul is mirrored in Revelation's statement that a certain number of deaths was required to fulfill some kind of cosmic lack (Rev 6:11). Even before historical Christians started to die, therefore, there was a very strong sense both that death was inevitable and that these deaths would be connected to the greater affairs of the cosmos: either because they served an instrumental purpose in the divine plan, or because they were the result of demonic intervention. There was, therefore, from the beginnings of the Christian mission in Asia Minor, a demonstrable interest in theologizing violence.

According to the traditional scholarly view, the text that galvanized an empire of Christians to become martyrs was the account of the death of Polycarp, the bishop of Smyrna (ca. 155 CE). This narrative is cited as the first martyrdom account and, with the letters of Ignatius of Antioch, as the harbinger of a new ideology of martyrdom. It is assumed to precipitate a shift in Christian understandings of their suffering and death and therefore is worthy of some consideration. As we might expect, the representation of the death of Polycarp in the *Martyrdom of Polycarp* drew heavily on earlier traditions that glorified suffering and death: on Pauline claims to imitate Jesus, on the exhortations of the gospels to follow Jesus to death, and on Hebrews's exposition of the sacrificial death of Jesus. Perhaps most deeply, however, the author of the *Martyrdom of Polycarp* drank from the intellectual well of Polycarp's older contemporary and mentor, Ignatius of Antioch, to whom we now turn.

The Letters of Ignatius

Ignatius was the bishop of Antioch sometime toward the end of the first century (Eusebius, *Hist. eccl.* 3.21–22) and died in the early part of the second century, likely during the reign of Trajan.[2] The details of his life are spotty, for Ignatius tells us nothing of his education or conversion, and Eusebius's interest is to put him into an apostolic context rather than a historical one. All that is known of Ignatius comes from his letters, purportedly written as he journeyed to Rome for trial and execution. Most scholars judge the account of his trial and execution, the *Acts of Ignatius,* to be a spurious fifth-century composition, but Ignatius's epistles are widely regarded as providing some of the first evidence for a theology of martyrdom and, certainly, for an enthusiasm on the part of Christians to be martyred.

Whatever Ignatius's place in the history of martyrdom, the textual history of his letters is remarkably complicated.[3] Of the thirteen epistles extant in the manuscripts, only half are deemed by scholars to be genuinely written by Ignatius. This core group is described in Eusebius:

> So when he came to Smyrna, where Polycarp was, he wrote an epistle to the church of Ephesus, in which he mentions Onesimus, its pastor; and another to the church of Magnesia, situated upon the Maeander, in which he makes mention again of a bishop Damas; and finally one to the church of Tralles, whose bishop, he states, was at that time Polybius. In addition to these he wrote also to the church of Rome, entreating them not to secure his release

from martyrdom, and thus rob him of his earnest hope. In confirmation of what has been said it is proper to quote briefly from this epistle. He writes as follows: "From Syria even to Rome I fight with wild beasts, by land and by sea, by night and by day, being bound amidst ten leopards that is, a company of soldiers who only become worse when they are well treated. In the midst of their wrongdoings, however, I am more fully learning discipleship, but I am not thereby justified. May I have joy of the beasts that are prepared for me; and I pray that I may find them ready; I will even coax them to devour me quickly that they may not treat me as they have some whom they have refused to touch through fear. And if they are unwilling, I will compel them. Forgive me. I know what is expedient for me. Now do I begin to be a disciple. May naught of things visible and things invisible envy me, that I may attain to Jesus Christ. Let fire and cross and attacks of wild beasts, let wrenching of bones, cutting of limbs, crushing of the whole body, tortures of the devil,— let all these come upon me if only I may attain to Jesus Christ." These things he wrote from the above-mentioned city to the churches referred to. And when he had left Smyrna he wrote again from Troas to the Philadelphians and to the church of Smyrna; and particularly to Polycarp, who presided over the latter church. And since he knew him well as an apostolic man, he commended to him, like a true and good shepherd, the flock at Antioch, and besought him to care diligently for it.[4] (*Hist. eccl.* 3.36.5–10)

This list of seven letters (*To the Ephesians, To the Magnesians, To the Trallians, To the Romans, To the Philadelphians, To the Smyrneans,* and *To Polycarp*), commonly known as the middle recension and transmitted in modern editions of Ignatius's letters, is a beguilingly simple proposal that severs, rather than unravels, a textual Gordian knot. The threads of manuscript tradition and textual attestation of the Ignatian corpus are as tightly interwoven as those of any early Christian author. In addition to the middle recension, there are both long and short recensions.[5] The former, believed to have been created during the fourth century, includes six additional writings (*Ignatius to Mary of Cassobola, Mary of Cassobola to Ignatius, Ignatius to the Tarsians, Ignatius to the Philippians, Ignatius to the Antiochians,* and *Ignatius to the Deacon Hero*) and interpolates the original letters with supplementary heresiological mate-rial.[6] These letters indicate that the figure of Ignatius, the famed bishop-martyr of Antioch, was a valuable spokesman in later doctrinal and ecclesiastical controversies. This long recension is extant in Greek and Latin, with the Latin containing some additional correspondence with the Virgin Mary and a letter to the disciple John.[7] The long recension circulated until the discovery of manu-scripts attesting the middle form by Ussher, Voss, and Ruinart.[8]

The short version, by contrast, is based on a Syriac tradition of Ignatius's epistles discovered by British scholar William Cureton and published in 1845.

This Syriac tradition, preserved in three manuscripts, contained versions of *To Polycarp, To the Ephesians,* and *To the Romans.* Cureton argued vociferously that the Syriac version, which he considered to be the genuine version, preserved the earliest version of the letters.[9] Cureton's thesis, however, failed to find favor among either his contemporaries or subsequent generations of church historians, and this corpus is widely treated as an abridgement of the middle recension.[10]

The discovery, reconstruction, and primacy of the middle recension as now generally accepted by modern scholars is written in the margins of the history of civil war Britain.[11] It was the royalist pro-episcopacy archbishop James Ussher who first sought out and published this collection of the letters of Ignatius. A consummate textual scholar, Ussher was guided by his conviction that Ignatius had written only seven letters and that these authentic epistles would confirm his claims to episcopal authority over and against the Protestant reformers of his time. Ussher's investigations led him to publish in 1644 a Latin edition of the middle recension with a Greek reconstruction that was supported by Isaac Voss's publication in 1646 of a Greek manuscript from Florence. This Florentine manuscript, which forms the basis for modern critical editions, contained versions of all the letters in the middle recension with the exception of *To the Romans.* Ruinart's edition, some thirty years later, included a Greek text of *To the Romans* from the tenth-century *Codex Parisiensis Colbertinus,* and with this manuscript the Greek middle recension was complete. Two caveats to note: first, as Kirsopp Lake has observed, the middle recension is excerpted from manuscripts that also contain either the inauthentic texts from the long recension or additional documents, or that have preserved the interpolated versions of the authentic letters.[12] Second, the famously pro-martyrdom letter *To the Romans* is nowhere found in Greek independent of the (likely) fifth-century account of the *Martyrdom of Ignatius.* Textually, *To the Romans* is a part of the later martyrdom tradition. Its excerption for inclusion with Ignatius's letters obscures the fact that it no longer exists as a separate letter.[13] The methodologically problematic manner in which the middle recension is spliced from the long recension and reconstituted as a textual unity has meant that the Ignatian corpus has continued to be challenged up to the present day.[14]

Whatever the history of their composition, Ignatius's letters are lines of communication in the social network that had developed between individual churches in early Christianity. Our extant evidence represents only a portion of this network. Polycarp was himself instrumental in the transmission and circulation of Ignatius's letters, and a number of scholars have credited him with assembling the letters in the first place.[15] The practice of writing letters to the churches in Asia Minor seems to have been for Ignatius a kind of *imitatio Pauli,* a way of casting himself as a deuteropauline martyr.[16] The salient point here is that Ignatius's letters were composed as he journeyed to Rome for martyrdom. In Ign. *Eph.* 12.1, Ignatius is arrested and condemned as a criminal. Although scholars debate the extent to which persecution existed in Antioch around the turn of the second century or whether a skirmish had led local authorities to ship Ignatius off to Rome, he was already condemned to death when he began his epistolary tour.

Many have condemned Ignatius's position on martyrdom as suicidal or pathological.[17] Even a more positive assessment of his legacy calls him "boastful."[18] There is no denying that Ignatius has an enthusiastic approach to death that cuts against the grain of the modern—and, to an extent, ancient—characterization of martyrs as humble. Yet modern prejudices should not color our assessment of Ignatius's views; his perspective on death is the logical conclusion of a broader, theologically grounded worldview.[19] In particular, his descriptions reveal martyrdom to be a communal event firmly grounded in eucharistic practices. In anticipating his arrival and execution in Rome, Ignatius paints a picture of a liturgically inspired entrance into the city. He will be surrounded by a choir singing praises to God (Ign. *Rom.* 2.2) as during the Eucharist (Ign. *Eph.* 4.1–2). He famously requests: "Let me be food for the wild beasts, through whom I can reach God. I am God's wheat, and I am being ground by the teeth of the wild beasts, that I might prove to be pure bread" (Ign. *Rom.* 4.1). The obliteration of his body will affect the quality of his discipleship: "Better yet, coax the wild beasts, that they may become my tomb and leave nothing of my body behind, lest I become a burden to someone once I have fallen asleep. Then I will truly be a disciple of Jesus Christ, when the world will no longer see my body" (Ign. *Rom.* 4.2).[20] Much of the language Ignatius employs is sacrificial. In a phrase reminiscent of Phil 2:17 and Roman *devotio* practices, he asks that he be allowed "to be poured out as an offering to God while there is still an altar ready so that in love you may form a chorus and sing to the Father in Jesus Christ" (Ign. *Rom.* 2.2).[21] When Ignatius succeeds in becoming a disciple and "imitator of the suffering of my God" (Ign. *Rom.* 6.3), he will be reborn into freedom.

The framing of Ignatius's death using a blend of imitative language and liturgical imagery overlays the passion narrative, martyrdom, and the Eucharist. Both martyrdom and the performance of the Eucharist function as imitations of the passion of Jesus and provide access to this communion with God. The use of liturgical language in turn ties the suffering and death of Ignatius to broader systems of community construction and sustenance. As a eucharistic sacrifice Ignatius's death is set within the framework of community regulation, and, like the Eucharist, it serves as a means to maintain and reinforce church unity.[22] In Ign. *Eph.* 20.2 Ignatius describes the Eucharist as "medicine of immortality" (φάρμακον ἀθανασίαζ). Given that the discourse of church unity and the discourse of martyrdom are coproduced in Ignatius, it is possible that he views his death as having a communal function. That is to say, Ignatius's death, like other forms of eucharistic offering, has a cathartic, healing effect on the church. The use of medical language again directs us to the communal, corporal nature of the church. By drawing upon medical discourse of healing and Pauline notions of the church as body (for example, 1 Cor 12: 12–22), Ignatius casts the eucharistic assembly as unifying catharsis.

At the same time and in addition to its communal function, Ignatius's martyrdom is a distinctly personal affair. Discipleship, imitation, and martyrdom are mutually explanatory. While imitation does not always involve suffering, Ignatius's statement that he will truly be a disciple of Christ when he is executed demonstrates that it is in death that his own potential will be realized. As he says in *To the Ephesians* (3.1), Ignatius is only beginning to be a disciple, as true discipleship will be attained in death. The language of mimesis permeates his writings. He asks permission to be "an imitator of the suffering of God" (Ign. *Rom.* 6.3). Death will have the immediate effect of transforming Ignatius into a disciple and also of replicating for him the effects of the death of Jesus: "I will be faithful when I am no longer visible to the world . . . for our God Jesus Christ is more visible now that he is in the Father" (Ign. *Rom.* 3.2–3). In a refusal of Roman structures that identified Christians merely by the attribution of the name, Ignatius writes that he does not want just to be called a Christian, he wants to be found to be one; and that, moreover, when he is obliterated, he, like Christ, will be more visible than he was when alive (Ign. *Rom.* 3.2). For Ignatius, being Christian is proved in the experience of martyrdom.

Ignatius's ideology of martyrdom, however, is not just a recapitulation of Christian eucharistic theology hermetically sealed from the power structures of the empire.[23] As with other facets of Ignatius's thought, his casting of martyrdom as sacrifice draws upon non-Christian practices and ideologies.[24] Ignatius portrays his journey to death as an imperial procession to the altar and contrasts unfavorably the role of the emperor to his own fate: "It is better for me to die for Jesus Christ than to rule over the ends of the earth" (Ign. *Rom.* 6.1). Utilization of the rhetoric of the imperial cult and the eucharistic assembly enables Ignatius to construct an idealized portrait of the Christian congregation contained in the person of the bishop.[25] In *To the Trallians* (1.1) he describes Polybius, bishop of Tralles, not as an individual but as a community embodied, a "whole multitude gathered" in him. The language of unity had both cosmic and practical, authoritarian consequences. The indivisible unity of the church allowed the assembled community to combat Satan (Ign. *Eph.* 13.1), but it also allowed Ignatius to insist on submission to the bishop (Ign. *Magn.* 13.2). The role of the bishop was grounded in the divine order: "therefore as the Lord did nothing without the Father, either by himself or through the apostles (for he was united with him), so you must not do anything without the bishop and the presbyters" (Ign. *Magn.* 7.1). The connection between ecclesiological order and divine order was itself a mirror of Roman imperial iconography.[26] By adapting the rhetoric and structures of imperial ideology to threefold Christian ecclesiology, Ignatius was able to trump Roman imperial order with a reconfigured heavenly order. The rhetorical grounding for this move (that is, the notion of the heavenly serving as the model for the earthly) had been laid by both Paul and Revelation—the former claims that his citizenship was in heaven, and the latter posits a heavenly order that mirrors the structures, iconography, and ideology of Roman imperial power. The place where these imperial and Ignatian models of divinely organized order meet is in Ignatius's discussion of martyrdom. By narrating his journey to death as an *imitatio Christi,* a eucharistic performance, and a kind of imperial procession, Ignatius is able to position himself as mediator between divine and ecclesiastical affairs.

For Ignatius, martyrdom serves a variety of interlocking purposes. It allows him to establish his own authority and status in the church. The liminal position occupied by the journeyer-toward-death allows Ignatius, as it does Paul, to position himself as mimetic mediator between the community and God. Drawing upon imperial structures, the sacrificial function of the passion narrative, and the Pauline epistles, Ignatius instructs his addressees in church order and unity. The rhetorical function of suffering and martyrdom is everywhere tied to notions of church unity, sacrifice, and imitation.

The Martyrdom of Polycarp

On a late April afternoon sometime in the second century, an elderly man was brought into the Roman amphitheater at Smyrna to be executed. Having initially evaded arrest, Polycarp had debated with Roman judges, risked the anger of the crowd, refused to offer sacrifice to the emperor, and hurried—with an injured leg no less—toward his death. The story of his death is adorned with biblical allusions and citations, miraculous events, and theological interpretations and is widely regarded as one of the more beautiful accounts of martyrdom that survives from the early church. The excitement one feels upon reading the *Martyrdom of Polycarp* is only amplified by the importance of its subject. Polycarp was no anonymous confessor whom bad luck, zealous legislation, or overconfidence had brought to the tribunal. He was a famed Christian bishop sought out by local police and an angry mob. As a correspondent of Ignatius of Antioch and, apparently, a student of John the evangelist, Polycarp is for some the vital link between the apostles and the apostolic fathers. As a historical figure he appeals to the romantic in even the most staunchly objectivist historian. Here in the person of Polycarp is the link between the Jesus movement and the early church, the first martyr, and the conduit of apostolic teaching.

More ink has been spilled over the dating of the *Martyrdom of Polycarp* than over any other early Christian martyr act. The attention this text has received is indicative of both the affection and the status it enjoys in scholarly circles. As a result of its literary artistry, the historical importance of its re-nowned protagonist, and its elegant presentation of martyrdom, the *Martyrdom of Polycarp* occupies the place of honor among the early Christian martyrdom accounts. Treated by scholars as the first martyrdom account and as a document that inaugurated a new genre, a new linguistic category, and a new ideology,[27] it has become the funnel through which pre-Christian noble death is channeled into Christian martyrdom.[28]

In the history of scholarship, the *Martyrdom of Polycarp* has almost always been treated as an authentic narrative of the death of an early Christian martyr. Although subjected to much examination and many tests during the rise of the Bollandists and their purge of spurious *acta*, the account has stood resolutely against historicist scrutiny. Given the pivotal role that the *Martyrdom of Polycarp* plays in histories of martyrdom as the "first example" of Christian martyrdom literature, it is worth dwelling on the circumstances of its composition—its integrity, authenticity, and dating.[29] For, if it was not composed in the second century, then the model for the emergence of Christian martyrdom must necessarily be rethought.

THE INTEGRITY OF THE ACCOUNT

The *Martyrdom of Polycarp* survives in two forms: one recorded, according to its epilogue, by Pseudo-Pionius, and one preserved in Eusebius's fourth-century *Ecclesiastical History.*[30] Although these two versions have a great deal in common, they also differ markedly and have been the subject of heated debate about the priority and antiquity of the textual traditions that they each represent. Eusebius preserves a shorter version of events in which the majority of the parallels between the death of Polycarp and the passion narratives do not appear. The differences between the accounts, especially the neat way in which certain themes are excised or added, raise the issue of their integrity.

Of the many scholarly arguments over stages of composition and the redaction of the *Martyrdom of Polycarp,* the interpolation theory of Hans von Campenhausen has been the most influential.[31] Taking the divergences between the Eusebian version and the menology (or Pseudo-Pionian) text as his starting point, von Campenhausen identifies four stages of redaction. First, noting that Eusebius does not include the parallels with the passion narratives, he posits a gospel redactor who introduced the parallels to the gospels that are not original to the text, but are rather, in his view, fourth-century additions. Second, he suggests that before Eusebius's incorporation of the text, the Quintus incident (*Mart. Pol.* 4) had been added to the account as an anti-Montanist polemic at the same time as the polemical sections on the veneration of relics (*Mart. Pol.* 17–18). Third, and also before Eusebius, a redactor introduced the miracles into the account (*Mart. Pol.* 5.2; 9.1; 15.2). Finally, chapters 21 and 22.2–3 are post-Eusebian additions.

Von Campenhausen's reliance on the divergences between the Pseudo-Pionian and Eusebian textual traditions has drawn considerable criticism.[32] Eusebius is known to have elsewhere adapted and modified his sources, and it seems possible that he here condenses a longer edition of the *Martyrdom of Polycarp* for his *Ecclesiastical History.* Furthermore, von Campenhausen's assertion that the imitation motif must derive from the fourth century seems to ignore the wealth of earlier texts in which martyrs were assimilated to Christ.[33] The arguments essential to his study, however, have marshaled admiration in W. H. C. Frend, Helmut Koester, and Gary Bisbee.[34]

The integrity of the account is a thorny issue. There are marked differences between the text in Eusebius and the Pseudo-Pionian version, yet the effect of these discrepancies is undercut if Eusebius is summarizing rather than copying.[35] From a literary perspective, the division into multiple layers of tradition seems unnecessary.[36] The single narrative seam in the menology text is Polycarp's double entrance into the stadium in *Mart. Pol.* 9; otherwise, the account hangs together beautifully: Quintus's brash self-offering, for instance, the most oft-cited example of interpolation as it interrupts a story about Polycarp, serves as a perfect counterpoint to Polycarp's martyrdom according to gospel. Given the perceptible literary unity of the account and the explanation for the differences between Eusebius's and Pseudo-Pionius's versions, it is interesting that scholars have tried to discern so many layers in the text's composition. Indeed, it may not be coincidental that the elements attributed to later stages of redaction—Quintus, the presence of relics, biblical parallelism—are precisely those that seem historically, rather than literarily, incongruous.

THE AUTHENTICITY OF THE ACCOUNT

For many, the dating of the *Martyrdom of Polycarp* has been grounded in the assumption that the text is an authentic eyewitness account written shortly after the events it describes.[37] If the narrative is eyewitness testimony, then the date of the execution can be used to anchor the date of the text. According to this view, several elements in the martyrdom account provide evidence for the date of the execution. First, during his trial Polycarp claims to have served Christ for eighty-six years (*Mart. Pol.* 9.3). The statement is ambiguous: does he mean that he has served Christ since his birth or since his baptism? If the latter, when was Polycarp baptized? As an infant or a young man? A second complicating issue, to be examined more fully below, is the reference to Quintus the Phrygian in *Mart. Pol.* 4. Quintus comes forward and offers himself for martyrdom only to apostasize at the last minute. If, as some scholars hold, Quintus is a member of the New Prophecy movement, then Polycarp's death must be dated after its emergence in the late 160s.

In some ways it is remarkable that such evidence is adduced for the dating of the text at all. These elements say more about the date of Polycarp's execution than about that of the composition of the martyrdom account. Methodologically, the argument is flawed: the reference to Polycarp's age at the time of his death would hardly under normal circumstances be considered evidence for the composition of the account, but rather merely for the date of the event mentioned. The assumption that permits this logical leap is the scholarly belief that the *Martyrdom of Polycarp* preserves an authentic eyewitness account of the death of the bishop of Smyrna. It is therefore worth reexamining in particular those sections whose composition in the first person suggests that their author was present at the events. The *Martyrdom of Polycarp* presents itself as a letter sent by the church at Smyrna to the church at Philomelium, a small, unremarkable town that had little to recommend it in the second century.[38] The letter opens in the first person and frames the subsequent narrative as an exemplary text that encourages its recipients to imitate the martyrs (*Mart. Pol.* 1.1–2). The use of the first person continues throughout the opening exhortation but ceases as the author transitions to the experiences of Germanicus, Quintus, and Polycarp. A number of authorial comments suggest a familiarity with these events, remarking, for example, upon the feelings of those men sent to arrest Polycarp: that "many regretted that they had come after such a godly man" (*Mart. Pol.* 7.3).

The use of the first person in a claim to eyewitness testimony, however, does not occur until Polycarp's trial in the arena and the appearance of a heavenly voice: "But as Polycarp entered the stadium, there came a voice from heaven:

'Be strong, Polycarp, and act like a man.' And no one saw the speaker, but those of our people who were present heard the voice" (*Mart. Pol.* 9.1). The miraculous intervention of a heavenly voice in conjunction with the abrupt reappearance of the first person is intriguing. Perhaps the note that no one else heard the heavenly exhortation is intended to strengthen the allusion to scriptural accounts of the baptism of Jesus in which it is unclear whether passersby heard the voice of God (Mark 1:11; Matt 3:17; Luke 3:22). The argument that the author intends to assimilate events in his narrative to events in the Jesus story hardly speaks to the authenticity of the account as a whole. Nor does biblical parallelism explain the sudden use of the first person. Functionally, the introduction of the first person places the authors of the letter in a privileged position vis-à-vis their audience. Their statement endows them with a particular kind of elite religious authority: they hear the voice of God. The claim legitimizes and authenticates an otherwise unattested miracle.

The same use of eyewitness testimony to validate the miraculous resurfaces toward the end of the account, at the lighting of Polycarp's pyre. The flames of the fire fan out like the sail of a ship to enclose the body of Polycarp, but only "we saw a miracle (we, that is, to whom it was given to see)" (*Mart. Pol.* 15.1). Once again, the first person authenticates a miracle that was otherwise indiscernible. The miracle is visible only to a chosen group who claim for themselves an unassailable rhetorical high ground: those who doubt the miracle are not part of the divinely appointed elite. The miracle itself and the olfactory delights it confers owe much to the idea prevalent in the cult of the saints that the bodies of the saints are fragrant and pleasing (for example, *Lyons* 1.35). The cultic interests of the implied eyewitnesses extend to the end of the work. The communal authors state that they were prevented from retrieving Polycarp's body by the adversary who prompted Nicetes to insist on its cremation. Nevertheless, the eyewitnesses retrieved the bones of the cremated Polycarp and set them somewhere appropriate for safekeeping and veneration. The letter concludes in the first person with the request that it be circulated to those farther afield.

The use of the first person and eyewitness testimony in the *Martyrdom of Polycarp* is selective and strategic. It validates otherwise unsubstantiated miracles—voices and visions indiscernible to the other witnesses—and accounts for the paucity of relics. The deployment of the first person is far from a guarantee of the early dating and authentic character of this text; on the contrary, it raises suspicions about the authenticity of the account as a whole. The appeal to eyewitness testimony in support of miracles is highly strategic; the rest of the account is narrated in the third person. If the account is not an eyewitness report, then it is worth considering afresh the evidence for its dating.

DATING THE *MARTYRDOM OF POLYCARP*

Even if the *Martyrdom of Polycarp* is not an authentic eyewitness account, the question of the date of the composition still remains. While we cannot and should not assume that the text is a second-century fabrication, this possibility must be entertained. When we examine the text, however, there are historical, literary, and conceptual reasons which suggest that the *Martyrdom of Polycarp* was composed sometime after the events described in it, potentially as late as the middle of the third century.

A number of elements in the *Martyrdom of Polycarp* seem historically implausible or outright inaccurate. One of its major peculiarities is the handling of the martyrs' trials. In place of a formal trial in a judicial basilica, Polycarp is both tried and sentenced in the stadium. If he was formally tried *pro tribunalis* (as the law would have decreed), no record of this event is contained in the *acta*. The content of the examination is similarly bizarre. If, as we would assume, the prosecutor followed the legal process outlined in the Pliny-Trajan correspondence, then the charge of atheism is out of place. This accusation and Polycarp's ironic response, "Away with the Atheists" (*Mart. Pol.* 9.2), seem more in keeping with the trial of Socrates than Roman legal process. The proconsul did not read out the verdict himself, as we would expect, and instead sent a herald into the stadium to announce that Polycarp had admitted to being a Christian.[39] The location of the trial in the amphitheater is startling. The clearest parallel for such an event also comes from the *Martyrdom of Polycarp*, in which the martyr Germanicus's conversation with the judge similarly takes place within the amphitheater. The affair is so ad hoc that the proconsul attempts to persuade Germanicus to recant even as the martyr stands within an arm's reach of a lion. If the *Martyrdom of Polycarp* is faithful to the historical events, the proconsul not only disregarded legal procedure in general, he was willing to take the risk that the sentence would be carried out before the trial was completed. It is difficult to believe that the "trial" of Germanicus bears any relationship to reality.

The chaotic, disjointed, and perfunctory feel of Polycarp's trial underscores the injustice of the event and emphasizes the parallels between the Roman prosecutor's trial of Polycarp and Pilate's address to the crowd. If the trial is not historical, this has ramifications both for the legal history of early Christian martyrdom and for our understanding of the account itself. The Roman proconsul does not so much veer off-script when it comes to Roman legal protocol as remain in gospel character. If Polycarp is assimilated to Christ and this assimilation shapes the record of his trial, then the legal situation envisioned in the narrative cannot be used to date the account.[40]

In addition to these legal incongruities, there is the highly literary and allusive character of the text itself.[41] The parallels between the passion narrative and the *Martyrdom of Polycarp* are apparent to the most cursory of readers.[42] Connections often cited include the delay in being handed over to the authorities (*Mart. Pol.* 1.2), the distance from the city at the point of arrest (5.1), the protagonist's prophesying of his own death (5.2; 12.3), the betrayal of the protagonist by someone close to him (6.2), the participation of a character named Herod in the events that lead to the death of the protagonist (6.2), the invocation of robbery as a motivating factor in the arrest and trial (7.1), the apprehending of the protagonist at night (7.1–2), the obedience to the will of God (7.1), entering the city on an ass (8.1), the Roman authorities' equivocation over the sentence of death (9.3–11.2), the intervention of the bloodthirsty Jewish crowd (12.2–13.1), the stabbing and flow of blood (16.1), and the timing of the protagonist's death around Passover (21).[43]

The self-conscious representation of Polycarp as Christly mimic coupled with the numerous allusions to scriptural narratives of Jesus's death certainly cast doubt on the text's status as an eyewitness report. Even if we are willing to grant that the historical Polycarp deliberately imitated the conduct of Jesus—as the account in turn encourages others to imitate Polycarp—we are still left with those elements outside of the control of the posited historical Polycarp that have a suspiciously scriptural ring to them. Yet for many scholars the literary ties between the passion narrative and the account of Polycarp's death are unproblematic. For Joseph Barber Lightfoot the preponderance of *imitatio Christi* in the acts of the martyrs and writings of Eusebius in fact supports (or at least does not discredit) the veracity of the events in the *Martyrdom of Polycarp*. If the presence of the *imitatio Christi* must be expressed in terms of genuineness, rather than in literary terms, then Lightfoot's argument is decidedly shaky. It seems questionable to say that because many authors could be indicted for fabricating a theological-literary theme, none of them should be. The phenomenon is widespread, as Lightfoot notes. If Lightfoot's point is that early Christians shaped the presentation of the martyrs using a Christly template, then it should be noted that there is a qualitative difference between the sustained and self-conscious *imitatio* in the *Martyrdom of Polycarp* and the *imitatio* in the examples Lightfoot produces.[44] The presentation of isolated elements of a martyrdom account (for example, Blandina's cruciform pose on the stake in the *Letter of the Churches of Vienne and Lyons*) as *imitatio* differs from the way in which the account of Polycarp's death is stretched over the frame of the passion narrative as a whole. The sustained presentation of Polycarp as *alter Christus* suggests that the entire story has been shaped by this concern.

Lightfoot's primary argument for viewing the parallelism as authentic, however, is his sense that the connections are forced and tenuous: "a fabricator would have secured a better parallel. We may say generally that *the violence of the parallelism is a guarantee of the accuracy of the facts.*"[45] Given the influence of his arguments, Lightfoot's assumptions about the act of fabrication bear some consideration.[46] In the first place, he assumes that if the parallelism is "inauthentic," then all elements of the narrative must stem from the genius of the author. In other words, either the author composed these parallels himself or the events actually happened. There is no room for accumulating oral traditions. More pressing is the assumption that the fabricator must be single-minded in his narration of events. Lightfoot's basic criticism—that the parallels aren't any good—fails to take seriously the aesthetic value of allusion and the author's possible supplementary goals. Even if we follow his argument that the parallelism is the ex nihilo creation of the author, Lightfoot overlooks the competing demands that biblical parallelism, verisimilitude, and—for want of a better term—polemical aims present to the author. For instance, he views the parallel between the two Herods—the Smyrnean police captain and the biblical king—as "faint" because their statuses and roles are not identical. This criticism assumes that the author is entirely at liberty to create parallels; but could he have invented a Smyrnean king or named his Roman procurator Herod without inviting a certain degree of suspicion from his audience? Furthermore, by calling the captain of the guard Herod, the author of the *Martyrdom of Polycarp* may be making a wry comment on the biblical Herod's function vis-à-vis Roman authorities. Given the anti-Jewish sentiment in the text as a whole, the identification of the guard with a Jewish leader also serves the larger program of the work. The parallelism both tarnishes those arresting Jesus by associating them with the Jews and reduces the biblical Herod to a subordinate role. The *imitatio* elicited by the parallel can be read as strategic and multifaceted.

Consideration of a more extended example of the augmentation of biblical parallelism by interpretation is worthwhile. The moment at which Polycarp refuses to be nailed to the stake and is instead bound can be understood as a break in the *imitatio Christi* motif. The divergence from the gospel script might be read, as Lightfoot would have us do, as a "violent parallel" indicating the authenticity of the event. Polycarp declines to be nailed because the historical Polycarp really was bound. This reading would, however, disregard the narrative effect of Polycarp's binding. Polycarp is bound not by accident but as the result of his own request; he states, "Leave me as I am; for he who enables me to endure the fire will also enable me to remain on the pyre without moving, even without the sense of security which you get from the nails"

(*Mart. Pol.* 13.3). Polycarp's emboldened, almost arrogant statement in some respects usurps the position and experience of Christ. Unlike Jesus, Polycarp does not require nails to hold him steady; he can stand by sheer will. A number of scholars have pointed out that the stoicism of Polycarp both here and elsewhere in the narrative casts him as a philosopher and assimilates him to Socrates.[47] This argument certainly has some merit and complicates the way in which we understand intertextuality to work in the account. *Imitatio Christi* and *imitatio Socratis* may be interwoven and fused. Another way of viewing the break in the assimilation to Christ is to connect the binding of Polycarp to early Christian interpretations that linked the death of Jesus to the binding of Isaac. When read in light of the narrator's description of Polycarp as a splendid ram (*Mart. Pol.* 14.1), it seems that the binding of Polycarp draws together sacrificial interpretations of Polycarp's death with a tradition that connected Isaac and Christ (for example, Irenaeus, *Haer.* 5.5.4). The binding of Polycarp therefore serves a concrete exegetical and theological purpose. The author may be working not only with multiple textual portraits of Jesus, but also with interpretive traditions, cultural tropes, and non-Christian exemplars. A deviation from the model of the passion narrative does not necessarily indicate that the events are authentic.

A further difficulty arises when we turn to the textual provenance for the story that is provided toward the end of the account. At the conclusion of the *Martyrdom of Polycarp* are two epilogues—the general epilogue and a separate anti-Marcionite epilogue found in the Moscow codex and Eusebius. The general epilogue provides an orthodox lineage to the work that traces the discovery of the text by Pionius, through Socrates and a copy by a scribe named Gaius, to the personal library of Irenaeus: "This account Gaius transcribed from the papers of Irenaeus, a disciple of Polycarp, who also lived with Irenaeus. And I, Socrates, wrote it down in Corinth from the copies of Gaius. Grace be with everyone. And I, Pionius, wrote it down again from the previously mentioned copy, after making a search for it (for the blessed Polycarp showed it to me in a revelation, as I will explain in the sequel). I gathered it together when it was nearly worn out by age, that the Lord Jesus Christ might also gather me together with his elect into his heavenly kingdom; to whom be the glory with the Father and the Holy Spirit forever and ever"(*Mart. Pol.* 22.2–3). The Pionius mentioned in the account is presumably the third-century martyr Pionius who was executed during the persecution of Decius around 250 CE. In his writings Irenaeus indicates that he is familiar with Polycarp's *Letter to the Philippians,* which he recommends as a powerful letter from which his readers can "learn the character of his [Polycarp's] faith," but he makes no mention of the account of Polycarp's execution (*Haer.* 3.3.4).

Irenaeus knows about Polycarp's death but appears not to have known about any letter detailing his execution. It would seem, therefore, that the textual history of the *Martyrdom of Polycarp* is fabricated. The construction of a literary heritage for the text serves to authenticate the account and endow it with a particular ancestry.

The reference to the author's revelation bears more than a passing resemblance to apocryphal narratives relating the discovery, or *inventio,* of corporeal or textual relics such as the *Apocryphon of James* and the *Apocryphon of John.*[48] Often, these texts are situated within a conceptual framework of secret and elite scribal traditions. The revelation was deliberately hidden and obscured from Christians in general. While the disclosure-via-vision of a previously unknown text may have its roots in these kinds of elite literary communities, later accounts such as the *Acts of Pilate* are directed not to an esoteric elite, but to all Christians.[49] In the *Acts of Pilate* the disclosure-via-vision guarantees the historical authenticity of the account. In those accounts directed to the entire Christian church, the discovery of the text is fashioned using the conventions of relic invention: a supernatural revelation discloses the location of a previously lost powerful religious artifact.[50] In the fourth and fifth centuries textual *inventio* appears to have garnered imperial and mainstream ecclesiastical support; Eusebius uses apocryphal letters from the library at Edessa (*Hist. eccl.* 1.13), and the emperor Theodosius himself opens the marble box containing the textual relic the *Apocalypse of Paul* (1–2). By the fourth century, and despite their condemnation of heretical apocryphal works, orthodox groups were also producing official accounts of the recovery of relics, be they textual or corporeal.

The use of the conventions of relic invention in the general epilogue to the *Martyrdom of Polycarp* does not offer concrete evidence for the date of composition. It does, however, cast doubts on an early dating. This narrative device functions in other early Christian texts not only to legitimize a new text, but also to account for the text's sudden appearance. If we see the same principle at work in the *Martyrdom of Polycarp*, it seems that the author is constructing a storied literary pedigree for a text that he composed. The vision explains the text's sudden appearance, and the need to explain this sudden appearance would seem to suggest that some time has elapsed between Polycarp's death and the letter's composition. If, as some have argued, the epilogue is a secondary addition to an already circulating account, then the vision seems unnecessary. Why would Pseudo-Pionius need to explain the discovery of a letter that was already well known? It seems more likely that the epilogue is part of the account. In this case, the vision serves either to authenticate the Pseudo-Pionian version (over and against some other version) or to account for the "discovery" of the letter long after the events it describes.

In addition to these literary peculiarities there are also conceptual anach-ronisms relating to the idea of martyrdom and knowledge of the cult of the saints presupposed by the author. If this is in fact the first martyrdom ac-count, it displays a remarkably sophisticated understanding of the role and status of the martyr. One striking feature is the text's unprecedented interest in the relics of the saint, in his physical remains. Whereas Ignatius of Antioch prayed that none of his body be left by the wild beasts so that he not be a bother to anyone (Ign. *Rom.* 4.2), the author of the *Martyrdom of Polycarp* exhibits a notable and refined interest in his subject's remains. After Poly-carp's death, the devil enters the action of the narrative to prevent the pre-servation of Polycarp's body: "But the jealous and envious Evil One . . . managed that not even his [Polycarp's] poor body should be taken away by us, although many desired to do this and to touch his holy flesh. So he put forward Nicetes, the father of Herod and brother of Alce, to plead with the magistrate not to give up his body, 'lest,' so it was said, 'they should abandon the crucified one and begin to worship this man'" (*Mart. Pol.* 17). All was not lost for the Christians. After the cremation of Polycarp's body, they col-lected together the remains and, according to the author, "laid them in a suit-able place; where the Lord will permit us to gather ourselves together . . . to celebrate the birth-day of his martyrdom for the commemoration of those that have already fought in the contest, and for the training and preparation of those that shall do so hereafter" (*Mart. Pol.* 18). This description is cited as the earliest example of relic collection in Christianity.[51] While antecedents of the Christian use of relics can be found in Greek hero cults, Jewish burial practices, and scriptural accounts,[52] the *Martyrdom of Polycarp* ostensibly contains the first instance of Christians treating the bodies of saints as loci of power. Concern for a proper burial was a commonplace in antiquity, but the author of the *Martyrdom of Polycarp* goes far beyond a mere interest in burial practices and bodily resurrection when he pronounces the bones of Polycarp to be "more valuable than precious stones" and describes their de-position in a suitable place where they are venerated (*Mart. Pol.* 18). The text envisions the housing of the bodies of martyrs in special locations where the *dies natales* of the martyrs are celebrated and where others are schooled in the practice of martyrdom. This construction presupposes a situation in which the cult of the saints is well established.

As early as the work of R. A. Lipsius in the nineteenth century, how-ever, scholars eyed the reference to Polycarp's remains with suspicion.[53] The widespread practice of collecting and venerating the bodies of the martyrs is unparalleled in second-century Christian literature. While concern for proper burial and the relationship between burial and resurrection are in evidence (see, for example, *Lyons* in Eusebius, *Hist. eccl.* 5.1.60–63), we should not confuse an interest in bodies with an interest in relics. Apart from the *Martyrdom of Polycarp,* the earliest text exhibiting a concern for the preservation of relics is the *Acts of Thomas.* These apocryphal acts are extant in Greek and Syriac, and both versions describe the mysterious disappearance and translocation of a leg bone of the saint around 232 CE.[54] Within nonapostolic martyrdom literature, references to the birthdays of the saints and the collection of their remains begin in Carthage around the turn of the third century (*Passio* 21.5; Cyprian, *Ep.* 76.2; *Acts of Cyprian* 5). The elements viewed as relics are comparatively unsophisticated. While Pudens's ring dipped in the blood of the wounded Saturus in the *Passion of Perpetua and Felicitas* can be deemed a *brandea* or second-class relic, this classification is rather retrospective; in the account itself the ring is a memento.

Most out of place in the *Martyrdom of Polycarp* is the anachronistic (or, perhaps better, prochronistic) apologia for the absence of relics. This explanation presupposes a cultural context in which the cult of the saints is not just emerging but fully formed—a situation in which the lack of relics was a problem, in which the cult of the saints was already booming. As already noted, however, the literary and material evidence suggests that, according to the traditional dating of the account, the *Martyrdom of Polycarp* predates other indications of the existence of a cult of the saints and of the collection of relics by around fifty years. Furthermore, the style of the explanation has much in common with later explanations for the absence of relics. The destruction of Polycarp's body is, in the world of the text, attributed to the devil. Yet the rationale of the Roman authorities is that the body should not be released "lest . . . [the Christians] should abandon the crucified one and begin to worship [Polycarp]" (*Mart. Pol.* 17.2). The same justification appears elsewhere in Eusebius's *Ecclesiastical History* where the bodies of martyrs are dug up and cast into the sea "lest any, as they thought, regarding them as gods, might worship them lying in their sepulchers" (*Hist. eccl.* 8.6.7). It is certainly possible, indeed probable, that Eusebius borrowed this concept from the *Martyrdom of Polycarp,* but it is notable that this justification for the eradication of relics appears only in the *Martyrdom of Polycarp* and these later texts. The fear that Christians might worship the martyrs "as gods" is more appropriate to the church fathers than to second-century Romans.[55] After all, to a Roman prosecutor the prospect that early Christians might abandon the crucified one is desirable. The threat here is not to Roman authority, but to ecclesiastical ability to control and regulate religious charisma. The situation described in the *Martyrdom of Polycarp* presupposes that the importance of martyrs is such that they might threaten the significance of Christ. The absence of relics provides the author with an opportunity to address an exalted view of martyrs that, in his eyes, goes much too far.

That the *Martyrdom of Polycarp* should be the first account to refer to relics and the cult of the saints is not completely implausible. After all, there has to be a first occurrence of everything. As we have seen, however, there are a number of reasons for suggesting that the account is not the first such reference: a considerable passage of time lies between Polycarp and subsequent references to the cult of the saints; the account presupposes a highly developed set of religious practices (bone gathering) for which there is little contemporary evidence; and the rationale for the text's apologia for the lack of relics fits with much later concerns about the status of the martyr.[56]

In a similar vein, there are passages in the text that presuppose a particularly developed understanding of martyrological orthopraxy (right practice). Throughout the account are references to the catholic church (καθολικῆς ἐκκλησίας) (*Mart. Pol.* 1; 8.1; 16.1; 19.1), and for the nineteenth-century German scholar Theodor Keim, the use of the phrase seems to betray a date much later than 157 CE.[57] The term resonates in a number of ways. In three of the four instances in which it appears, the sense of the passage conveys nothing more than the notion of a unified community. A similar usage is found in Ignatius's *Letter to the Smyrneans,* in which he writes that wherever the bishop appears, there also is the catholic church (8.2). In *Mart. Pol.* 16.1, however, the use of the term is different, for here the text describes Polycarp as "bishop of the Catholic Church in Smyrna" (ἐπίσκοπος τῆς ἐν Σμύρνη καθολικῆς ἐκκλησίας). The textual evidence for καθολικῆς is slightly complicated as in two manuscripts (m L) the term ἁγίας appears in its place. The weight of the manuscript evidence (a b h p Eus) supports the use of the term "catholic," which is retained in recent critical editions of the *Martyrdom of Polycarp.*[58] The nuance of the word, therefore, demands additional reflection. Whereas other uses of the term in the *Martyrdom of Polycarp* appear to refer to the universal church in general, the specification of the church in Smyrna seems to connote a sense of proto-orthodox conformity. The use of the phrase suggests a contrast between Polycarp's Catholic Church and other Christian communities in Smyrna,[59] in which case we must ask, To which Christians does the author refer?

Reinhard Hübner tentatively hypothesizes that the phrase rises from a situation of conflict between the "catholic church" and Valentinians.[60] He argues that the *Martyrdom of Polycarp* is polemic directed against the elitist

Valentinians and also contains a positive egalitarian message in presenting a vision of Christianity for everyone.[61] While it seems likely that the author of the *Martyrdom of Polycarp* has a group of Christians in mind, it seems extraordinary to suggest that this group is a cohort of Valentinians. This argument fails to account both for the numerous first-century scriptural texts that present suffering and martyrdom as means of following Jesus and for more moderate orthodox positions on martyrdom such as that of Clement of Alexandria.[62] This argument is grounded in a stereotype of Gnosticism as elitist and anti-martyrdom over and against the orthodox, populist appeal of martyrdom.[63] The binary is simplistic and reductionist, and it relies on an outdated stereotype of Gnosticism; recent work on Gnosticism has deepened our view of the extent to which attitudes to martyrdom intersect with orthodoxy.

More importantly, if the *Martyrdom of Polycarp* seems directed against a specific form of Christianity, surely the starting point for information about the identity of this group of Christians should be the martyrdom account itself. When we look to the text, the most likely candidate for this kind of implicit criticism would be the Phrygian Christians personified by the antitype Quintus. If the account was composed in the third century, it functions as a subtle denouncement of orthodox stereotypes of Montanism; otherwise, the association may be entirely accidental. Alternatively, the reference to the Catholic Church in Smyrna may be directed to those outside of Asia Minor as a means of suggesting Smyrna's conformity to orthodoxy in general. The author presents the work as something of an encyclical, addressing the letter not only to Philomelium, but to all the churches everywhere (*Mart. Pol.* 1.1). The use of the term "Catholic Church" is, therefore, here a statement of conformity. The addressees can be sure that they are receiving a communiqué from the universal church in Smyrna, not from some suspicious regional variety.

To a rather developed notion of the Catholic church we can add an awareness of heterodox practice of martyrdom. One of the rubs for the dating of the *Martyrdom of Polycarp* has been the presence and apostasy of Quintus, a Christian from Phrygia in Asia Minor, in *Mart. Pol.* 4. According to the narrative, a certain Quintus rushed to offer himself for execution only to fall away at the last moment: "Now there was one man, Quintus by name, a Phrygian recently arrived from Phrygia, who, when he saw the wild beasts, turned coward. This was the man who had forced himself and some others to come forward voluntarily. The proconsul, after many appeals, finally persuaded him to swear the oath and to offer the sacrifice. For this reason therefore, brothers, we do not praise those who hand themselves over, since the Gospel does not so teach" (*Mart. Pol.* 4.1 [trans. Holmes, *Apostolic Fathers*]). The function of Quintus's spectacular failure has not been lost on scholarly interpreters of the martyrdom. While some have viewed *Mart. Pol.* 4 as a later insertion, it is clear that Quintus's eager attempt to secure glory and death for himself contrasts narratively with the patient self-restraint of the *Martyrdom of Polycarp*'s episcopal hero. Where Quintus is brash and active, Polycarp is restrained and quiet. In the words of Michael Holmes, Polycarp's martyrdom "is a matter of divine calling rather than human accomplishment or initiative."[64] The contrast between Quintus and Polycarp is an integral part of the narrative and cannot be easily excised. If, as Holmes and others have argued, the contrast between Quintus's unevangelical self-offering and the model of martyrdom "in accordance with the gospel" presented in the figure of Polycarp is a motivating force for the composition of the account, Quintus takes on a greater significance.[65] If one of the author's purposes is to condemn the kind of martyrdom and kinds of martyrs that Quintus represents, the character of Quintus provides a valuable insight into the historical context of the *Martyrdom of Polycarp*'s composition.

When it comes to the significance of Quintus for the dating of the account, a number of possibilities present themselves. Quintus may represent a form of behavior—either potential or actual—that the author wished to discourage. Some scholars classify Quintus's conduct as a form of "voluntary martyrdom."[66] According to the narrative, Quintus had "forced himself and some others to come forward voluntarily." His eagerness and self-offering are connected to his subsequent cowardice and apostasy. In contrast to Polycarp, who held back and held fast, Quintus offered himself for martyrdom and then retracted his confession. The critique that the author offers is not of apostasy, a general threat envisioned in the writings of a number of early Christian authors, but of coming forward to volunteer for death. Apostasy is the black mark used to condemn volunteerism. This much is evident in the author's concluding statement that it is "for this reason [the apostasy of Quintus], therefore, brothers, we do not praise those who hand themselves over." Offering oneself for martyrdom requires both an ideology that values suffering and death and also a political and legal system in which it is possible to volunteer for execution.[67]

Even as Quintus personifies a type of martyrdom that the author of the account wishes to avoid, it is possible that he also represents a particular ancient Christian group. In martyrdom scholarship some have interpreted the description of Quintus as a Phrygian as a veiled allusion to the New Prophecy, the ecstatic religious practice popular in Asia Minor and Carthage in the third century.[68] Adherents to the New Prophecy, or Montanists as they are often known, have traditionally been portrayed as eager and enthusiastic believers in martyrdom whose reckless, provocative conduct led to their executions.[69]

The debate over Quintus's association with Montanism revolves around the assumption that the practice or group embodied in Quintus is an accurate portrayal of late second- or third-century Montanists. Quintus's portrayal should cohere with what we can learn from other sources about the nature of Montanism.[70] William Tabbernee's important work on Montanist inscriptions, for instance, has demonstrated that Montanists were no more eager to seek out martyrdom than were the "orthodox."[71] In practice, then, discussions about the identity of Quintus center on the extent to which Montanists were or were not voluntary martyrs—if they were, the identification of Quintus as a Phrygian who offered himself for martyrdom is a fairly secure reference to the Montanists; if they were not, then the reference to Phrygia is an incidental detail turned scholarly red herring. Whether or not Quintus is supposed to be understood as an adherent of the New Prophecy, his depiction tells us something about the date of the account. The presentation of the "wrong" approach to martyrdom in the person of Quintus suggests that at the time of the text's composition, the experience was fairly well known.

PLACING POLYCARP AMONG THE MARTYRS

The idea that the *Martyrdom of Polycarp* is an eyewitness account seems untenable. To this improbability we can add a number of other unlikely events: the seemingly illegal trials, one of which, that of Germanicus, is conducted in the physical presence of a lion; the ease with which the people are able to gather firewood for Polycarp's pyre in the stadium; and the similarities with the death of Jesus. The anachronisms, implausibilities, and historical inaccuracies discount the possibility that the account was written, as claimed in *Mart. Pol.* 18.3, within a year of the bishop's death. Unless one wishes to fillet the narrative into a multistage composition that allows the attribution of such anachronisms to later redactors and editors, the account should be treated as a single work. The question, then, is when the *Martyrdom of Polycarp* was written. As it stands, the text is a highly sophisticated and detailed exposition on the correct form of martyrdom, on martyrdom "according to gospel." The author distinguishes between different kinds of martyrdom and offers a subtle polemic against the enthusiastic volunteerism embodied in Quintus. The distinction presupposes that at the time the account was written, various competing ideologies and practices of martyrdom already existed that the author then engaged. Similarly, the author's concern that some might confuse Polycarp with Christ makes sense only in a context in which the status of the martyr was well established. It is difficult to imagine that the text is, as has sometimes been claimed, the first important writing on martyrdom, the first text to use *martys* unambiguously to refer to someone who dies for his or her beliefs,[72] the first text to warn against the practice of voluntary martyrdom, and the first text to refer to the cult of the saints. In the *Martyrdom of Polycarp,* the practice of martyrdom has been extensively theorized.

Rather than inaugurating the genre and ideology of martyrdom, the *Martyrdom of Polycarp* assertively enters into a preexisting debate about the nature of martyrdom and the status of martyrs, a debate that assumes the existence of the cult of the saints, the collection of relics, catechesis for martyrdom, the Catholic Church as a distinctive entity, the practice of voluntary martyrdom, and the high estimation of the martyrs. The first text that can confidently be said to have known the *Martyrdom of Polycarp* is the *Martyrdom of Pionius,* a third-century martyr act from Smyrna with literary and thematic connections to the *Martyrdom of Polycarp.* The account's protagonist is assumed to be the same Pionius who appears in the epilogue to the *Martyrdom of Polycarp.* Pionius's connection to Polycarp is accentuated by the date of his death, "on the anniversary of the blessed martyr Polycarp, while the persecution of Decius was still on" (*Mart. Pionius* 2.1). In a further assimilation to the death of Polycarp, the date of Pionius's arrest is twice referred to as the "great sabbath" (*Mart. Pionius* 2.1; 3.6; cf. *Mart. Pol.* 8.1).[73] Neither of these elements in the *Martyrdom of Pionius* necessarily refers to a literary account of the death of Polycarp, but if Polycarp's death was commemorated on a certain day, then it seems plausible that literary acts accompanied this act of memorialization. The execution of Pionius took place during the persecutions of Decius, and thus the account of Pionius's death cannot be dated before 250 CE.[74] In all probability, therefore, the *Martyrdom of Polycarp* was in circulation in the first half of the third century.

The uncertainty regarding the precise purposes and circumstances of the composition of this text aside, it is worth reflecting on its function. Even without a firm foothold in ecclesiastical history, it is still possible to consider the ways in which the death of Polycarp is understood in this account. Of particular importance here is the manner in which the *Martyrdom of Polycarp* functions within the larger context of third-century martyrological theologies and practices. Once the account ceases to be trumpeted as the herald of an international movement and is recast as one voice among many, we can hypothesize about the relationship between the highly nuanced martyrological theory of the *Martyrdom of Polycarp* and other treatments of martyrdom in the third century.

A distinctive feature of the presentation of martyrdom in both Ignatius and the *Martyrdom of Polycarp* is the characterization of the martyr as model and *imitator Christi.* Polycarp's death is described as taking place "according to gospel." The characterization of this death as evangelical is deliberately and repeatedly contrasted with the unevangelical death of Quintus, who not only came forward of his own accord, but encouraged others to do so before apostasizing out of cowardice. The distinction between forms of martyrdom is carved with amorphous notions of scriptural conduct and gospel-led life. This is in turn overlaid by the designation of Polycarp and the addressees as "Catholic." The three binaries—patient martyrdom/enthusiastic martyrdom, evangelical/unevangelical, Catholic/non-Catholic—are stacked upon one another to the effect that true, gospel-shaped martyrdom becomes irrevocably associated with the Catholic Church in Smyrna. That this select group are the only ones capable of discerning the miraculous events in the narrative is not only a means of authenticating and authorizing the character of Polycarp's death, it places at one remove the traditional notion that miracles are accessible to those of faith. Not only miracles, but also the ability to discern them, are available only to insiders. If the author of this account is familiar with the Johannine saying that links *semeia* (miraculous events) to the production of faith ("these are written that you may believe"; John 20:30–31), then a subtle shift takes place here. Explicitly and implicitly, the author narratively crafts two positions: the miracle-filled, scripturally guided, patient death of the Catholic bishop and the rushed, unevangelical, cowardly life of Quintus.

This characterization of Polycarp certainly contrasts Polycarp to Quintus, but it also, as the author repeatedly notes, presents Polycarp as an imitator of Christ. As we have already seen, the details of Polycarp's imitation are often used as a gauge for the authenticity of the text. It is important to remember, however, that biblical parallelism is rarely an end in itself. With respect to dating, Lightfoot's error is to have assumed that the author's intent is to produce the best possible literary parallel rather than to use the parallelism to a particular effect. The presentation of Polycarp as imitator of Christ is a reading of Jesus traditions but is also productive: Polycarp models sets of behaviors and attitudes that the author wishes his audience to reproduce. In other words, the paradigm Polycarp embodies is held up to the audience as a target for emulation. In his grand study of martyrdom in the early church, von Campenhausen argues that biblical parallels inculcate a set of values in the audience. Polycarp's exemplary function is grounded in the ecclesiastically normative concept of imitating Christ.[75] Holmes has made a similar argument that the account presents a moderate take on martyrdom grounded in gospel.[76] Quintus, in turn, becomes an antitype whose example is to be avoided and heeded as a warning. The Christly attitude to martyrdom, as portrayed in Polycarp, is not to offer oneself for martyrdom, but to embrace it eagerly once the opportunity is presented.

The account of Polycarp's martyrdom explicitly identifies its hero as a model to be emulated and imitated. The model presented by Polycarp, however, is about more than just imitating Jesus; it re-creates the Jesus narrative itself. The moment when Polycarp refuses to be nailed to the stake can be read, following Irenaeus or the *Gospel of Peter,* as an *imitatio Christi,* but it also serves to emphasize Polycarp's masculinity.[77] If a central theme slips into and binds these texts together, it is the manliness of the punctured hero. The frail and elderly Polycarp, steeled by hours of prayer at his arrest, grows ever more potent throughout the account. He eagerly disembarks from his carriage and refuses the reinforcement of nails. This robust portrayal of the good death draws upon Greco-Roman discussions of the masculine virtues and narratives of manly courage. Just like Gaius Marius in Cicero's *Tusc.* 2.22.53, Polycarp does not need to be nailed, for he is a true *vir.* That the heavenly voice of *Mart. Pol.* 9.1 exhorts Polycarp to "play the man" directs us to the manner in which martyrdom in this text is about the performance of masculinity. In allowing these cultural and scriptural intertexts to echo in our reading of the text, it is not necessary to adjudicate between the various models or designate one intertext regnant over the others. On the contrary, the confluence of these traditions in the person of Polycarp augments the interpretation of each intertext with the nuances of the other. Thus, even as Polycarp is explicitly described as imitating the model of Jesus, his masculine *imitatio* in turn alters the way in which the audience interprets the death and person of Jesus and, if they catch the allusions, the death and person of Socrates. The interpretations of both Polycarp and Jesus are altered by the practice of reading these figures together.[78]

Conclusion

We have reconsidered the evidence for dates of martyrdom literature from Asia Minor. The repositioning of the *Martyrdom of Polycarp* as a third-century text radically alters our understanding of the emergence of martyrdom in early Christian communities. If, as we have seen, the account was not composed and circulated in the middle of the second century, then histories of martyrdom have to be reconfigured. Moreover, and perhaps more important, even if the *Martyrdom of Polycarp* were a second-century account, this would not automatically render it influential. As we have noted, the *Martyrdom of Polycarp* did not appear to influence other early Christian thinkers until the composition of the *Martyrdom of Pionius* in the middle of the third century. The evidence for the *Martyrdom of Polycarp*'s reception in the second and early third centuries is negligible. We must conclude that it is not the fountain-head of early Christian martyrdom writ large—and we may question whether in fact such a fountainhead exists at all.

We have also identified a particular martyrological tradition in Asia Minor. There is a certain cohesion to the presentation of martyrdom in both the letters of Ignatius and the *Martyrdom of Polycarp*. Irrespective of the date of the *Martyrdom of Polycarp*, both bodies of literature portray martyrdom as the mimetic and sacrificial death of a disciple of Christ. Polycarp is a fusion of Christ figure and Greco-Roman heroic male, and his death is, similarly, a medley of both sacrifice and ekphrastic pedagogical moment. In the flames of the executioner's pyre, the author of the *Martyrdom of Polycarp* welds notions of sacrifice and exemplarity, masculinity and mimesis. In his letter to the Romans, Ignatius crafts his death as an imperially styled sacrificial offering. The eucharistic undertones reverberate in both texts; the bodies of both martyrs become bread for public consumption. In both cases, the depiction of suffering and death is related to the correct performance of and posture toward martyrdom, ecclesiology, and church unity. This depiction is not just ecclesiastically introspective; it is positioned in opposition to Roman structures of power. Both authors describe martyrdom as functionally sacrificial in a manner that apes the sacrificial practices of the Roman household and empire and mimes the self-offering of Christ. The dual focus of the sacrificial language—in undermining Roman structures and establishing Christian ones—illustrates the richness of these texts and their multifaceted objectives. Ideologies of martyrdom may function in similar contexts elsewhere in the Roman empire, but their contours and content are not rendered identically.

3

Rome:
Contesting Philosophy

The Jesus movement came to Rome in the mysterious pre–New Testament period, and by the time of Irenaeus's visit in the final quarter of the second century, the group there had become the largest assembly of Christians in the empire.[1] The paucity of information about this period means that the contours of early Christian history in Rome can be only lightly sketched. Like other religious movements, it is reasonable to assume that members of the Jesus movement entered Rome, sometime in the 40s CE, via the trade routes that passed through the port of Puetoli.[2] While there is considerable scholarly debate about the substance of Christianity's presence in the empire's capital and the identity of its earliest leaders, some terse, ambiguous evidence suggests that as early as the time of the edict of Claudius (ca. 49 CE), members of the Jesus movement were being identified as troublemakers. The evidence is problematic, but it seems that by the time of the fire of Rome in 64 CE, Christians had attracted enough attention to be labeled arsonists by Nero. According to Tacitus (*Ann.* 15.38–44), it was not only their odious character that made them such suitable candidates; the dense population of Christians in Trastevere—an area spared by the fire—appeared suspicious.[3] If the followers of Jesus had not conceived of themselves as a discrete group before the fire of Rome, Nero's dramatic response forced them to define themselves as Christians. The memory of this event continued to shape the perception and self-perception of Roman Christians long after Rome had been rebuilt. That Christian identity was forged in flames is not merely the rhetoric of later apologists.

In the imagination of subsequent generations of Christian authors, Rome became the home of martyrs. It was here, they imagined, in the very heart of the oppressive empire, that the great apostles Peter and Paul had died. For later authors, the victimization of Christians had begun during this period, when Nero famously labeled them arsonists and used them as human torches to illuminate Rome. Although no specific legislation was in place promoting persecution, the memory of this experience fostered the creation of a narrative in which Christians portrayed themselves as a persecuted community.[4] At the same time, this memorialization allowed Christians in Rome to restructure the city itself, and the cosmos as a whole, as a grand amphitheater in which to perform Christianity.

We focus here on the motif of the philosophical martyr in early Christian discourse in second-century Rome. It was not only in Rome that Christians read their experience of persecution in concert with philosophical examples of noble death, but philosophical topoi found a particular home here in the writings of educated Christian instructors. The relationship between philosophy and martyrdom is complicated. The death of the philosopher, most notably Socrates, hovers in the background of the description of Eleazar in 4 Maccabees, of Jesus in Luke, and in a number of early Christian martyr acts.[5] The casting of Jewish and Christian martyrs as Socratic figures is a way to harness the cultural value and positive connotations of the philosophical death and use these values to interpret the deaths of Jews and Christians.

If the reuse of cultural icons such as Socrates is well established in martyrdom scholarship, the adaptation of philosophical ideals and language in the context of Christian persecution is the subject of greater debate. Alexandrian Christians Clement and Origen are often treated as the inaugurators of philosophical-martyrological pedagogy. Robin Darling Young writes that Alexandrian Christian paideia instructed Christians how to "detach themselves from the body and sensible world and to prepare them to offer their bodies in a certain state of calm that resembled . . . an attachment to the transcendent realm familiar already in the Platonic tradition."[6] Young proposes that these authors "add a philosophical element that was not present before; they envision a long period of intellectual training and of ascetic self-discipline in order to lead a Christian about to give public testimony to the requisite ability."[7] That Clement and Origen place a particularly philosophical spin on the deaths of Christians cannot be contested. The claim that these authors are responsible for inaugurating this philosophical trend, however, may be too forceful. In an article on preparation for martyrdom, Nicole Kelley argues that early Christian martyrdom literature in general adopted and adapted the techniques of philosophical training as a means of preparing early Christians for martyrdom.[8] She intimates that philosophical pedagogical strategies and ideals were used to inculcate martyrological values in early Christian groups as early as the second century. If Kelley is correct, then it will come as no surprise to find philosophically infused martyrdom in other quarters of the empire.

When we turn to Rome and to the writings and martyrdom traditions associated with Justin Martyr, it becomes clear that many in Rome framed their understanding of Christian martyrdom with the tradition of the philosophical noble death and doused their heroic subjects with an air of self-possessed clarity. For some, the application of the title "philosopher" to Justin may seem inappropriate, as in the history of ideas, Justin has not enjoyed a great reputation as an intellectual. Nor have martyrdom stories been viewed as erudite literature. The questions of whether Justin is a philosopher or martyrdom literature is philosophy rest largely on assumptions about what philosophy was in the ancient world. More often than not, it is reified into an elite intellectual practice that operated in splendid isolation from the rest of society. The portrait of the philosopher as steel-headed and grey-haired is reinforced by ancient aesthetics and extant sculpture, but this image obscures the extent to which philosophical concepts were more broadly diffused in ancient society. We have to look no farther than the Greek playwright Aristophanes's lampooning of Socrates in *The Clouds* to see that the figurative busts of intellectual icons that have come down to us from ancient Athens were in their day brightly colored and eye-catching. Moreover, philosophical values and ideals nurtured the cultural imagination, just as wider social values informed philosophy. Those not formally educated by tutors may have had some familiarity with philosophical concepts, values, and maxims, even if they were not well versed in the metaphysical theories on which they were based.

In scholarship, the chasm between philosophy and martyrdom widened further under pressure from another stereotype—the construction of martyrdom as a literary subset of apocalyptic literature. The pervasive assumption that martyrdom is essentially apocalyptic and that apocalypticism and philosophy are antithetical systems of thought has scuppered the fruitful comparison of philosophy and martyrdom. Examinations of the interdependence and mutual influence of philosophical texts and martyrdom literature have remained largely superficial.[9] Comparisons between the philosophical death and the death of the martyr have been content to consider literary reproduction or elementary conceptual borrowing.[10] The presence of other elements of philosophy and the function of philosophical values in martyrdom literature have been mostly overlooked. Rare exceptions have been made in the cases of Clement and Origen, whose philosophical credentials are respected, but Justin, whose writings are often viewed with disdain, does not garner the same kind of attention.[11]

In exploring philosophical representation, identification, and topoi in the discourse of martyrdom in Rome, it is not necessary to assume that the authors or their audiences were philosophers in a strict sense. The presence of philosophical maxims does not necessarily imply philosophical training; ample evidence suggests that many people were familiar with general principles and slogans.[12] Our exploration suspends hoary questions about what qualifies as philosophy in the ancient world and focuses instead on how philosophical categories and conventions structure martyrological discourse in Rome. As part of this task, we examine the ways in which martyrdom constructs a particular sense of Christian identity, beginning with the figure and writings of Justin, Christianity's first acclaimed philosophical pedagogue, and then moving to the multiple literary traditions associated with Justin's death.

Justin Martyr

From Rome, most of the evidence for Christian attitudes to martyrdom emerges from traditions associated with the Christian philosopher and "apologist" Justin Martyr (ca. 103–165 CE). Almost all of our information about him is derived from his own writings, particularly from the opening of *Dialogue with Trypho* in which he narrates his journey through the various schools of Greek philosophy to the one true philosophy—Christianity. Justin was born in Flavia Neapolis in Samaria, most likely of Greek parents, but traveled to Asia Minor to receive his education. His first Stoic tutor was quickly abandoned for a Peripatetic; he then progressed to a Pythagorean whose demands that Justin master geometry, music, and astronomy proved unappealing. Finding himself drawn to the transcendental mysticism of Plato, Justin acquired a Platonist tutor, and it was while meditating on the seashore at Ephesus that he first learned of Christianity. According to the autobiographical section in *Dialogue with Trypho,* Justin encountered an old man who raised some objections to the Platonic view of the soul and began to instruct him in the prophecies about the coming of Jesus.[13] Conversion, as Arthur Darby Nock has shown, was for many in the ancient world a matter of philosophical realignment, not a question of religious affiliation.[14] In this way

Justin's conversion to Christianity was part of his philosophical quest for the vision of God.

After his conversion, Justin continued to live in much the same philosophical vein as previously. He established himself as an independent teacher of Christian philosophy, attiring himself with the cloak of a professional philosopher, and may have traveled to Alexandria before settling in Rome. In the city Justin's philosophical school may well have been above the baths of Myrtinus, as he says in the *acta*, but the location cannot be reliably identified as the manuscript tradition is corrupt. Of Justin's students we know very little. Apart from the notable apologist Tatian, we can identify only the students mentioned in the *Acts of Justin*, whose names have a suspiciously symbolic ring to them. If, however, we can trust that Justin's fellow martyrs are representative of the members of his school, then we should note that his students comprised men, women, foreigners, slaves, and Christian converts.

Martyrdom in Justin's Writings

Discussion of the persecution and execution of Christians in Rome comes mostly from Justin's so-called *Apologies,* two texts (or perhaps a single text extant in two parts) purportedly directed to the emperor Marcus Aurelius.[15] Among modern scholars there is considerable debate surrounding the audience of apologetic literature such as Justin's. The *Apologies* themselves claim to offer an explanation of and justification for the existence and behavior of Christians. Whereas older scholarship maintained that apologetic literature was directed at Roman intellectuals and authorities, more recent studies have argued that apologetic literature utilizes the conventions of Greco-Roman protreptic in order to solidify group cohesion.[16]

Justin's *Apologies* are examples of this philosophically styled literature, in which Christians utilized Greco-Roman rhetorical forms and conventions to launch defenses of Christianity. The critical point is that—in Rome at least—the genres and ideologies of martyrdom and apologetics were mutually influential. The narrative presentation of the deaths of Christians in a particular and distinctive manner was part of dressing Christianity in the trappings of Roman ideology and literary conventions. Styling the martyr as philosopher was a way to draw upon cultural values that prized the endurance, calm, and courage of the ethical, imperiled philosopher. By harnessing this icon, Justin is able to present an image of Christians as unjustly targeted. At the same time, as we will see, he uses suffering to define what it means to be Christian.[17] The phenomenon of martyrdom becomes a way to distinguish Christianity from other groups: both the Jews who are cast as "persecutors" and those Christians who are excluded as "heretics." Even as he uses martyrdom to sever ties with Judaism, Justin frames his argument with analogies and values drawn from contemporary philosophy.

PERSECUTION FOR THE NAME

Throughout the *Apologies,* Justin complains that Christians are being executed merely for being Christians, or, as he puts it, "for the name" (*1 Apol.* 4.4).[18] The majority of the scholars who have discussed this theme in Justin have treated it as evidence for the historical and legal situation that led to the persecution of Christians in the second century.[19] To be sure, this idea is present outside of the writings of Justin: the Pliny-Trajan correspondence, as well as that of other early Christian apologists, indicate that Christians had begun to be identified and to identify themselves as a socially distinct group. Yet as Clifford Ando has ably demonstrated, Romans were not especially interested in the names or identities of local deities, or in religious practices of regional groups.[20] The Roman attitude to preexisting legal and religious structures in the provinces was beneficently to allow these antique and traditional practices to continue. It was the social and religio-political nonconformity of early Christians, their novelty, and their challenges to established social order and power structures that made them repulsive to Roman authorities. Thus, while Christians may have been denounced merely for being Christian, the reporting of this phenomenon by apologists such as Justin also reflects Christians' interest in the significance of the identifier "Christian."

In Justin's writings, the name "Christian" and the notion of persecution for the name have a strategic and rhetorical function. They enable him to draw together the concept of embodying Christianity with the experience and practice of martyrdom and, accordingly, to use martyrdom to define what it means to be Christian. In *1 Apology,* Justin describes two groups within the Christian community whose identification with the name "Christian" is of central importance. In the first instance there are Christians who are prosecuted merely for bearing the name "Christian":

> Now, something is not judged to be either good or bad by the name it is called without consideration of the actions which are associated with that name. In fact, in so far as you can draw anything from the name alleged against us, we are most kind hearted. We do not think that it is right to ask to be released on account of our name if we are proved to be wicked. Given this, in the event that, with respect both to our name and to our behavior, we are found to do no wrong, you should take great care not to become liable to just punishment for unjustly punishing those who have not proved to be guilty. For neither commendation nor punishment could reasonably be based on a name unless

actions can show something to be virtuous or wicked. And, in point of fact, you do not punish all of those who are accused in your court before they are proved to be guilty. But with us you take the name as proof, though, so far as the name goes, you should punish our accusers instead. (*1 Apol.* 4.1–4)

Here Justin sets up a contrast between, on one hand, being accused and convicted on account of the name and, on the other, being convicted for wickedness. This condemnation of Christians merely for their name, is, for Justin, unjust. He implores the Roman emperor to conduct the trials of Christians on the basis of their lifestyle.

In the second instance, in chapter 16 of *1 Apology*, Justin discusses the importance of abstaining from swearing. Citing a number of passages from Matthew, he connects Jesus's injunctions against swearing with prohibitions against idolatry. These passages form the basis for his argument that swearing an oath is incompatible with Christian devotion to God. Here the initial appeal to justice is modified by a shift in Justin's attention. We might expect to find him again criticizing Roman persecution, but instead he rounds on a new group in the Christian community, who, he says, are Christian in name alone:

> And whoever are not found living as he taught are not to be recognized as Christians, even if they speak the teachings of Christ with their tongues. For he said that not those who only speak but those who also do the works will be saved. For he said this: "Not everyone who says to me 'Lord, Lord,' will enter into the Kingdom of Heaven, but the one who does the will of my Father who is in Heaven. For he who hears me and does what I say hears the one who sent me. And many will say to me, 'Lord, lord, did we not eat and drink and work miracles in your name?' and then I will say to them, 'depart from me, workers of wickedness.' Then there will be weeping and gnashing of teeth, when, while the just shine like the sun, the unjust are sent to the eternal fire. For many will come in my name outwardly clothed in the skins of sheep but inwardly being ravenous wolves; from their works you will know them. And every tree which does not produce good fruits is cut down and thrown on the fire." And we request that those who do not live according to his teachings, and are only called Christians, be punished by you as well. (*1 Apol.* 16.8–14)

Given that Justin introduces this group within the context of a discussion of swearing oaths, we might expect that these "wolves in sheep's clothing" would be apostates who denied being Christians when brought to trial. If this was a problem, as well might be inferred from *1 Apol.* 4, then it is not raised here. Fire and brimstone aside, Justin's focus is on the ethical conduct of these wolves, or to put it in Justin's philosophical terms, on the kind of life they lived. The introduction and condemnation of this group of people who were

Christian "in name alone" sets up a contrast with those Christians persecuted "for the name." The contrast is delineated along the lines of lifestyle. Justin chastises those who are only nominally Christian for failing to live a life that corresponds to the identity they had claimed. There is a biting irony to his words. The Romans persecuted Christians for the name alone (regardless of lifestyle), and Justin also chastises and invites heavenly judgment on those who are Christian in name only. The structures and logic of condemnation are essentially identical. Justin wants the Romans to evaluate the Christians as he does, by focusing on the life led by the supposed Christians, not on the names by which they are called.

In *1 Apol.* 26 the targets of Justin's polemic step out of the metaphorical shadows. He catalogs those groups of individuals who presented themselves as Christians but were not persecuted by the Romans (*1 Apol.* 26.1–5). Justin acknowledges that these people are called Christians but contends that they are in fact "heretics" and casts them as magicians. This genealogical ancestry is intended to force the later generations of faux Christians, most notably Marcionites, outside the boundary of what can be called Christian. According to Justin, if these heretics bear witness to anything, it is to blasphemy. As Judith Lieu has noted, Justin's attribution of confessional language to the Marcionite blasphemy contrasts the witness of his Christians with the witness of the heretics.[21] Justin concludes this section of the apology by reiterating his point that though called Christian, these groups are frauds: "And all those springing from them [these heretics] are, as we said, called Christians, just as among the philosophers those who do not share the same doctrines do have the common name of philosophy predicated of them . . . But that they are not persecuted nor killed by you—at least because of their doctrines—we are sure" (*1 Apol.* 26.6–8). For Justin, the authenticity of claims to Christian identity is proved by the experience of persecution. These other groups are excluded from Christianity because they do not experience persecution, suffering, or martyrdom. Conversely, they are not persecuted because they are not truly Christian. Membership in Justin's philosophical club not only entails, but also requires, that the Christian suffer.[22] The experience of persecution serves both as proof of authentic Christian identity and as the constituting element of Christian identity itself.

JEWS AS PERSECUTORS

In Justin's *Dialogue with Trypho,* blame for persecution is often laid at the feet of the Jews. Jewish antagonism in his own time is for Justin a rehearsal of a prophetic script in which the Jews have always persecuted the righteous. He writes: "For you [the Jews] murdered the righteous one and the prophets before him. And now you reject those who put their hope in him and in God, the almighty and creator of all, who sent him" (*Dial.* 16.4). In appealing to the examples of murdered prophets, Justin inserts the experiences of his contemporaries into a scripturally grounded tradition of rejected and persecuted messengers of God (Isa 57:1; Luke 6:23; Matt 23:29–31; Luke 11:49). To modern readers schooled in the discourse of the suffering exemplar, the rhetorical appeal to biblical precedent is common to the point of banality. Yet Justin pushes this theme in a number of directions, highlighting continuity and forcing disjunction. On one level, the construction of and appeal to a historical thread of persecution make his claim to continuity with Jesus concrete. In the same way as the gospel authors had woven biblical allusions to rejection and persecution into a historical tapestry of suffering, Justin extends the history of persecution into his own day. This continuity is expressed through appeals to a common enemy; just as the Jews had persecuted the prophets and bayed for the blood of Jesus, now they lurk unseen in the background of Christian persecution (*Dial.* 16.4). The effect of identifying adversarial forces as Jews is to align Justin's contemporaries with Christ. Christians are identified with Christ by virtue of their shared opponents.

At the same time, on another level, Justin presents martyrdom as one of the ways in which Christianity can be differentiated from its religious forebears and cultural ancestors. Christians and Christians alone are willing to entertain the prospect of martyrdom. Moreover, according to the *Dialogue with Trypho*, the Jews are grandfathered into a history of persecution that links Jew and Roman. The power of Justin's rhetoric is forcefully felt in the writings of modern scholars who have been seduced by the familiar, if perhaps unfounded, narrative of Jewish persecution of Christians.[23]

In the writings of Justin, then, martyrdom serves two related purposes with respect to his rhetorically constructed Jews. On one hand, it enables Justin to define Christianity as distinct from Judaism. We detect here in Justin a coarsening of Christian discourse in which boundary marking is facilitated by the coproduction of the terms "Christian" and "martyr": the category of the martyr is invoked in order to patrol the borders of the related category of Christian. On the other hand, even as Justin constructs an image of Christianity, he creates a counterpoint—Judaism. Their relationship is complicated and multidirectional. Various aspects of difference and continuity are emphasized in the service of specific discussions. The adoption of prophecy as a point of shared heritage, and hence continuity, is brought into a new focus by Justin's insistence that only Christians have martyrs.

Conceptually, in the Roman administration of torture, witness to death had served as an identifier of truth.[24] Martyrdom, a unifying signifier of truth, bolsters Christian claims to possess piety and to define Christianity through the exclusion of others. Justin severs ties with other groups using the persecutor's sword. He is by no means the first author to use resistance to torture and obstinacy until death to carve group identity. In Antiochus's cauldron, concrete notions of Judaism and Jewish identity bubbled to the surface of the Maccabean literature. Shelly Matthews has discussed the extent to which the protomartyr Stephen's prayer of forgiveness subtly, but effectively, posits radical discontinuity between Jewish and Christian martyrdom traditions.[25] In a variety of contexts, therefore, martyrdom was used to tear hybrid cultures limb from limb. It is noteworthy that the articulation of what it meant to be a Christian is for Justin best made by appeals to similar problems within philosophy. This presentation is consistent with his characterization of Christianity as good philosophy. He draws this point out farther in *1 Apol.* 4.8, where he writes, "For of philosophy, too, some assume the name and the garb who do nothing worthy of their profession; and you are well aware, that those of the ancients whose opinions and teachings were quite diverse, are yet all called by the one name of philosophers." In truth, for Justin this is not an analogous problem at all; it is one and the same. Christianity is everywhere presented as a form of philosophy, or rather, the best and truest form. In philosophy, as in Christianity, the task of identifying the true members is a question of both lifestyle and diversity of belief. The characterization of the true Christian as philosopher shapes Justin's literary description of the martyr, to which we now turn.

ACTS OF PTOLEMAEUS AND LUCIUS

The earliest extant martyrdom account—if it can be called a martyrdom account at all—is extracted from Justin Martyr's *2 Apology.* The *Acts of Ptolemaeus and Lucius,* as this narrative is known when removed from its immediate literary context, is a brief account of the circumstances of the arrest of the Christian teacher Ptolemaeus. The brevity of the text makes it difficult to categorize or analyze as an example of the martyrdom genre. To many, the material fits more readily with the apologetic literature popular among Christian rhetoricians and teachers, yet there is something haphazard and disorganized about the current form of *2 Apology.* Added to the *Acts of Ptolemaeus and Lucius* are a stock pedagogical topos drawn from ancient Greek literature (*2 Apol.* 11.2–5; cf. Xenophon/Lucian, *Somnium* 6–17), a story based on Genesis 6, a description of Justin's troubles with the Cynic Crescens, some allusions to Socrates, and a petition to the emperor, or *libellus.* In a recent article, Paul Parvis has ingeniously suggested that *2 Apology* is a collection of fragmentary texts drawn together and edited by Justin's students after his death as a means of memorializing their teacher.[26] The process of collecting and assembling may seem reminiscent of later hagiography, but it also resonates with philosophical literary practices. The titling of Justin's work and presentation of his literary progeny as apologies is a deliberate posthumous attempt to shape Justin as a philosophical, Socratic figure. Parvis's theory justifies the treatment of the *Acts of Ptolemaeus and Lucius* as a separate literary entity.

In light of its distinctive literary form, it is interesting to note the brevity of Justin's account. Almost no information about the protagonist Ptolemaeus or the content of his teachings is provided. Following the argument of Adolf von Harnack, Ptolemaeus has been identified as Ptolemy, the Valentinian Roman teacher who authored Ptolemy's *Letter to Flora*.[27] The suggestion is intriguing if only because it unravels another common assertion—that Valentinians were not martyred. While there are some striking coincidences between these two accounts, the truth is that no evidence connects the two figures. Instead, Justin recalls the events that precipitated Ptolemaeus's arrest. He narrates the reform of a formerly hedonistic woman under the influence of Ptolemaeus's teachings and her subsequent rejection of her persistently licentious husband. The rejected husband files a complaint with the emperor first against his wife and then against Ptolemaeus. This leads to Ptolemaeus's arrest, his admission that he is a Christian, and his execution.

The theme of the pious woman betrayed by her embittered spouse or fiancé was common in ancient literature, but it is nonetheless interesting to note how Justin couches his account in the language of philosophical ethics and generally accepted standards of good conduct.[28] He cleverly opens this portion of 2 *Apology* with a comparatively lengthy description of the reform of the woman's character: "A certain woman was living with a husband who was licentious, and she had once been licentious herself. But when she learnt the teachings of Christ she came to her senses, and tried to persuade her husband to come to his, reporting what she had been taught, and telling him of the punishment in eternal fire that will come to those who live senselessly and not according to right reason" (2 *Apol.* 2.1–2). The presentation of Christianity in this section is remarkably bland. Ptolemaeus, like Justin himself, is an instructor in Christian teachings. As the content of these teachings goes unnoted, we must infer them from Justin's summary of the woman's beliefs. So far as her stated practices go, these appear to be twofold: first, she cautions her husband that those who do not live lives of self-restraint (σωφροσύνη) or sound logic are destined for eternal fire; second, she resolves to divorce her husband on the grounds that he does not live in accordance with either justice or natural law.

To be sure, self-restraint, reason, and justice are biblical themes, and it is possible for us to view Justin's inclusion of them here as references to a life lived in accordance with scripture. This interpretation seems improbable, however, when we consider the lack of distinctively Christian ideas in the account. There is no mention of details of the Jesus story or the resurrection, or of liturgical practices such as baptism. Instead, the woman's "conversion" to Christianity is described as a reformed way of living. The conversion to "the teachings of Christ" uses pedagogical rather than religious language. Christ provides instruction about how to live. The content of the unnamed woman's instruction, moreover, has much in common with philosophical maxims. Appeals to justice and living in accordance with right reason formed a substantial part of discussions of Stoic virtues (Diogenes Laertius, *Lives* 8.87). The principle of living "according to nature" was particularly associated with Cynic and later with Stoic ethics and played an integral part in the formation of Roman jurisprudence.[29]

When confronted by the Roman prefect Urbicus, Ptolemaeus admits to being Christian and to participating in "the school of divine virtue" (2 *Apol.* 2.13). The unusual terminology identifies Ptolemaeus as a philosopher and pedagogue.[30] The content of his confession is modified only by Justin's statements that he is a lover of truth who had come to a personal knowledge of "the good" (2 *Apol.* 2.11, 13). Such general statements would have resonated with broadly held philosophical notions of what constituted the good life. By presenting Ptolemaeus in this way, Justin mounts a defense of Christian teachers that presents them as philosophers and pedagogues who participated in educational structures rather than as seditious outsiders who sought to undermine order.

We do not need to conclude from this detail that Ptolemaeus's particular brand of Christian philosophy was in some sense a philosophical school in the style of the Peripatetics. The presentation of Ptolemaeus's teachings as a nonthreatening and nondescript philosophy is explicable given the context of the work, which is ostensibly addressed to Marcus Aurelius, a Roman Stoic, and more probably was heard by Roman Christians saturated in the kinds of commonly held Stoic beliefs exhibited by the woman. Justin is able to appeal to both of these audiences, to potential Roman opponents and to Christians more comfortable with the maxims of Chrysippus than of Christ. Presenting the condemned Christian as the teacher of socially acceptable and philosophically derived ethical principles served a clear rhetorical aim, one dictated by the apologetic macrogenre of 2 *Apology*.

Acts of Justin and His Companions

That the *Acts of Ptolemaeus and Lucius* is oriented toward the concerns of the apologist rather than the hagiographer should not surprise us. After all, it is embedded within a piece of protreptic literature designed to engage with Roman styles of argument. What is often overlooked, however, is how the *Acts of Ptolemaeus and Lucius* sets the tone for the philosophically styled martyrdom accounts produced in Rome during the second century. The *Acts of Justin and His Companions* contains the same elements: a philosophically styled protagonist, a presentation of Christianity as philosophy, and a close association with apologetic trends current in Roman Christianity.

As Justin seems to have anticipated at the end of 2 *Apology,* his teachings about Christianity eventually attracted the attention of authorities in Rome. According to Eusebius, the Cynic philosopher Crescens reported Justin to the Roman governor (*Hist. eccl.* 4.16.8). Conflict between Justin and Crescens is recorded in 2 *Apology,* but Eusebius had derived this information from Justin's fellow Christian apologist Tatian (*Oration to the Greeks* 19). Tatian's version presents an alternative view of Justin's death that to some extent replicates the motif of the unfairly betrayed teacher found in the *Acts of Ptolemaeus and Lucius.* This information, however, is not parleyed in the *Acts of Justin.* Writing after Justin's death, Tatian's reduplication places himself in a literary mimetic relationship with the martyred Justin. Like Justin, he narrates the unjust death of an early Christian teacher. Following the conventions of Greek philosophical lineage, he reproduces the literary practices of the martyred philosopher-apologist, thereby becoming disciple, literary heir, and imitator. Already, therefore, we can see the construction of patterns of philosophical conduct. In relaying the circumstances of Justin's death, Tatian imitates a philosophical literary paradigm perpetuated by Justin himself.[31]

The account of Justin's trial, the *Acts of Justin,* is preserved in three distinct recensions: A, B, and C.[32] The earliest version, commonly referred to as recension A or the short version, contains an extremely brief account of Justin's trial and is viewed by most scholars as the earliest and most authentic.[33] Recension B, the vulgate or middle recension, is the text most commonly used by scholars.[34] Recension C, which closes with prayers for the emperor and refers to Mary as *theotokos,* is widely acknowledged to be the latest, having been composed long after the other versions.[35] The *Acts of Justin* suggests that Justin was arraigned with seven of his students before the illustrious Stoic Roman governor Quintus Iunius Rusticus on 14 April 165 CE. Despite his name, Rusticus was no rough and simple-minded magistrate. He is best known as the friend and instructor of the emperor Marcus Aurelius, to whom

Justin addressed his *Apologies*. In the list of acknowledgments that make up the first book of his *Meditations*, Marcus Aurelius credits Rusticus with shaping his view of character and discipline: "From Rusticus I received the impression that my character required improvement and discipline; and from him I learned not to be led astray to sophistic emulation, nor to writing on speculative matters, nor to delivering little hortatory orations, nor to showing myself off as a man who practices much discipline, or does benevolent acts in order to make a display" (*Med.* 1.15).[36] In the *Acts of Justin,* therefore, and unlike the majority of martyr acts, not only the protagonist but also his accuser were well known to the audience. That Justin's judge was both a famed Stoic thinker and also a former tutor of the emperor to whom Justin had addressed his *Apologies* is very suggestive. Although all the extant traditions suggest that the historical Justin was tried by Rusticus, this does not exclude the possibility that Rusticus serves as a narrative philosophical foil to Justin, an emblem of Stoic philosophy, and a verbal sparring partner for the beloved Christian philosopher.

In keeping with the philosophical tone of the account, the *Acts of Justin* opens with a discussion about the good life, a topos in philosophical discourse. The prefect Rusticus begins his interrogation of Justin with the question "What sort of a life do you lead?" (*Ac. Justin* A 2.1). Justin's reply that he leads a blameless life that everyone would agree is without condemnation is in keeping with the view contained in the *Apologies* that Christian conduct is good. This account of Justin's beliefs does not paint as exalted a picture of Jesus as do Justin's *Apologies*:

> [This is the doctrine that] we hold reverently towards the God of the Christians, whom alone we hold to be the craftsman of the whole world from the beginning, and [also regarding] Jesus Christ, the servant of God, who was proclaimed in the prophets as one who was about to come to the race of humankind as a herald of salvation and teacher of good doctrines. What I say is insignificant in comparison to his divinity, but I acknowledge the power of prophecy, for proclamation has been made about him whom I have just now said to be the Son of God. For know that in earlier times the prophets foretold his coming among men. (*Ac. Justin* A 2.5–7)

The creedal formula is retained precisely in recension B.[37] Justin employs language that resonates within Platonic and Pauline circles. Jesus is both the craftsman of the *Timaeus* and the servant of God from Philippians; he instructs others in good doctrines and, in keeping with Justin's argument in the *Dialogue with Trypho,* was the one foretold in the prophets. The creedal statement here is in some respects an epitome of the views expressed in Justin's writings.

CONTESTING PIETY IN THE JUSTIN TRADITION: RECENSION B

Rusticus's antagonism toward Christianity and the contestation of philosophical terms and virtues are only sharpened by the editor of recension B. Throughout this edition are a number of instances in which the εὐσέβεια, or reverence/piety, shown by the Christian heroes to Christ is juxtaposed with εὐσέβεια to the emperor. At the very outset, recension B introduces this contrast into the text by locating the martyrdoms within the context of "impious decrees posted against the pious Christians" (*Ac. Justin* B 1.1). This initial designation of the Roman decrees as impious and the Christians as pious informs our understanding of the subsequent usage of the terms in the text.

The contrast between piety and impiety reverberates throughout the account as the editor of recension B systematically incorporates additional language of εὐσέβεια into Rusticus's interrogations of the martyrs. Rusticus and Liberian appear to talk at cross-purposes. The redactor alters the text so that in response to Rusticus's question "Do you also refuse to be reverent?" Liberian responds, "I *am* reverent toward . . ." (*Ac. Justin* B 4.9).[38] Clearly, Rusticus and the Christian martyr have different understandings of what it means to be reverent. The contrast highlights both the ironic misunderstanding by the Roman prefect who himself propounds the "impious decrees" (*Ac. Justin* B 1.1) and the way in which the monodirectional piety of the Christians trumps Roman εὐσέβεια. The climax of this discussion comes in an unparalleled passage toward the end of recension B where we arrive at the crux of the matter. Rusticus asks Justin whether he will sacrifice to idols, and Justin replies that "no one of sound mind turns from piety to impiety" (*Ac. Justin* B 5.4). This response further clarifies the position of the martyrs that Christian εὐσέβεια is incompatible with Roman notions of εὐσέβεια to the point that to show εὐσέβεια to anyone but Christ is considered impious.

To the modern reader the exclusivity of Christian piety may seem obvious; after all, monotheism precludes the possibility of worshipping other deities. The key to understanding the nuances of these exchanges lies in the ancient understanding of εὐσέβεια.[39] In its non-Christian use, εὐσέβεια was an ambiguous term denoting reverence or respect for the orders of the domestic, national, and cosmological spheres. The vagueness of its meaning required that the term often be combined with prepositions in order to clarify to whom εὐσέβεια was being shown; in other words, εὐσέβεια denotes proper conduct toward any established order, not solely one that is religious. In recension B, Rusticus and Justin wrestle over the limits and specificity of reverence, and the narrator reworks Roman *pietas* into Christian self-exclusion.

If we consider the argumentation of recension B in light of ancient notions of εὐσέβεια and *pietas,* we see why Rusticus and the martyrs talk past one another. To a Roman administrator it would not have been apparent why Christians could not show εὐσέβεια to both Christ and the emperor, not only because the Romans were accommodating of long-standing indigenous religious traditions, but also because Roman εὐσέβεια implied a network of social allegiances and duties. The gestures of deference and articulations of power implied in the discourse of piety were not exclusively religious but encompassed all manner of social and identity-grounded responsibilities. Displays of reverence reinforced social relations and regulated networks of power. It is not the case, as Frend has noted, that "what was εὐσέβεια to the pagan was ἀσέβεια to the Christian and vice versa."[40] The situation was more nuanced, for the Romans *pietas,* or εὐσέβεια, to the emperor was compatible with *pietas* to the gods or one's parents. Only to Christians did the two seem mutually exclusive and diametrically opposed.[41] Rusticus's horror at Christian "impiety" (*Ac. Justin* B 2.1) is a result of that impiety's resistance to and transgression of the established social order.

Just as Christian and Roman notions of piety are contrasted, so too adherence to the decrees of Rome is contrasted with the proscriptions of Christ. In recension A, Rusticus's first question to Justin concerns his manner of life— "What kind of life do you lead?" (*Ac. Justin* A 2.1)—to which Justin replies that his life is "blameless and without condemnation in the eyes of all people" (*Ac. Justin* A 2.2). The editor of recension B postpones Rusticus's question and replaces it with a command to obey the gods and emperor. As a result, obedience to the impious decrees of Marcus Aurelius is contrasted with obedience to the commands of Christ (*Ac. Justin* B 1.1). Justin's response—that "there is no blame or condemnation in obeying the commands of our savior Jesus Christ" (*Ac. Justin* B 2.1–2)—initially reads as a non sequitur. Rusticus has asked Justin a straightforward question, and Justin's response is evasive. Frend interprets this passage as a quintessentially apologetic response intended to draw attention to the lawfulness of Christian conduct and highlight the injustice of persecuting Christians on the basis of name alone.[42] His reading is persuasive, but only for recension A, where Justin's reply fits the question. In recension B, Justin's response moves the conversation away from the question of sacrifice to idols and to the nature of Christian doctrine and identity. Rusticus will be unable to draw the conversation back to the sacrificing to idols until halfway through the interrogation (*Ac. Justin* B 5.4).

The change in the opening of the tribunal serves a number of purposes. First, the editorial alteration reinforces the portrait of Justin as the emboldened philosopher who cleverly evades the interrogations of his persecutors.[43]

Second, the linguistic mirroring of the terminology of obedience in *Ac. Justin* B
2.1–2 gives recension B "an enhanced literary color" and contrasts obedience
to the gods (and emperor) with obedience to Christ.[44] This juxtaposition and
the legal motif suggested by the exchange are resumed in *Ac. Justin* B 5.6 where
Justin will contrast the tribunal of Rusticus with the eschatological trial before
Christ. The subordination of earthly laws and punishments to eternal ones
demonstrates the inevitability and non-choice that Justin and his companions
face—they answer to a superior heavenly authority that outclasses the threat
of earthly punishment.

The editor of recension B amplifies the rhetorical force of the confessional
formula "I am Christian" so that it negates other forms of social identification.
This interest lies behind the expansion of the dialogue between Euelpistus and
Rusticus during the interrogations. In recension B, Euelpistus is clearly identified as an imperial slave and attributes his freedom to his new Christian identity: "Euelpistus, an imperial slave, answered, 'I am also a Christian. I have been
freed by Christ and share in the same hope by the grace of Christ'" (*Ac. Justin*
B 4.3). This passage, which plays with Pauline metaphors of freedom from slavery (1 Cor 7:21–24; Gal 5:1), could equally be rendered, "Euelpistus answered,
I am an imperial slave, and I also am a Christian . . ." Christian duty removes
the constraints of social conventions and the obligations (εὐσέβεια) that Euelpistus should feel toward his imperial master.

The negation of identity is paralleled in a number of other acts of the martyrs.[45] In these texts it is notable that when the accused are questioned regarding their names, places of origin, and social status, their self-identification as
Christian supersedes other identity markers. As Peter Brown notes, "friendship
with God raised the Christians above the identity they shared with their fel-
lows. The *nomen Christianum* they flaunted was a 'non-name.' It excluded the
current names of kin and township."[46] While recension B does not propagate
the idea that the martyrs lack all forms of identity, clearly kinship with Christ
entails freedom from the constraints of social reverence.

LANGUAGE OF CONFESSION AND WITNESS

Whereas the *Martyrdom of Polycarp* incorporates a description of the
execution of its protagonist, the *Acts of Justin and His Companions* almost
shies away from death altogether. The author of recension A merely remarks
that the martyrs were scourged and executed in accordance with the laws (*Ac.
Justin* A 5.6). The focus of the concluding remarks is on the dual role of confession and testimony/martyrdom: "Then the holy martyrs, glorifying God,
went out to the customary place and completed their testimony [ἐτελείωσαν
τὸ μαρτύριον] by their confession of our Savior [ἐν τῇ τοῦ σωτῆρος ἡ μῶν],

to whom is glory and power with the Father and the Holy Spirit now and forever. Amen" (*Ac. Justin* A 6). The specific valence of μαρτύριον (witness, testimony, or martyrdom) in this context is contested. Following the traditional dating of the *Acts of Justin* as later than the *Martyrdom of Polycarp* and the pathological model of martyrdom, most scholars have assumed a fixed notion of martyrdom in the former text. Herbert Musurillo, for instance, translates ὁμολογία (confession) as "act of faith," an editorial decision that redefines ὁμολογία entirely.[47] Here the "martyrdom" is "perfected" or "completed" by the "confession of the Savior" at the moment of death. For the author of recension A, verbal testimony is an important component of μαρτύριον. The notion that martyrdom is perfected at the end of the martyr's life may lead some to conclude that the author views death itself as an important constitutive element of martyrdom. This said, the notion that a person's actions and life can be analyzed and evaluated only at his or her death is a persistent element in Greek literature and culture. If, as Solon declares, no man can be called happy until he is dead, how much more so can he not be judged a good witness until the opportunity for recantation is withdrawn? Certainly, the logic of the noble death of the philosopher, as we recall, sets a seal on the authenticity and veracity of the philosopher's argument. Continued adherence to a logical position even to death guarantees that there was no change of mind. In some contexts before Christianity, death and witness are coterminous because death can serve as a kind of witness.

Any ambiguities that the modern reader finds in the use of the term *martyrdom* in recension A are hardly resolved by the conclusion to recension B. Here the redactor clarifies the method of execution but leaves the formula of recension A otherwise unchanged: "Then the holy martyrs, glorifying God, went out to the usual place, and being beheaded they completed their testimony by their confession of our Savior. Some of the faithful secretly took their bodies and buried them in a suitable place, the grace of our Lord Jesus Christ working in them, to whom is glory forever. Amen" (*Ac. Justin* B 6.1–2). That the phrase is retained, with a slight emendation that adds greater emphasis on the perfecting function of beheading, indicates that its presence is purposeful. The presentation of confession as a part of martyrdom is preserved. The lack of clarification does not speak to the meaning of the term *martys* in the way that we might hope. The expectation that a later edition of the story would somehow solidify the meaning of the term is a modern one. The editor's concern is not to redefine *martys* or police the use of μαρτύριον, but to adapt its nuances for a particular purpose. As in recension A, the presentation of the language of *martys* serves a specific rhetorical function: here it validates the legitimacy of Justin's philosophical views.

Stoic Ekpyrosis *in the Roman Martyrdom Tradition*

Both Rusticus and Marcus Aurelius were well-known Stoics. Much of the dialogue and contrast between Justin and Rusticus takes on a new significance when read within the context of Roman Stoicism. The account does not so much present the trial of Justin and his followers as provide a setting in which Stoic philosophical principles and the philosophical life can be tried, tested, and contested. As the narrative progresses, the noble Rusticus grows increasingly anxious and uncontrolled. Unlike Justin, Rusticus becomes angry and his frustration palpable, which is arguably understandable in the face of obstinate Christian inflexibility but is out of keeping with his reputation as a Stoic philosopher.

It is not only in the dialogue between Justin and Rusticus that philosophical imagery lingers. A common theme in both the *Acts of Ptolemaeus and Lucius* and the *Acts of Justin and His Companions* is the consummation of the world by fire (2 *Apol.* 2; *Ac. Justin* A 5; *Ac. Justin* B 5). The earliest two versions of the *Acts of Justin* utilize the Stoic idea of ἐκπύρωσις to describe the eschaton.[48] In the course of his examination of Justin, Rusticus asks the accused whether he believes he will ascend to heaven if he is beheaded. Justin responds: "I have confidence from my perseverance, if I endure. Indeed, I know that for all those who live a good life there awaits the divine gift even to the consummation [μέχρι τῆς ἐκπυρώσεως]"(*Ac. Justin* B 5.2). Fiery scenes of eschatological destruction are a common enough element of early Christian literature, and it is perhaps for this reason that the Stoic undercurrent in these texts has been overlooked.[49] Yet given the preponderance of Stoic imagery and gestures throughout the rest of the account, it is worth reading this reference as conflagration.

Ancient Stoic eschatology used the term ἐκπύρωσις to refer to the eventual consumption of the cosmos by fire. In the majority of descriptions of the conflagration, the world would, as a phoenix from the ashes, be reborn from the destruction and the cycle would begin again. An important article by J. Albert Harrill demonstrates the variety of opinion among ancient Stoic writers about the nature of ἐκπύρωσις and proposes that in some authors the cycle was not repeated.[50] Moreover, as Harrill shows, one strain of thought links the theme of ἐκπύρωσις to the Stoic philosophy of the sage as stable, controlled, holistic self. This theme was not unique to Stoicism but was present throughout Greek and Roman medicine and culture. Harrill argues that this notion of the stable self surviving until the conflagration informed 2 Peter. His argument that self-stabilization and knowledge of the properties and mechanics of cosmic order which could lead the believer to a moral position that allowed him or her to experience eschatological renewal applies equally to the *Acts of Ptolemaeus and Lucius* and the *Acts of Justin*. In the former, the reference to eternal fire seems like transparent sycophancy; the connection between morality, judgment by fire, and salvation is unclear. Following Harrill's reading, however, a substantive link between ethical self-control and eschatological deliverance emerges.

In the *Acts of Justin*, as already noted, Justin maintains that if he endures and leads a just life, he will remain even to the conflagration of the world (*Ac. Justin* A 5). The language of perseverance (ὑπομονή), commonplace in martyrdom literature, recalls the characterization of the sage. While the term summons values of steadfastness and resolute endurance so familiar from characterizations of the martyr, it also confers a sense of bodily and pneumatic stability, permanence, and firmness. Read in light of Harrill's work on ἐκπύρωσις, Justin rehearses a Stoic notion that the holistic/stable self survives until the conflagration. Justin's stability is underscored by his confidence and the quality of his commitment to the notion of heavenly ascent. As he says to Rusticus in recension A, he does not think he will ascend to heaven; he is firmly assured of it (οὐχ ὑπονοῶ, ἀλλ' ἀκριβῶς πέπεισμαι). Justin's vocabulary invokes epistemological categories in order to relate his complete, rigid certainty. *Acts of Justin* B 5.3 fortifies the language of epistemological certainty even further. Justin responds to Rusticus's question about ascending to heaven by stating that he is not only fully convinced that he will ascend to heaven, he has accurate knowledge (an *episteme*) of it (οὐχ ὑπονοῶ, ἀλλ' ἀκριβῶς ἐπίσταμαι καὶ πεπληροφόρημαι). Justin's self-control invokes Christian immovability, Greco-Roman masculinity, and Stoic stability. His unyielding will not only exemplifies the correct posture with respect to the Roman empire, but also models a bodily/pneumatological practice of self-regulation. Justin embodies the holistic, stable self. This stability both explains the logic of his statement that he will remain until the conflagration and provides an example of exercised philosophy.

Paul

Not every text pertaining to martyrdom in Rome is concerned with philosophical debate and rhetorical contests. In addition to the martyrdom traditions associated with Justin Martyr, we have a cluster of Roman texts that refer to the execution of the Apostle Paul.[51] According to tradition, Paul was executed in Rome (ca. 64 CE) during the reign of Nero. An anonymous letter from the church in Rome to the church in Corinth, commonly known as *1 Clement,* briefly describes the execution of Peter and Paul and proposes them as moral exemplars for the audience. The text uses the death of the apostles to extol the audience to endure in faith despite opposition based on envy (*1 Clement* 5).[52] The use of heroic figures as moral exemplars is a commonplace in antiquity among both Christian and non-Christian authors. We should not be surprised, therefore, to find that Tertullian uses the examples of Peter and Paul in the same way (*Prescription against Heretics* 32). Paul, and especially the death of Paul, is used as a reference point for later moral exhortation.

In addition to the references in *1 Clement* and Tertullian, there is the account of Paul's death relayed in the *Martyrdom of Paul,* the final component of the tripartite text the apocryphal *Acts of Paul.* In the late-second-century *Martyrdom of Paul,* Paul travels to Rome as part of his missionary work (*Mart. Paul* 1).[53] There he is greeted by Luke and Titus and hires a barn outside the city to teach the word of truth. According to the account, Paul won many converts, including those from the house of Caesar (cf. *Ac. Justin* B 4.3). The inevitable conflict with the emperor arrives in the form of Nero's cup bearer, Patroclus, who comes to hear Paul speak, falls asleep in a window, falls out of the window, and dies (*Mart. Paul* 1–2; cf. Acts 20:9–12). Paul and his fellow Christians pray for Patroclus and revive him, but not before word reaches the emperor that the boy is dead. When a shocked Caesar finds Patroclus alive, he is horrified to hear him exhorting the merits of Christ, a new king who will destroy all the kingdoms. The result of the exchange is that, having learned that many members of his household are "soldiers of Christ," Nero orders decrees against the Christians (*Mart. Paul* 2).

Paul is arrested and tried by Caesar. In his response to the accusation that he recruits soldiers from Nero's province, Paul responds: "Caesar, not only from thy province do we enlist soldiers, but from the whole world. For this charge has been laid upon us, that no man be excluded who wishes to serve my king. If thou also think it good, do him service! For neither riches nor the splendor of this present life will save thee, but if thou submit and entreat him, then shalt thou be saved. For in one day he will destroy the world with fire" (*Mart. Paul* 3). When Paul finally appears before Nero, he states that if he is beheaded, he will rise again and appear to Nero as proof of his resurrection. The statement alludes to the resurrection appearances of the gospels and has echoes of Justin's defiant statement that he will be raised from the dead when he is executed. When he is finally executed, Paul stands facing the east with arms outstretched. Miraculously, milk, rather than blood, spurts from his neck when he is beheaded (*Mart. Paul* 3). Milk had been a symbol for instruction in Paul's writings (1 Cor 3:2) and directs us to the pedagogical point: the death of Paul is exemplary.[54]

To be sure, the author of the *Martyrdom of Paul* is familiar with the narrative of the canonical Acts of the Apostles and the Pauline and deuteropauline epistles. It is interesting, however, that while the generic features of the novelistic *Martyrdom of Paul* differ, there are many thematic similarities with the *Acts of Justin and His Companions.*[55] The idea that the world will be consumed by fire and the contrasting debate about life after beheading resonate with Justin's conversation with Rusticus. It is not the thematic elements themselves but the manner in which they are presented that is suggestive. It is difficult to press too firmly on the connection between these two accounts. The scholarly consensus maintains that the *Martyrdom of Paul* was composed around 180 CE in Rome, dating it to fifteen years after the death of Justin. The chronological proximity of the two accounts (if recension A was composed during this period) means that the lines of textual dependence and conceptual influence cannot be fully parsed. We should not be seduced into thinking that, because Paul has been historically more important than Justin Martyr, the traditions about Paul predated and influenced those of Justin. Nor is it necessary to come down decisively on the matter. A number of suggestive family resemblances point to a shared martyrological grammar and eschatological perspective.

Conclusion

One of the most striking aspects of martyrdom literature in Rome is its dissimilarity to the evidence from Asia Minor. If the Acts of the Apostles was composed in Rome in the early part of the second century, it is possible that the philosophically styled death of Jesus in Luke and the controlled, forgiving death of Stephen in Acts influenced the presentation of martyrs as philosophical figures.[56] Justin's hagiographer does not set his subject in a history of suffering heroes or frame his death in terms of Christly imitation. If literary connections are intimated, they gesture to the persecution of Socrates and writings of Paul. The figure of the philosopher martyr as cipher for good Christian conduct emerges out of Socrates's shadow.

Philosophy helped early Christians articulate their ideas and provided moral exemplars of values upon which to hang the martyr's persona, yet the effect of this reading of the martyr is more pronounced than just conceptual assonance. Martyrdom as a facet of Christian behavior and marker of Christian identity is used to divorce Christians from heretics and Jews. The juxtaposition of the multiplicity of eponymous sects and the singular truth of Christianity is punctuated and reinforced by the construction of martyrdom as an exclusively Christian practice. The resonance with philosophical traditions enables Justin and members of his circle to usurp Socrates's position as privileged outsider besieged by unjust authorities.

Justin's canon was shaped by his students after his death to become a literary corpus defined by the corporeality of his death and read with memories of Socrates. His anonymous students acted as artisans, shaping pedagogical matter into martyrological apologetics. Apologetics, hagiography, and philosophy are here inextricably linked. Writing as apologist is an act of consolation framed by philosophical literary memorialization. As Sara Parvis's work on Justin has ably demonstrated, the *Apologies* formed the textual basis for the writings of later authors.[57] The reuse and reworking of Justin's writing on the desks of Tertullian and Melito of Sardis demonstrate that the greatly controversial task of apologetics was shaped by literary traditions associated with Justin, and, by extension, with Justin's death. If Justin is said to be at the very heart of Christian apologetics, then this statement must be made with the caveat that the presentation of Justin as apologist is formed by his experience of martyrdom. It is in death that Justin truly becomes an apologist. It would not be an overstatement, therefore, to see the birth of Christian apologetics in the death of the first great apologist. The emergence of martyrdom and apologetics in Rome in the second century does not appear to owe much to the rich symbolism of Revelation or to mimesis of the life of Jesus. Nor do those composing and shaping these texts root themselves in scriptural antecedents. The portrayal of Polycarp, weighed down with sacrificial metaphors and dripping with scriptural allusions, seems to have had no influence on ideas of martyrdom that clung to the figure of Justin. If Justin's views share familial resemblances with other ideologies of Christian martyrdom, they are with those of Clement and Valentinus. In Rome, martyrdom serves as proof of the veracity of Christianity, the true philosophy.

4

Gaul:
The Victors of Vienne and Lyons

By the middle of the second century, Gaul, previously something of a cultural wasteland and backward outlier of the Roman empire, had begun to prosper. Lugdunum (Lyons), the capital of Gaul, had been founded as a Roman colony by Plancus in 43 BCE. The town subsequently became a bustling metropolis, and inscriptional evidence demonstrates its trade ties with the rest of the Roman world.[1] The province was agriculturally rich, which gave rise to a thriving community that in turn attracted immigration and trade. The arrival of Christianity is shrouded in obscurity. Our only textual and material evidence from the second century is the anonymous *Letter of the Churches of Vienne and Lyons* (ca. 177) and the writings of Irenaeus, to which can be added a single inscription from Marseilles.[2] There are no archaeological data to provide evidence of the presence of Christians in Gaul before the reign of Constantine. Sulpicius Severus's fourth-century *Chronicon* suggests that a Christian community had been established shortly before the persecutions of 177 CE (2.2), and Henri Leclercq has followed this line, arguing that the statement "those through whom especially our affairs had been established" (καὶ δἰ ὧν μάλιστα συνεστήκει τὰ ἐνθάδε) suggests that the founders of the community were themselves among those arrested in 177 CE.[3] Yet even Sulpicius Severus, the earliest source to refer to these persecutions, was greatly removed from the events. Grammatically, the statement may just imply that the leaders of the church (that is, those responsible for arranging their affairs) were arrested.[4] The *Martyrdom of Paul,* a text associated with the Apostle Paul and the city of Rome, refers to the evangelist Luke's having come from Gaul (*Mart. Paul* 1), and an early Christian manuscript tradition for 2 Timothy asserts that Paul's associate Crescens was sent as a missionary to Gaul.[5] These texts bear witness to an interest in establishing apostolic roots in Gaul, but it is impossible to state with any confidence either a date for the arrival of Christianity in Gaul or that we have any sources for Gallic Christianity in the second century. It is thus with some trepidation that we proceed.

The relationship between Lyons and Asia Minor and Phrygia as presumed from the *Letter of the Churches of Vienne and Lyons* is easier to establish. A sizable number of immigrants from Phrygia appear to have worked in Lugdunum, and it is likely that Christianity also arrived in Gaul via the trade route from Asia Minor to Massillia (Marseilles) and then moved up the Rhône valley to the capital.[6] References in the *Letter* to Alexander, "a Phrygian by race" (*Lyons* 5.1.49), and to Attalus, a Roman citizen from Pergamum (*Lyons* 5.1.17), indicate that some of the Christian martyrs were from Asia Minor. Writing in the nineteenth century, historian William Simpson suggested that the churches of Lyons and Vienne had been founded by missionaries dispatched by Polycarp himself.[7] There is no evidence that the ties between the two communities were instigated by Smyrna's most famous bishop, but it is possible that Christians relocated to Gaul from Asia Minor to join their compatriots.[8] An alternative suggestion by Charles Phipps, which has fallen largely out of favor, holds that Christianity arrived from Rome.[9] Much has been made of the Greek and Asiatic names of some of the martyrs (Attalus, Alexander, Vettius Epagathus, Biblis, Elpis, Ponticus, and Alcibiades), but we should be wary of pressing too hard on this evidence. Even if some of the Christians are tied to Asia Minor, others have Romano-Gallic connections (Blandina, Maturus, and Sanctus).[10] It is important that the influences of Roman and Gallic religion and culture not be overlooked.

A further question concerns the number of Christian communities in Gaul. The *Letter* is purportedly sent from both the church of Vienne and the church of Lyons, and members of both communities are arrested at the same time, presumably in Lyons. The combination raises the question "Did Lyons and Vienne form a single community or were there discrete congregations?"[11] Eusebius's statement, with reference to the Easter controversy, that Irenaeus was the presbyter of the "parishes in Gaul" (*Hist. eccl.* 5.4.1), suggests that there was only one bishop in the region. His description may, however, be an anachronistic gloss. The status and organization of episcopacies in the second century are far from clear, and Eusebius's information about the history of Christianity in the West is even murkier. It is likely that Eusebius here neatly solves an untidy problem. Ideological, rather than logistical, divisions are evident in Irenaeus's own descriptions of Christianity in Gaul. He refers to the wealthy disciples of the "Gnostic" Marcus, who was apparently active in the Rhône valley (*Haer.* 1.13.5). We might reasonably infer that these wealthy Christians sponsored their own house churches or meetings, of which Irenaeus was not a part, and that there was likely more diversity than the *Letter* suggests. Even if the communities were conceptually and ideologically unified, liturgical unity is a historian's romance. Lyons and Vienne were twenty miles apart; there would have been several congregations in each city meeting in separate house churches. All of these questions assume, of course, the authenticity of the *Letter.* This, as we will see, is far from certain. Without the *Letter* our knowledge of Christianity in Gaul dwindles to scraps of information, and the racket of the mob is replaced by silence.

Here we undertake an analysis of the literary evidence and character of early Christian literature from Gaul. Of the "regional forms" of Christianity identified by scholars, Gallic Christianity has received the most limited attention.[12] As we will see, some doubts overshadow the provenance of the *Letter of the Churches of Vienne and Lyons,* and, as already noted, it is difficult to know precisely how Christianity arrived in the region. These have not been the reasons, however, that the ideological distinctiveness of Gallic Christianity has been overlooked. In histories of Christianity, Gaul has been cast as the impoverished offspring of Asiatic Christianity. This may be part of the larger scholarly trend that views the spread of Christianity as evolutionary, or perhaps a sense that given the dearth of literature and Irenaeus's ties to Asia Minor, Gaul has little character of its own. When we read the sources carefully, however, we will see that this literature contains distinctive thematic elements. This distinctiveness suggests that they are evidence for Gallic Christianity. This does not mean, of course, that Gaul was not part of a system of social networks that spanned the empire, or that Christianity did not arrive from another region bearing some preexisting characteristics, but that we should give thought to the possibility that there is such a thing as Gallic Christianity.

Letter of the Churches of Vienne and Lyons
DATING AND AUTHORSHIP

While the history of Christianity in Gaul is largely a matter of deduction, the *Letter of the Churches of Vienne and Lyons* stands out from the rest of second-century literature. The anonymous text describes the arrests, trials, and tortures of a group of Christians in Gaul in the later second century. Unlike other early martyrdom accounts, the *Letter* has not left much of a textual imprint in the early church. The account of the persecution takes the form of a letter composed by "the servants of Christ residing at Vienne and Lyons, in Gaul" and directed to "the brethren throughout Asia and Phrygia" (*Lyons* 5.1.3). The letter is preserved exclusively and only partially by the fourth-century church historian Eusebius in his *Ecclesiastical History* (5.1.1–5.3.4) and is otherwise unattested as a separate document until the medieval period. Evidence for the incidents it describes is not found outside of the letter, and even then Eusebius's own inconsistencies make the events recorded by this single source difficult to date: in the *Chronicon,* he dates the persecutions to 166–167; in the *Ecclesiastical History,* to 177. Of these two dates the latter is the more widely accepted.[13]

The date of the events is of less concern than the authorship and provenance of the letter. If it was not written in Gaul, it ceases to be of much use for our study of the region. As it stands, the *Letter* is attributed to anonymous "churches" rather than to the hand of an individual. Its epistolary form and purpose are both curious.[14] The only other extant examples of letters composed in the name of a church are *1 Clement* and the *Martyrdom of Polycarp.* The latter begins, "The church of God which sojourns at Smyrna to the church of God which sojourns in Philomelium and to all the communities of the holy and catholic church sojourning in every place" (*Mart. Pol.* 1). Although the epistolary framework of the *Martyrdom of Polycarp* is, as we saw in chapter 2, similarly suspect, it does suggest a generic quality to the martyrological letter. All three accounts are concerned with martyrological examplars—*1 Clement* with the deaths of Peter and Paul, the *Martyrdom of Polycarp* with the eponymous protagonist, and the *Letter of the Churches of Vienne and Lyons* with the communities of Vienne and Lyons.

If, as Eusebius suggests, the original letter contained the names of all of those members of the Christian community who survived the persecution (*Hist. eccl.* 5.5.3), then Eusebius appears to have refashioned the account to conform more fully to the genre of *1 Clement* and the *Martyrdom of Polycarp.* The shift refocuses the reader's attention on the cities rather than on their constituting members. Historically, Lyons and Vienne were feuding towns (Tacitus, *Hist.* 1.65), so there is something suggestive about their literary collaboration. In the conclusion of the account, the historical rivalry between the two cities is buried in order to promote unity in the church; the rhetorical effect of their union here is to suggest that civic patriotism is subordinated to ecclesiastical unity. Even if we did not have Eusebius's editorial admission, his hand would be readily apparent in the letter.

It seems quite impossible that Eusebius composed the letter ex nihilo. Of the swathes of material from the Latin West, only the *Letter of the Churches of Vienne and Lyons,* the writings of Irenaeus, and Tertullian's *Apology* are cited in his *Ecclesiastical History;* Eusebius's marked preference for material about churches in the East is most likely due to his discomfort working with Latin sources.[15] Despite his linguistic limitations, Eusebius does not invent texts or traditions in order to fill the lacunae in his knowledge of Christianity in the Latin West. It would strain credulity to suggest that he created a story of persecution in Gaul in 177 CE and did not invent other such accounts to supplement his history. The challenge, then, is to assess how aggressively Eusebius edited the text he had received and to determine how much of the version he included in his *Ecclesiastical History,* if any, can be traced back to the second-century Gallic churches.

Traditionally, and in agreement with the tenth-century author Oecumenius, Irenaeus is the putative author of the *Letter*.[16] Oecumenius has been followed by Pierre Nautin, who suggests that Irenaeus was head of the community in Vienne and assumed the episcopacy of Lyons after the execution of Pothinus, one of the martyrs described in the letter.[17] This interpretation is supported by the placement of Vienne before Lyons in the title (*Lyons* 5.1.3), a surprising sequence given that Lyons was the more important city, and by the somewhat vague terms used to describe Pothinus's role in Lyons (*Lyons* 5.1.29).[18] To be sure, one function of the letter is to shore up the reputation of the bishopric in Lyons. The presentation of Pothinus as a martyr-bishop par excellence at the beginning of the work polishes the episcopal seat to which Irenaeus ascends. Yet the placement of Vienne ahead of Lyons remains surprising.

It is certainly true that Irenaeus was an enthusiastic writer of correspondence. There are also thematic similarities between Irenaeus and the *Letter*. Both share an interest in love (*Lyons* 5.1.9, 10, 17, 23, 49; *Haer.* 4.44.9) and peace (*Lyons* 5.2.7; *Haer.* 3.9.2), and the authors employ similar technical language for the clergy and ranks of martyrs.[19] This does not prove Irenaean authorship of the *Letter*. We might choose to view these common features as evidence of a particularly Gallic form of Christianity, rather than as the product of a single author or as evidence of Eusebius imitating his sources. The conjecture that Irenaeus is the author of the *Letter* is grounded in two assumptions: first, that he possessed a copy of the *Martyrdom of Polycarp* and composed his letter using this model, and second, the fact that few members of the small communities in Vienne and Lyons would have possessed the skills necessary to compose such an account.[20] With respect to Irenaeus's supposed reliance on the *Martyrdom of Polycarp,* no literary evidence supports this claim. With respect to literacy among Christians in Gaul, both the author of the *Let-*

ter and Irenaeus himself indicate that the communities in Gaul had a number of wealthy members. Add to this the social ties that many other members of the Gallic churches had with Asia Minor and it is not strictly necessary to place the *Letter* under the stylus of Irenaeus. If, as Eusebius leads us to believe, the original text contained the names of the members of the churches responsible for sending the letter, and if Irenaeus humbly places himself among them, then it is extraordinary that Eusebius would have omitted his name altogether.[21]

Segments of the *Letter* are unlikely to have been composed by Irenaeus. In 5.2–3, the authors specifically mention visiting the martyrs in prison and showing them their compositions. The imprisoned martyrs apparently berated their visitors for calling them martyrs when the title should be applied exclusively to Christ. The account presumes a formal distinction between "martyr" and "confessor" that emerges out of the Confessors Controversy in Carthage in the mid-third century.[22] This portion, and presumably the sections that follow, must be later commentary on the martyrs.

A more general objection to Irenaean authorship arises out of the dating of the events. In the first place, no evidence suggests that Irenaeus was present in Gaul during the persecutions. Nautin is forced to redate the persecutions in order to place Irenaeus at the scene. Of greater note is the rhetorical character of this text. The *Letter* states that the churches in Lyons and Vienne have composed other correspondence denouncing Montanism and condemning strife in the community (*Lyons* 5.3.4).[23] These brethren at Gaul are concerned to ground their statements on orthodoxy and on heresy in the martyrs themselves. The interweaving of heresiology and hagiography is rhetorically powerful. If Irenaeus really is the author of the *Letter*, it is peculiar that he does not utilize the same strategies in *Against the Heresies*, for while there are points of contact between his writings and the *Letter*, Irenaeus does not use martyrs to refute heretics. Eusebius, by contrast, is especially fond of presenting his martyrs as proto-heresiologists, as is certainly apparent in his account of the martyrdom of Polycarp and his presentation of Justin Martyr. It seems likely, therefore, that Eusebius is responsible for at least editing 5.2–3, the concluding portion of the *Letter*. For the reader of Eusebius, an encounter with the *Letter* produces a certain déjà vu. The opening assertion that the martyrdoms are "worthy of undying remembrance" (*Lyons* 5.1.1) is an expression Eusebius used in *Martyrs of Palestine* (2.28) and *Ecclesiastical History* (3.4.4). His statement that the *Letter*'s value is not only historical but also instructive resonates strongly with his assessment of Clement of Alexandria (*Hist. eccl.* 3.24.1). These literary flourishes, coupled with the anachronistic interests of certain portions of the letter, may suggest that Eusebius has been a heavy-handed editor and is responsible not only for the opening pre-face, but also for shaping later portions of the account (*Lyons* 5.2–3) that fit well with his pro-martyrdom, anti-rigorist stance. Eusebius, however, was not given to fabricating his sources. We can only assume that the bulk of the *Letter*—the section that describes the arrest, torture, and execution of the martyrs (*Lyons* 5.1)—derives from Eusebius's source.[24] In light of the paucity of material evidence for the existence of Christianity in the Rhône valley dur-ing the second century, the lack of further reference to persecution in Gaul during this period, the highly literary character of the account, and the indi-cations of third-century redaction, it is still with considerable suspicion and caution that we proceed to a literary analysis of the text.

CIRCUMSTANCES OF ARREST

The details of the arrest of the martyrs of Lyons are improbable. Accord-ing to the text, during the summer of 177 animosity built up against the Chris-tians, who began to be excluded from certain social spaces—the baths and the market places, in particular, but also, apparently, even their own houses (*Lyons* 5.1.5). After an indeterminate period, an enraged mob attacked the Christians physically and dragged them to the forum, where they were questioned by the tribune and city authorities (*Lyons* 5.1.7–9). The reasons for the targeting of the Christians are difficult to ascertain: the text does not supply a historical pretext, and the Christians of Lyons do not appear to have been a socially co-hesive group. The social status of Christians ran the gamut of possibilities (slave, free, wealthy, citizen, noncitizen, male, female, young, educated, and old), and it is difficult to deduce exactly how they would have been regarded by their non-Christian peers. What would have distinguished Christians from their contemporaries was their noncompliance with the social rituals that served as markers of conformity. In the world of the text the situation is re-versed: what marks these socially disparate individuals as a unified social unit is their conformity to the will of God.

J. H. Oliver and R. E. A. Palmer have suggested that the instigators of the violence were wealthier citizens of Lugdunum looking for cheaper gladiators for the arena.[25] In 176 CE the Roman senate had issued measures to relieve landowners of part of the burden of financing gladiatorial games by allowing them to use condemned criminals at a fraction of the cost of professional gladiators. In the senate proceedings, a Gallic nobleman had served a critical role, praising the measure as a sign of progress and referring to the ancient use of *trinqui* in his own country. Precisely what *trinqui* were is unclear—although the language used in the proceedings has a sacrificial tone—but the senatorial act offers evidence for how Christians came to be used as gladiators. The argument that the landed classes in Gaul were acting behind the scenes to instigate violence against the Christians in order to acquire criminals for the arena is inspired but based largely on circumstantial evidence.

After their initial arrest and examination in front of the crowd, the martyrs are imprisoned pending the return of the governor. With the governor's entry into the account, the individual martyrs start to take shape. When Vettius Epagathus, a lawyer, attempts to defend the accused Christians, he is denounced and confesses that he is also a Christian (*Lyons* 5.1.9). His imprisonment initiates a search for Christians that culminates in the arrest of a number of individuals from Vienne. The terminology used here is that the arrested were collected together out of the two churches (ὥστε συλλεγῆναι ἐκ τῶν δύο᾽ Ἐκκλησιῶν πάντας τοὺς σπουδαίους). Taken literally as a reference to a physical location, the passage presents a distinct legal problem: Vienne, part of the *provincia Narbonensis,* lay outside the jurisdiction of the *legatus* of Lugdunum.[26] Interestingly, the slaves of the Christians were also arrested. The account does not say that the slaves were tortured, but rather that, fearing they would be tortured, they accused the Christians of incest and cannibalism (*Lyons* 5.1.14). The accusations made against the Christians are stylized and peculiar.[27] Similarly fantastical slurs were leveled without evidence against adherents of Bacchus several centuries earlier.[28] It seems unlikely that slaves would have been rounded up and then not tortured. Moreover, their false witness serves a narrative function as a foil for the true witness of the tortured Christians.

The literary character of the details of the arrests extends into the trial. At each step of the process the anger of the mob, the governor, and former friends of the Christians grows. The revelations of the non-Christian slaves only exacerbate the situation. This wrath is then directed against Sanctus (a deacon from Vienne), Maturus (a recent convert), Attalus (from Pergamum), Blandina (a slave girl), and Blandina's unnamed mistress (*Lyons* 5.1.17). To their number is later added Alexander (*Lyons* 5.1.49), a Phrygian physician whose sympathy for the accused Christians betrays his own religious allegiance, and Ponticus, a fifteen-year-old youth who is executed with Blandina. With the initial arrests, the stage is set for an athletically styled contest between the martyrs of Christ and the representatives of Rome (the governor and the torturer). This contest of will and bodily strength serves as a microcosm of the cosmic battle.

TORTURE AND SPECTACLE

One of the distinctive aspects of the *Letter of the Churches of Vienne and Lyons* is its voyeuristic focus on torture and bodily degradation.[29] The author delights in the licking of whips, dissolution of bodily parts, and contortions of the body. The martyrs' bodies become locations for a cosmic battle between Satan and Christ, amorphous vessels for Christ to inhabit, and sites of victory and triumph. Throughout the account there remains a dual focus on both the torturers' efforts to subjugate the Christians and the impotence of these endeavors. If in the world of the text the martyr's body is the site for cosmic battle, in Greek and Roman cross-examinations the body of the tortured subject (a slave) is a locus for truth. According to this system the slave cannot resist the truth-extracting structures of torture. The artifice of human interaction is destroyed by torture: the slave cannot help but give truthful witness in this state. The inextricability of torture and truth meant that the slave body was open to excavation and could be mined for truth.[30] In the *Letter,* as in other accounts, this notion is harnessed by the hagiographer. The account reproduces the notion of torture as truth as a means of guaranteeing Christian authenticity—the martyr's inflexibility and stubbornness under torture serve as markers of truth for the Christian audience. At the same time, lingering beneath the surface of these descriptions of torture is a fear of apostasy. Blandina's mistress worries that she is not strong enough to maintain her confession, and the martyr Biblis is at first "feeble and weak" and blasphemes (*Lyons* 5.1.18, 25). The author offers an explanation: those who recant under torture have been seduced by the devil (*Lyons* 5.1.27). The delicate balance between torture as test and torture as truth preoccupies much of the account.

For those whose bodies remain immune to physical demonic pressure, their resilience combats the secondary aim of torture, to denaturalize and deidentify their subjects.[31] From a historio-sociological perspective, one purpose of torture is to force the tortured to acknowledge and defer to the claims of the torturer. In the process, the identity of the individual is lost in the blurred experience of pain. The narrative of the *Letter,* however, tells a very different story. Even as the author takes pleasure in the brutality of the examinations, the true martyrs resist attempts to subjugate them:

> But Sanctus also endured marvelously and superhumanly all the outrages which he suffered . . . There arose therefore on the part of the governor and his tormentors a great desire to conquer him; but having nothing more that they could do to him, they finally fastened red-hot brazen plates to the most tender parts of his body. And these indeed were burned, but he continued unbending and unyielding, firm in his confession, and refreshed and strengthened by the heavenly fountain of the water of life, flowing from the belly of Christ. And his body was a witness of his sufferings, being one complete wound and bruise, drawn out of shape, and altogether unlike a human form. Christ, suffering in him, manifested his glory, delivering him from his adver-

sary, and making him an example for the others, showing that nothing is fearful where the love of the Father is, and nothing painful where there is the glory of Christ. (*Lyons* 5.1.20–23)

Sanctus appears to feel no pain: he is "unyielding," "unbending," and "firm in his confession." He is a model of Roman masculinity. The truth of his testimony is reinforced by the fact that he clings to it even to death.[32] If Sanctus's masculinity is expressed in his stiffened resolve and the firmness of his confession, it is immediately undercut by the newfound shapelessness of his body. This shapelessness forces a blurring of identity, as it is precisely those anatomical features that have marked Sanctus's body as masculine that have been rendered indistinguishable and without form. At this moment Christ suffers in him and delivers him from the adversary. Torture here succeeds in denaturing Sanctus's body, but the identity he acquires in its place is the elevated association with Christ:

> For when the wicked men tortured him a second time after some days, supposing that with his body swollen and inflamed to such a degree that he could not bear the touch of a hand, if they should again apply the same instruments, they would overcome him, or at least by his death under his sufferings others would be made afraid, not only did this not occur, but, contrary to all human expectation, his body arose and stood erect in the midst of the subsequent torments, and resumed its original appearance and the use of its limbs, so that, through the grace of Christ, these second sufferings became to him, not torture, but healing. (*Lyons* 5.1.24)

Despite the torturers' best efforts, the application of additional sufferings only fortifies and reconstructs Sanctus's body. Supplementary torture serves a similar function in the case of Biblis, which follows immediately after this description of Sanctus. Within the context of audience reception, the narrative eradication of pain serves both consolatory and exhortatory purposes. The account consoles the relatives of those who have suffered for Christ that their loved ones did not experience pain. In a broader sense, if Augustine is to be believed, the painlessness of suffering for Christ consoles those grieving in general.[33] Furthermore, the denial of pain encourages those who were scared of or intimidated by the prospect of martyrdom to fear nothing. The presentation of pain as healing reassures those who otherwise would be inclined to avoid suffering for Christ that suffering can be painless. In fact, in the case of Biblis, renewed tortures recompose the martyr's body and rouse her from apostasying slumber (*Lyons* 5.1.24, 26). The author creates a literary trompe l'oeil in which bodily suffering is rendered impotent by Christly analgesic and the administration of pain solidifies the martyr's body.[34]

The bifurcation of pain and suffering in the account is noteworthy. Historically, suffering and pain have been viewed as synonymous and equally negative entities. Yet in the logic of the *Letter,* they are clearly demarcated from one another.[35] We might reasonably infer that Sanctus enjoys the experience of suffering for Christ, but it is not necessary, or even appropriate, to categorize his experience as masochistic. Masochism is the enjoyment of *pain,* but Sanctus does not feel any pain. Suffering for Christ is painless. Sanctus's experience and the narrative's denial of pain gesture to ancient constructions of masculinity: we might recall Arria's protestation that plunging the dagger into her abdomen "doesn't hurt" (Val. Max. 4.6.5). At the same time, in the narrative, Sanctus's denial of pain resists the structures of torture. Rather than being denatured by pain, Sanctus enjoys himself; his focus on his confession is sharpened by torture, and the process of torture itself is short-circuited. Moreover, deidentification allows Sanctus to assume a new identity—Christ. The physical eradication of Sanctus's shape, his *morphe,* allows Christ to inhabit his body. Paradoxically, the elimination of Sanctus's identity permits him to assume a better one. In this way, the author of the *Letter* layers the descriptions of torture with modes of resistance. The objectives of the torturers are at every turn frustrated: torture is depicted as exaltation, painless, and communion with Christ.

The ambitions of torture are supplemented by the rituals of the amphitheater, which are intended further to denigrate and animalize the criminal in a public forum. Just as torture is rendered futile, so too the spectacle of exposure to the beasts is subverted. The martyrs resist the constraints and expectations of amphitheater ritual and reconfigure the hierarchies of the execution ritual itself.[36] Although the process was designed to place the deaths of the martyrs on display, it is not the martyrs but the audience members who become the spectacle. The martyrs Maturus, Sanctus, Blandina, and Attalus were led into the amphitheater "to be exposed to the beasts and to give a public spectacle of the heathen inhumanity" (*Lyons* 5.1.37), but the crowd, not the martyrs, grows angry and uncontrolled and is reduced to the status of beasts: "Once again they [the martyrs] ran the gauntlet of whips (according to the local custom), the mauling of animals, and anything else that the mad mob from different places shouted for and demanded. And to crown all they were put in the iron seat, from which their roasted flesh filled the audience with its savor. But that was not enough for them, and they continued to rage in their desire to break down the martyrs' resistance" (*Lyons* 5.1.38–39). The maddened mob with its cannibalistic yearning to taste the flesh of the martyrs is exactly the opposite of the civilized observers they were supposed to be. Attalus himself condemns the crowd, saying that they are eating human flesh

(*Lyons* 5.1.52). That Attalus responds in Latin is a marker of his citizen status (*Lyons* 5.1.43) and, at the same time, a gesture to the social status of those whom he addresses, for they are Romans. In the background echoes a subtle jab at Roman civility in Gaul: the Romans had officially deemed human sacrifice illegal and barbaric, but in the *Letter of the Churches of Vienne and Lyons* they themselves delight in the perverse sacrifice of Christians.

A number of the martyrs remain silent throughout their execution. Alexander, for instance, "uttered no groan or cry at all but simply spoke to God in his heart" (*Lyons* 5.1.51). Alexander's self-control is a display of good Roman masculinity: he is strong, resolute, and controlled. Once inside the arena, the female martyr Blandina was "hung on a post and exposed as bait for the wild animals that were let loose on her" (*Lyons* 5.1.41). She remains composed in prayer, and the wild animals never approach her; she is unhooked from her perch and returned to prison. The animals that will not touch her are, following the conventions of the apocryphal acts, domesticated. The crowd, by contrast, is enraged by the martyrs' calmness and composure. It is the behavior of the martyrs that has caused them to become mad—that is, to become bodies without rationality, the very condition to which they had come to watch the martyrs reduced.

By the end of the account the crowd has become fully animalized, "wild and barbarous," "enflamed [by] their bestial anger," and raging and grinding their teeth (*Lyons* 5.1.57, 58). The conduct of the martyrs subverts the expectations of the spectacle; instead of the martyrs being animalized by the process of execution, their silence and acceptance disorient the crowd. The condemned become civilized, while the civilized become barbaric. Just as with torture, the narrative reversal of ritual expectations articulates the martyrs' resistance.

BIBLICAL REENACTMENTS

The martyrs' display of self-control in the face of an increasingly rabid crowd is reminiscent of both the self-control of the Lukan Jesus and the stoic composure of the Maccabean martyrs before the passionate Antiochus.[37] Biblical reminiscences go even farther as the characters of the *Letter of the Churches of Vienne and Lyons* are assimilated to a cast of scriptural actors. Upon occasion the comparison is explicit: the attorney Vettius Epagathus is compared by the author to Zachary, the father of John the Baptist (*Lyons* 5.1.9). In other cases the allusions are more discrete and ambiguous, gleaming with interpretative possibility. The characterization of the aged Pothinus, the bishop of Lyons, is reminiscent of the Maccabean Eleazar and the aging bishop Polycarp: "The blessed Pothinus, who had been entrusted with the bishopric of Lyons, was dragged to the judgment seat. He was more than ninety years of age, and very infirm, scarcely indeed able to breathe because of physical weakness; but he was strengthened by spiritual zeal through his earnest desire for martyrdom. Though his body was worn out by old age and disease, his life was preserved that Christ might triumph in it" (*Lyons* 5.1.29). Like Eleazar, Pothinus is energized by the desire for martyrdom. The allusion to the Maccabean hero reframes Pothinus's conduct within biblical history. It amplifies the theme, present in the description of Sanctus's tortures, that the bodies of the martyrs are vivified by divine power despite their weaknesses. Here, Pothinus is sustained by "spiritual zeal" and is preserved, providentially, in order to serve as a location for Christly triumph. The Maccabean allusions reappear toward the end of the account where Blandina is styled as the Maccabean mother, a "noble mother" who encourages and dispatches her spiritual "children" to God before finally being executed herself (*Lyons* 5.1.55–56).[38] The references to the Maccabees provide a narrative and conceptual framework for the *Letter*. As in 2 and 4 Maccabees, the torture and death of the other martyrs are buttressed by the deaths of an aging leader and an exemplary mother.

The comparison of Blandina to the Maccabean mother is amplified by the use of the plural noun *tekna* (children). Blandina is paired only with the youth Ponticus, rendering the plural *tekna* suggestively metaphorical. Blandina does not have a biological relationship with Ponticus, nor is she depicted as abandoning her children. Casting Blandina as the Maccabean mother both feminizes her and invokes a Pauline-styled fictive kinship in which the family was constituted of martyrs and, perhaps, other Christians. Even if the ambiguously plural "children" is an allusion to 4 Maccabees, it suggests to the audience that Blandina has other, unnamed children. That Ponticus is also described as her sibling calls to mind Paul's portrayal of Christians as brothers and sisters in Christ, again invoking the notion of a Christian family, rather than a biological one. Blandina's exemplarity functions not only to invite the audience to join the cohort of martyrs in battle, but also to invite them into her Christian family. The audience can become children of Blandina through martyrdom and also through participation in the broader Christian community. In this respect, Blandina's conduct does not model familial abandonment but, rather, creates a Christian family within the world of the text.[39]

The death of Blandina, however, resonates with multiple biblical models.[40] She is introduced into the account as the very least of the Christians. Socioeconomically she is an ugly female slave, one of the dregs of society. Whatever the ancient stereotypes, her appearance and social status belie her true worth. In the words of J. Albert Harrill, "In a physiognomic reversal, the *eidos* of

Blandina's slave body—cheap, ugly, and contemptuous—turns out, in the end, to be the most beautiful and prized spectacle of divine power (*dynamis*), the real 'autopsy' and direct sighting of God."[41] Blandina's conduct is implicitly contrasted with that of the pagan slaves who had betrayed their Christian masters: the pagan slaves were not tortured and provided a false witness; Blandina was tortured and provided an authentic testimony (*Lyons* 5.1.17). Like Sanctus and Pothinus, however, Blandina's strength and testimony are grounded in Christ and her ability to perform Christ: "Blandina was hung on a stake and set as food before the beasts driven in the arena. Because she was seen hanging in the form of a cross and on account of her energetic and unceasing prayer she stirred up great enthusiasm among the contestants. During the contest they looked with their eyes through their sister to the one who was crucified for them so that he convinced those who believe in him that everyone who suffers for the glory of Christ will have eternal fellowship with the living God" (*Lyons* 5.1.41). Assuming the form of the cross is paralleled in other early Christian narratives. Thecla voluntarily climbs the pyre and extends her arms in a cross before God quenches the flames (*Acts of Paul and Thecla* 3.22).[42] Fructuosus stretches out his arms in prayer (*Martyrdom of Fructuosus* 4.3-4). In Blandina's case, her ability to perform Christ has both a soteriological effect and a startling narratological one.[43] Blandina herself disappears, and in her place and in her physical form only Christ is apparent. The transformative quality of her imitation of the crucifixion is so strong that she vanishes; her identity is transformed into and subsumed by that of Christ. In a manner similar to the apocryphal acts and the *Martyrdom of Polycarp*, Blandina is presented as following in the footsteps of Christ and imitating his passion. That she is described as the most cheap and worthless of people amplifies the effect of corporeal cohabitation. At the same time, unlike other early Christian martyr acts, here imitation elides identity: Blandina recedes into the background of the text and is supplanted by Christ. The nature of the martyr's imitation adapts Pauline notions of the body and reverses them so that the body of the martyr becomes a site for Christly occupation. The characterization of Blandina is a tapestry of biblical reenactments: she is the Maccabean mother encouraging her children, the biblical Daniel turned courageous Thecla whom animals do not dare approach (*Lyons* 5.1.42), and an imitator of Christ.

THE DEVIL

Just as Christ co-opts the bodies of the martyrs and moves into the foreground of the narrative, his adversary, the devil, plays a prominent role as the villain of the piece. The devil appears in many early Christian martyrdom accounts, sometimes as a secondary character, but mostly as a rhetorical trope, a shadowy force that is responsible for persecutions, tortures, and evil that plague Christians but whose involvement is largely superficial. In the *Letter of the Churches at Vienne and Lyons,* by contrast, the devil is the primary antagonist. Christly possession of the martyrs is paralleled by the devil's occupation of the governor and of the governor's efforts to lead the martyrs astray. The narrative is replete with references to demonic interference in the world, so much so that the devil even becomes an actor in the narrative, complete with thoughts, suppositions, and assumptions. The role of Satan in the account is both general, in that he orchestrates the torture and execution of Christians, and personal, in that he is embroiled in individual struggles with martyrs.[44] In narrating these encounters, the author employs military and athletic imagery derived from the Maccabean literature, the writings of Paul, and the book of Revelation to describe the struggle of martyr and devil and to foreshadow the eventual victory of the former.

The crumpled body of the martyr becomes the locus for Christ's struggle with his adversary. In the description of the tortures of Sanctus, noted above, the conquest of Satan is expressed as a victory of Christ. Simultaneously, Sanctus is an agent in this victory, as his bodily sufferings earn glory and serve as a pattern for others.[45] Throughout the account, the deaths of the martyrs are interpreted as both exemplary and inspirational and as victories over Satan. The language of victory is most consistently connected to the defeat of Satan. The death of Blandina in particular serves a dual function as both example and triumph. Her torture in a cruciform pose incites the admiration and excitement of bystanders. The efficacy of this pose is summed up: "Thus for her victory in further contests she would make irreversible the condemnation of the crooked serpent, and tiny, weak, and insignificant as she was she would give inspiration to her brothers, for she had put on Christ, that mighty and invincible athlete, and had overcome the Adversary in many contests and through her conflict had won the crown of immortality" (*Lyons* 5.1.42). The fusion of athletic imagery and biblically derived elements of the cosmic myth is apparent in the description of Blandina as dressing in the invincible athlete Christ. The incarnation of the devil as the crooked serpent could be understood either as an allusion to the fall of humanity in Genesis or as a reference to the primordial beast Leviathan (Isa 27:1). The former reading would place the work of Christ in Blandina firmly within the scope of salvation history. The curse brought about by the serpent is fulfilled and subverted by the martyr's death.[46] Blandina crushes the serpent and dismantles the primordial events that led to the existence of the curse. Relating Blandina to events in Genesis gives her death a cosmic significance. The permanency of the effect of her death is highlighted as of great cosmic importance.

Imagery of cosmic conflict persists to the end of the work. The devil is a voracious and gluttonous beast who eagerly seeks to consume the Christians. Just as reciprocal love was instrumental during the tortures of Blandina and Sanctus, it also functions to vanquish the devil in a more fundamental sense: "Because of the sincerity of their love this became the greatest of all the contests which they waged against the Demon, to the end that the throttled Beast might be forced to disgorge alive all those whom he at first thought he had devoured" (*Lyons* 5.2.6). The language of consumption is striking here: not only does the beast consume the martyrs, but their love forces him to vomit them back up. The victory over evil is accomplished through love and also by virtue of Christly possession. The martyrological anthropology that permeates the text and the cosmic battle that preoccupies the author are related concepts. The presence of Christ in the bodies of the martyrs is a sign that victory over Satan has been won.

The martyrs are described as being scented with "the sweet savor of Christ" as they go out to the arena.[47] The multilayered image evokes a handful of rich interpretations. One reading, delicately described by Susan Ashbrook Harvey, draws upon the invocation of bridal imagery in the passage:[48] "For the first went out rejoicing, glory and grace being blended in their faces, so that even their bonds seemed like beautiful ornaments, as those of a bride adorned with variegated golden fringes; and they were perfumed with the sweet savor of Christ, so that some supposed they had been anointed with earthly ointment" (*Lyons* 5.1.35). From this Harvey argues that the imagery anticipates the translocation of the martyr at death to the heavenly bridal chamber, a preview, so to speak, of the postmortem rewards that the martyrs can expect. On the other hand, the description of the aroma as a proprietary aspect of the countenance of Christ suggests a bodily proximity to Christ. The aroma of the martyrs gestures to the Corinthian correspondence and signifies life (2 Cor 2:15).

Another interpretation of "the sweet savor of Christ" invokes a different complex of ideas. Ancient constructions of scent often maintained that it was exhaled, thus associating it with breath.[49] The association of breath, the martyr's triumph in death, and victory over Satan may allude to 2 Thess 2:8 where the "lawless one" is conquered by "the breath of his [Christ's] mouth" (τῷ πνεύματι τοῦ στόματος). The idea of martyrdom as conquest of Satan weaves together the language and imagery of military battle, athletic endurance, and Christly possession. By utilizing a biblical narrative of fall and conquest and the Pauline concept of Christ inhabiting the bodies of Christians, the author of the *Letter* both constructs a narrative of salvation and encourages the audience to strap on armor and step into salvation history.

Irenaeus

The conclusion to the *Letter of the Churches of Vienne and Lyons* dissolves into Eusebius's *Ecclesiastical History* to the extent that it is unclear where the letter ends and Eusebius begins. He furnishes further excerpts describing the modified asceticism of one Alcibiades during his imprisonment and Alcibiades's condemnation of the followers of Montanus. These excerpts are typical of Eusebius, who frequently uses martyred Christians as mouthpieces for orthodoxy. In one of his final comments on the Gallic correspondence, Eusebius notes that the martyrs had composed a letter supporting Irenaeus's assumption of the episcopacy of Lyons:

> The same witnesses also recommended Irenaeus, who was already at that time a presbyter of the parish of Lyons, to the above-mentioned bishop of Rome, saying many favorable things in regard to him, as the following extract shows: "We pray, father Eleutherus, that you may rejoice in God in all things and always. We have requested our brother and comrade Irenaeus to carry this letter to you, and we ask you to hold him in esteem, as zealous for the covenant of Christ. For if we thought that office could confer righteousness upon any one, we should commend him among the first as a presbyter of the church, which is his position." (*Hist. eccl.* 5.4.1–2)

This passage is an institutionalizing account that gives Irenaeus the blessing of the martyrs, including, presumably, that of Pothinus, the previous ecclesiastical leader. For Eusebius, a committed admirer of Irenaeus, the excerpt serves to bolster Irenaeus's authority further. Not only did Irenaeus learn the faith from Polycarp himself, but his assumption of office was suggested by the very best kind of Christians: dead, holy ones.[50] At the same time, the recommendation helps create the narrative of episcopal succession that Eusebius is constructing. The recommendation of Irenaeus supports the illusion that leadership and structure have always been a part of the universal church. According to Eusebius, Irenaeus, on one hand, and the martyrs of Lyons and Vienne, on the other, had always been linked. The latter played a role in promoting the former, and, if Nautin is to be believed, Irenaeus himself wrote the letter detailing the sufferings of these martyrs.

Apart from his supposed personal connection with the story of the deaths of the martyrs of Lyons, Irenaeus is aware that Justin Martyr (*Haer.* 1.28.1), the otherwise unknown Telephorus (*Haer.* 3.3.3), and Polycarp (*Haer.* 3.3.4) have been executed, although he does not appear to be familiar with the narratives of their deaths. He does, however, quote without attribution the famous epistle of Ignatius *To the Romans,* in which Ignatius states that he wants to be ground into wheat by the wild beasts (*Haer.* 5.28.4).[51] These epistolary and personal connections have led some scholars to speculate that Irenaeus's perspectives on martyrdom were, in one sense or another, Asiatic.[52] Such conclusions depend on the assumption that Irenaeus derived his ideas about martyrdom from others. Even if the deaths of Justin and Polycarp and the writings of Ignatius left an imprint on Irenaeus's thinking, we should not assume that he replicated their opinions entirely without augmentation. We must also note that Irenaeus uses the fact of their executions, rather than literary descriptions of them, to put forward his own views.

STEPHEN

Somewhat unexpectedly, early Christians were not that interested in Stephen the martyr. The exception to this rule is Irenaeus's use of the martyrdom of Stephen (Acts 7) in *Against the Heresies.* Irenaeus repeatedly refers to Stephen as "the first to follow the footsteps of the martyrdom of the Lord" and "the first that was slain for confessing Christ" (*Haer.* 3.12.10), which is particularly significant because until the fourth century early Christians were not especially interested in Stephen.[53] The Apostolic Fathers, apologists, Nag Hammadi corpus, and extant early Christian apocrypha do not refer to Stephen at all. The sixth-century Gallic *Decretum Gelasianum* mentions a spurious work about Stephen, the *Revelatio, quae appellatur Stephani, apocrypha,* but this has been identified by P. von Winterfeld as a Palestinian text written by the priest Lucian in 415 CE.[54] There is only one second-century non-Gallic reference to the great protomartyr. Eusebius mentions a sect of the Nicolaites, Nicolas being one of the seven Hellenists elected to service in Acts 6:5 (*Hist. eccl.* 3.2.1). The connection with Stephen here is somewhat strained; it would not be an overstatement to say that his death takes on exegetical significance only in Gaul. Stephen's heroism and exemplary function are highlighted both in the *Letter of the Churches of Vienne and Lyons,* in which the martyrs, like Stephen, pray for forgiveness for their persecutors (*Lyons* 5.2.5), and in the writings of Irenaeus (*Haer.* 3.12.10; 3.12.13; 4.15.1), where Stephen serves as a model for orthodoxy and good conduct.

Irenaeus uses Stephen's courage and martyrdom to accentuate the harmony of the views of the earliest Christians, as "both the apostles and their disciples thus taught as the Church preaches, and thus teaching were perfected" (*Haer.* 3.12.13). It is for this purpose and in this context that Irenaeus mentions

Stephen's martyrdom.[55] Stephen's death is a fulfillment and perfection of doctrine and a copy of the death of Jesus, whom Irenaeus calls "the leader of martyrdom" (*Haer.* 3.12.13). Irenaeus highlights Stephen's forgiveness of his executioners and the boldness of his proclamation as evidence of his doctrinal orthodoxy and authenticity. This emphasis underscores the rhetorical function of martyrdom for Irenaeus: martyrdom is evidence of true doctrine.

MARTYRDOM AND ORTHODOXY

When addressed in the writings of Irenaeus, martyrdom is placed squarely within the context of the author's condemnation of his opponents. The martyr's imitation of Christ and the gospel accounts in which Jesus exhorts his followers to embrace suffering and persecution are invoked in order to define correct belief. In *Against the Heresies,* Irenaeus formulates a catena of scriptural citations connecting the practice of martyrdom to the resurrection of the body and, finally, to the humanity of Christ:

> If, however, he was himself not to suffer, but should fly away from Jesus, why did he exhort his disciples to take up the cross and follow him,—that cross which these men represent him as not having taken up, but [speak of him] as having relinquished the dispensation of suffering? For that he did not say this with reference to the acknowledging of the Stauros (cross) above, as some among them venture to expound, but with respect to the suffering which he should himself undergo, and that his disciples should endure, he implies when he says, "For whosoever will save his life, shall lose it; and whosoever will lose, shall find it." And that his disciples must suffer for his sake, he [implied when he] said to the Jews, "Behold, I send you prophets, and wise men, and scribes: and some of them you shall kill and crucify." And to the disciples he was wont to say, "And you shall stand before governors and kings for My sake; and they shall scourge some of you, and slay you, and persecute you from city to city." He knew, therefore, both those who should suffer persecution, and he knew those who should have to be scourged and slain because of him; and he did not speak of any other cross, but of the suffering which he should himself undergo first, and his disciples afterwards. For this purpose did he give them this exhortation: "Fear not them which kill the body, but are not able to kill the soul; but rather fear him who is able to send both soul and body into hell"; [thus exhorting them] to hold fast those professions of faith which they had made in reference to him. For he promised to confess before his Father those who should confess his name before men; but declared that he would deny those who should deny him, and would be ashamed of those who should be ashamed to confess him. And although these things are so, some of these men have proceeded to such a degree of temerity, that they even pour contempt upon the martyrs,

and vituperate those who are slain on account of the confession of the Lord, and who suffer all things predicted by the Lord, and who in this respect strive to follow the footprints of the Lord's passion, having become martyrs of the suffering one; these we do also enroll with the martyrs themselves. For, when inquisition shall be made for their blood, and they shall attain to glory, then all shall be confounded by Christ, who have cast a slur upon their martyrdom. (*Haer.* 3.18.5)

Irenaeus's opponents are those who presume that the Lord was not actually crucified. He poses the question of why Christ would have exhorted his followers to take up their crosses and follow him (Mark 8:34; Matt 16:24) if Jesus was not himself present at the crucifixion. He then reflects the prophesized mimetic experience of Jesus's followers onto Jesus himself—those who denied Christ in tribunals would be denied by Christ at the heavenly tribunal (Matt 10:33). Irenaeus's opponents, in his view, are also guilty of this crime because in denying the crucifixion of Christ, they also deny martyrdom. That Irenaeus exploits the functional and formal connections between martyrdom and the death of Jesus to indict those he opposes is not altogether unexpected. That it is martyrdom that is used to shore up the death of Christ (rather than the death of Christ supporting the validity of martyrdom) demonstrates the rhetorical power of martyrdom for Irenaeus's audience and opponents.

CREATION AND COSMIC BATTLE

Just as in the *Letter of the Churches of Vienne and Lyons,* Irenaeus views martyrdom as entering into a cosmic battle with the devil. His description of the victory over Satan achieved through the death of Jesus bears more than a passing resemblance to the description of the torture of Blandina in the *Letter*: "For the law never hindered them from believing in the Son of God; no, but it even exhorted them so to do, saying that men can be saved in no other way from the old wound of the serpent than by believing in him who, in the likeness of sinful flesh, is lifted up from the earth upon the tree of martyrdom, and draws all things to himself, and vivifies the dead" (*Haer.* 4.2.7). Irenaeus's portrait of the death of Jesus weaves together elements of both Genesis and Revelation. Jesus is a martyr (Rev 1:4) whose death operates as part of a cosmic battle with Satan to heal the primordial wound. That Irenaeus and, presumably, his audience in Gaul cast the death of Jesus as martyrdom on a tree that repairs the wounds inflicted by the serpent in the garden of Eden only intensifies the force of Blandina's *imitatio.* Like Jesus, Blandina is a martyr hung on a tree whose death has a direct role in crushing the serpent-devil. The presentation of Blandina as *imitatrix Christi* seems directly related to this particular reading of the death of Jesus. It is significant that Blandina herself participates in the cosmic battle with Satan; her death resembles that of Jesus in function as well as form.

Conclusion

The *Letter of the Churches of Vienne and Lyons* and the writings of Irenaeus offer many thematic parallels with one another. These thematic correspondences have been traditionally understood as an indication of shared authorship rather than as the product of a common cultural context. The idea of a Gallic or even Lyonnais Christianity is problematic as it assumes a regional uniformity predicated upon artificial boundaries. This argument, however, is not cited as the reason for the neglect of Gallic Christianity. The reluctance even to speak of Irenaeus and the *Letter* as examples of second-century Gallic Christianity is remarkable when contrasted with the frequent descriptions of Irenaeus as an example of Asiatic Christianity. That Irenaeus and, consequently, the *Letter* are categorized as Asiatic even though they are located in western Europe discloses an inconsistency in the way regional forms of Christianity are constructed. Whereas other regional forms are identified with the regions themselves, Gallic Christianity is identified with Irenaeus, who, in turn, is viewed as the heir of the Johannine evangelist because he was born and raised in Asia Minor. The disappearance of "Gallic Christianity" reveals an assumption in the way that the history of early Christianity is narrated: first, that it is difficult to separate individual authors from their communities and cultural contexts; and second, that a particular model of character formation is embedded in the genealogical approach to the history of Christianity. Irenaeus lived in both Rome and Gaul and yet for a cradle Christian childhood influences are assumed to have been dominant. To be sure, there are many reasons for treating Irenaeus as an Asiatic Christian—for example, he uses texts from Asia Minor and corresponds with Christians there. It is worth asking, however, why, if Irenaeus wrote in Gaul, about events in Gaul, and for people in Gaul, his literary productions are not viewed as representative of Gallic Christianity.

Regardless of how we might choose to interpret the similarities between Irenaeus and the *Letter of the Churches of Vienne and Lyons*—as evidence of Gallic Christianity or as the literary product of Irenaeus—it is clear that there is a distinctive theology of martyrdom in Gaul. This does not altogether discredit the notion of literary and cultural ties to Asia Minor, as many of these shared thematic interests are drawn from Revelation and the Pauline epistles, but the use of these texts is highly distinctive and unlike the Polycarp tradition into which the *Letter* is often assimilated. Whereas Irenaeus and the *Letter* both display an interest in Revelation and the Gospel of John, two texts with strong ties to Asia Minor, they are the only second-century accounts to focus on Stephen as protomartyr. As imitator of Christ who follows in Christ's footsteps, Stephen is prototypical for the martyrs in the *Letter*. These martyrs are also cast as imitators of Christ and vessels for Christ to inhabit. Yet this portrayal is distinct from the *imitatio* of Polycarp, in which the mimetic hierarchy between Polycarp and Christ is constantly reinforced. Here in the *Letter*, and in a manner analogous to the Pauline epistles, the bodies of the martyrs house both Christ and the battle with Satan. The prominent role played by love as analgesic and reciprocal relationship between Christ and the martyrs is a distinctive feature of these Gallic texts.

5

Roman North Africa:
Apocalyptic Ascent

The history of Christianity in North Africa in the second century is shrouded in mystery. Carthage, the capital of the Roman province of Africa (*Africa Proconsularis*) and the epicenter of Christian literature, was a bustling city by the time of Christianity's arrival.[1] Perched on the Bay of Tunis, the city's location made it a valuable center of commerce, trade, and administration from the Punic period onward. In contrast to the origins of Christianity in other major urban centers, for Carthage there are not even myths of apostolic foundations to eye with suspicion; almost abruptly, with the writings of the prolific author Tertullian in the third century, Christianity appears. While scholarly theories about Christianity's arrival in North Africa have proposed connections with Asia Minor and Italy, these hypotheses are based largely on logical deduction from trade routes and on comments made by later authors.[2] The names of the Christians included in the first piece of Christian literature from North Africa, the *Acts of the Scillitan Martyrs* (ca. 180 CE), includes the typically indigenous name Nartzalus. This evidence suggests that by the time we encounter textual records of Christianity in North Africa, Christianity is no longer limited to an immigrant population.

Despite the paucity of Christian literature, evidence suggests that Christianity had arrived in proconsular Africa long before the composition of the *Acts of the Scillitan Martyrs*. Fronto, a famed polemicist from Cirta, lampoons the Christians in his diatribe *Against the Christians* (ca. 162–166 CE).[3] If the Christian identification of the baker's wife in the North African Apuleius's *Metamorphoses* is correct (9.14.5), then he also sees the Christians as distorters of religious tradition.[4] To these we might add Tertullian's statement from around 196–198 CE that Christians had "filled every place among [the pagans] . . . cities, islands, fortresses, towns, market-places, the very camp, tribes, companies, palace, senate, forum" (*Apol.* 37.4). Tertullian is likely exaggerating and, further, exploiting fears that Christians had infiltrated all areas of society, but the force of his polemic rests on its verisimilitude: his assertion would not be credible if there were not a sizable group of Christians in Carthage. Archaeological evidence further corroborates their presence in Africa as early as 150 CE. The catacombs at Hadrumetum (Sousse), 150 miles south of Carthage, contain Christian images and inscriptions, including depictions of the good shepherd, the dove, and the fish, that date to circa 150 CE. The presence of Christian iconography and burial sites around the middle of the second century implies that at least some kind of established Christian community was at Hadrumetum before these burials. This deduction aside, it is not possible to say how long Christians had been there or to use these data to reconstruct the date of Christianity's arrival in Africa.[5] While we can be sure that Christians lived in North Africa before the advent of martyrdom, their social location, the contours of their religious traditions, and the cadences of their day-to-day lives are hidden from view.

In the absence of clear evidence, the character of early Christianity in proconsular Africa has been connected to local Phoenician religious practices. A number of the Christians in the *Acts of the Scillitan Martyrs* have Punic names, so it is likely that some Christians were deeply embedded in Punic culture. Of the many facets of Punic religion, the sensational practice of child sacrifice has captured the attention of modern commentators.[6] The evidence from Carthage is hotly debated. According to the scholarly narrative, child sacrifice arrived in North Africa with the Phoenicians. The Hebrew Bible often refers to instances of or prohibitions against child sacrifice among the ancient Israelites. These practices appear to have died out in the eastern Mediterranean after the seventh century BCE, but evidence suggests that Phoenicians imported child sacrifice to North Africa, where the practice continued long after it had ceased elsewhere. Archaeological excavations of a children's cemetery known as the *tophet* by the port in Carthage led to the discovery of a cache of urns and stelae of children[7] that has in turn led to the theory that at this site parents would offer their infants to the gods Baal-Hammon and Tanit in fulfillment of a vow or as a response to divine favor. The theory garners further support from ancient writers Diodorus of Sicily, Plutarch, and Tertullian.[8] The arresting idea of parents sacrificing their infants to a deity has contributed to the view that Punic religion was austere, sacrificial, and bloodthirsty.

The common element of unusual human death has led a number of scholars to assume that child sacrifice in North Africa is a conceptual key for understanding martyrdom in the region.[9] There is, however, a puzzling ambiguity about how, precisely, child sacrifice flavored Christian martyrdom. More often than not, scholarly references to the influence of austere Punic religion on austere Carthaginian Christianity refer to Tertullian rather than to the early martyr acts. In his sketch of Christianity in the third century, John Henry Newman wrote, "there was the priest of Punic Saturn, the child-devourer, a sort of Moloch, to whom the martyrdom of Christians was a sacred rite."[10] Newman is composing fiction, but he and many of his contemporaries seem to have thought that Christians were being sacrificed to a Punic deity. This line of reasoning is curious given that Christians were tried and sentenced by Romans and executed by beheading or in the arena. The notion that Christians were willing to be martyred because of some indigenous predisposition for human sacrifice lacks nuance and perspective. Any assertion to this effect needs to rest on a careful analysis of the terms in which the deaths of Christians are described. Language of sacrifice is strikingly absent in the *Acts of the Scillitan Martyrs* and the *Passion of Perpetua and Felicitas*. While the reference to Saturn in the *Passio* 18.4 may well invoke local religious practices, the structures of ritual execution in the amphitheater do not replicate the structures of child sacrifice. We might infer that the author of the *Passio* attempts to condemn the Romans by aligning their persecution of Christians with human sacrifice, but this rhetorical move would not imply that anyone—Roman, Christian, or noncitizen African—viewed the deaths of Christians as analogous to child sacrifice.

As this book has argued throughout, the influence of local religious, social, political, and economic structures on the articulation of martyrdom is a critically important and often overlooked feature of histories of martyrdom. Setting Tertullian, for example, in his African context is essential.[11] At the same time, the eagerness with which scholars have fixated upon child sacrifice and used it to characterize indigenous religious practice makes the non-Roman inhabitants of proconsular Africa seem exotic and subtly barbaric. The connection between child sacrifice and martyrdom is based on the common characterization of both practices as austere, unnatural, and ritualized.[12] That human beings are killed in the service of a deity binds the two phenomena together more concretely. As we saw in our survey in chapter 1 of traditions of noble death, however, it is not necessary to view martyrdom as unnatural. There are many nonsacrificial contexts in which the premature death of a human being is deemed appropriate. Given that depictions of the deaths of Christians in proconsular Africa shy away from sacrificial language and imagery, we should be wary of assuming that Christian martyrdom emerged out of this particular religious convention. If child sacrifice was practiced in Carthage, it was only one of many Punic and Roman intellectual, religious, and cultural traditions that could have shaped the understanding of martyrdom in the region.

Here we consider the ideologies of martyrdom that emerged in the second century in proconsular Africa, focusing on the *Acts of the Scillitan Martyrs* and the famous *Passion of Perpetua and Felicitas.* The richness of these accounts, the sophistication of the contemporary Christian writer Tertullian's rhetoric, and the vividness of Perpetua's visions make it impossible to track down every cultural intertext and explore every image. Thus we focus on two specific themes: the ways in which North African ideologies of martyrdom can be termed enthusiastic or apocalyptic and the ways in which Pauline traditions support specific communal practices. The latter interest is built on the argument that Pauline traditions, and especially the *Acts of Paul and Thecla,* played an important role in the communities producing these accounts. Despite this dual focus, the chapter is ordered chronologically and treats the texts individually. The intent is to describe features of a rugged ideological landscape.

Acts of the Scillitan Martyrs

The earliest evidence for both Latin Christianity and North African martyrdom is an unassuming record of the trials of the martyrs of Scilli. With the composition of this account, Roman Africa steps into the pages of Christian history. The references both to the proconsulship of C. Bruttius Praesens and Claudianus and to P. Vigellius Saturninus, the *proconsul Africae,* date the events to July 180 CE. The martyrs are arraigned, but not in the judicial basilica in the forum. The setting of their trial is the *secretarium,* an office within the proconsul's residence where business affairs were conducted. Although still public, the trial and eventual executions do not have the spectacular quality of dramatic official trials and public executions *ad bestias.*[13] The martyrs were summarily executed after the trial. The location of Scilli is unknown.

The simplicity of the account and its apparent lack of artifice lead Musurillo to label the *Acts of the Scillitan Martyrs* as one of the most authentic of the extant martyr acts.[14] The assimilation of simplicity to authenticity has meant that this narrative has been treated more often as a historical record of events and a resource for social history than as part of the discourse of martyrdom. Even while the assumed historical veracity of the *Acts of the Scillitan Martyrs* has been praised, some scholars have dismissed the source as hardly worthy of an interpretive focus.[15] A closer reading, however, reveals a text laden with suggestive dialogue and scriptural subtexts. The latter are highlighted by the *acta* itself: when questioned, Speratus, the most prominent member of the group, admits to possessing "books and letters of a just man Paul" (*libri et epistulae Pauli uiri iusti*) (*Ac. Scilli.* 1.13).[16] The term *libri*, usually translated as "books," although it could equally be rendered "the books," gleams with possibility for scholars interested in the formation of the canon.[17] What are the *libri Pauli* to which Speratus refers? Adolf von Harnack's view that the *libri* are scrolls of the Old Testament seems unlikely given the explicit reference to Paul.[18] Later versions of the account offer more formal and canonical interpretations of the term: the longer Latin version (Codex Parisinus Latinus 2179) supplies *libri evangeliorum,* and the Greek (Codex Parisinus Graecus 890) reads "our customary books, and the epistles of Paul, the devout man, which belong with them."[19] While a number of noncanonical letters have been attributed to the apostle, the reference to *libri* (books) in opposition to *epistulae* (letters) might signal a distinction between the two and a departure from the generic form in which Paul is known to have written. Perhaps Speratus has in his possession both letters written by Paul and books *about* Paul, either the canonical Acts of the Apostles or the apocryphal *Acts of Paul.*

The reference to Paul here is evidence of his status in the Christian communities at Carthage and of the status of literature associated with him. In both cases it is clear that the martyrs of Scilli view themselves as standing in continuity with Paul and Pauline scriptural traditions. The centrality of the reference to the letters of Paul is further demonstrated in the work of David Eastman, which identifies a chiasmus in this section of the account:[20]

> A "I am a Christian." And they all agreed with him.
> > B "Do you want time to deliberate?" "In a just matter like this, there is no deliberation."
> > > C "What are the things in your box?" "Books and epistles of Paul, a just man."
> > B' "Have a delay of thirty days and think it over."
> A' "I am a Christian." And they all agreed with him.

From the fourth century onward, when the legislation of the emperor Diocletian forced Christians to hand over religious books, references to scripture become increasingly common. It is highly unusual, however, for a pre-Diocletian account to make an overt reference to Christian literature, much less to use chiasmus to highlight its importance structurally. For such a brief account, it is an exquisite detail that should not be passed over without thought. Perhaps the reference to Paul is supposed to serve as a hermeneutical key to the account and, short though it is, the text should be read in light of the Pauline corpus.

There are a number of points in the text at which the martyrs' statements—completely disjunctive in the context of the pronconsul's questions—make veiled allusions to the Pauline corpus and hint at a more sophisticated understanding of what is at stake. Toward the beginning of the account, Saturninus interrogates Speratus about the nature of Christianity. The exchange is peculiar, for Saturninus almost seems to offer an apology for Roman practices and to justify his position to the accused Christian: "Saturninus the proconsul said: 'We too are a religious people, and our religion is a simple one: we swear by the genius of our lord the emperor and we offer prayers for his health as you also ought to do.' Speratus said: 'If you will give me a calm hearing, I shall tell you a simple religious doctrine'" (*Ac. Scilli.* 3–4).[21] The juxtaposition of competing notions of simplicity underlies the exchange. Roman claims to simplicity, an attribute prized by Roman rhetoricians and society, are undercut by the simple mystery of the Christians.[22] Simplicity is a prominent feature in Roman rhetoric that connected complexity and excess or luxury with theatricality and unreliability. This rhetoric was inlaid with ethnic stereotypes: simplicity of speech, for instance, which was often associated with the Attic, was preferred over the showy, theatrical styles of the Asiatic (Cicero, *Brutus* 51), even though, generally, the Greeks were similarly condemned for their luxurious and unreliable nature and "Asiatic" is merely a synonym for bad writing. By the second century simplicity had become valorized as a virtue and a "catchword" in aristocratic and imperial circles.[23] The rhetoric of simplicity here functions both to defend Christianity against charges of *superstitio* (an excess of religion) and to indict the Romans for practicing a religion of excess.[24] Despite Saturninus's protestations, it is clear that Roman claims to religiosity have no basis in rhetorically powerful simplicity. Simplicity is here a marker of truth. Simultaneously, the suggestively Pauline terminology of mystery may take us farther. Speratus's simple doctrine (*mysterium simplicitas*) is likely baptism, the simple act of which is contrasted with the grandeur of its effect, resurrection. Yet Speratus never gets to explicate the content of the religious doctrine. For those in the know, the allusion to the resurrection hangs in the air as a promise for the martyrs (and, by extension, the audience) and a foreshadowing of the conclusion of the account.

he *Acts of Justin and His Companions*, Speratus and Saturninus talk
another. When Saturninus offers Speratus the pardon of the emperor,
s sets his gaze beyond the courtroom to heaven and states, "we [the
ans] hold our emperor in honor" (*Ac. Scilli.* 2). Speratus's emboldened
ɪ_ɹ_ on of Roman authority, however, is modified by his position on economic tribute: "Speratus said: 'I do not recognize the empire of this world.
Rather, I serve that God whom no man has seen, nor can see with these eyes. I
have not stolen; and on any purchase I pay the tax for I acknowledge my Lord
who is the emperor of kings and of nations' " (*Ac. Scilli.* 6). Speratus's response
places the Roman emperor in a subordinate position to God, the emperor of
kings. That Speratus pays taxes on account of his recognition of divine authority subordinates the Roman emperor to Speratus's God. The thought here is
very close to Rom 13:6 in which Paul instructs the community at Rome to pay
taxes because the authorities have been appointed by God. At the same time,
Speratus is clear: Roman authority is subject to God, and temporal authority
is trumped by the celestial, universal empire of God.

The distinction between the Roman emperor and the universal emperor
passes Saturninus by, but references to the superior authority of God and to
parallel celestial affairs continue throughout the account. Cittinus protests
that the martyrs have nothing to fear but their Lord God who is in heaven
(*Ac. Scilli.* 8), and, modifying the gospel maxim to rank secular and sacred
affairs, Donata says, "Pay honour to Caesar as Caesar; but it is God we fear"
(*Ac. Scilli.* 9; cf. Matt 22:21). Most famously, after the sentence has been
pronounced, the martyr Nartzalus states: "Today we are martyrs in heaven.
Thanks be to God!" (*Ac. Scilli.* 15). The declaration has been read both as evidence that martyrs go directly to heaven and as evidence that the term *martys*
refers, in this account and period, to someone who dies for Christ.[25] Nartzalus's words may, however, also continue the interest in superior heavenly structures of power by reflecting Paul's assertion that the citizenship of Christians is
in heaven (Phil 3:20), a statement that views structures of power in heaven as
direct parallels to our own. Read in light of Pauline discussions of heavenly
citizenship and the repeated references to parallel heavenly affairs throughout
the account, Nartzalus's declaration may locate the martyrs as witnesses in a
heavenly court. Heaven as a setting for future judgment is a commonplace in
early Christian literature but plays a distinctive role in Roman African accounts (for example, *Martyrdom of Marian and James* 6.6–10).[26] This interpretation modifies the range of meanings for the term *martys*. The term is relocated
from the earthly courtroom, but not from a legal context altogether, and it still
denotes a legal witness. The rhetorical effect of the heavenly imperial court is
to trump the powers of the earthly Roman courtroom. Paradoxically, by re-

producing Roman structures of power and authority in the celestial sphere, Christians tried under that very power and authority are able to render the Roman government impotent.

The responses of the individual martyrs supplement one another. The martyrs finish one another's sentences and inject themselves into each other's examinations. Donata's adaptation of Matt 22:21 to develop Speratus's claims that he pays taxes but does not recognize the Roman empire rearticulates Speratus's point in a more developed way. The contributions from Cittinus, Donata, Vestia, and Secunda follow immediately from one another almost as if they were a single accused person. Their rapid, unsolicited responses convey not only their excitement and eagerness, but also their singularity of purpose. The phrase "they all agreed" appears repeatedly in order to express the unity of the Christians. Concern to maintain the solidarity of the accused may account for legal and textual problems that appear at the end of the account. Only six martyrs are explicitly identified in the introductory preface (*Ac. Scilli.* 1) as having confessed to being Christian (Speratus, Nartzalus, Cittinus, Donata, Vestia, and Secunda), but a larger number are sentenced to death (the previous six plus Felix, Aquilinus, Laetantius, Januaria, Generosa, and Vesta). If this is a legal text, the disparity is highly problematic. How could these martyrs have been executed without having made individual confessions? A number of text-critical explanations have been developed to account for the inconsistency.[27] Whatever the accuracy of these reconstructions, within the world of the extant Latin text that presents the martyrs as one voice (or, in Pauline terms, as a single body), this apparent disparity is unproblematic. All the martyrs agreed, and therefore all the martyrs are sentenced. They are, after all, one body. Despite claims that the *Acts of the Scillitan Martyrs* appears unedited and authentic, it is hardly likely that a Roman governor would have tolerated the legal chaos the work depicts. If this account has any relationship to a court document, this legal source has been edited to express the single-mindedness of the martyrs and their indebtedness to Paul.

Passion of Perpetua and Felicitas

The *Passion of Perpetua and Felicitas* is one of the most-discussed and well-loved early martyr acts. It tells the story of the arrest and execution of a group of Carthaginian martyrs—Revocatus, Saturninus, Saturus, Secundulus, Perpetua, and Felicitas—around the turn of the third century during the reign of the emperor Septimus Severus (ca. 202–204 CE).[28] In its current form, the text is a composite work produced by at least three authors: in addition to an editorial introduction and conclusion, the account contains a

diary-visionary section purportedly written by Perpetua and a visionary report attributed to her fellow martyr Saturus. The scholarly affection enjoyed
by the account is due in no small part to the enigmatic and beguiling "prison
diary" that forms its centerpiece. Perpetua's diary, as it is often called, is, if
authentic, the first example of Christian women's writing. The intriguing and
exciting possibility that a martyr's own words, written in her own hand (*Passio* 14.1), have been preserved by history has elicited wonder and admiration
from many quarters. Yet before we can admire Felicitas's courage or Perpetua's passion, we must first consider the nature of the literary evidence.

DATING AND TEXTUAL PROBLEMS

The textual history of the *Passion of Perpetua and Felicitas* is remarkably complicated. In addition to the Latin text, there exist both a rather loose
Greek translation and a shorter version known as the *Acta minora*. The scholarly consensus maintains that the Latin *Passio* is the earliest version of the
story, redacted and translated by subsequent generations of readers.[29] The
Greek version has a great appreciation for the details of gladiatorial combat,
amplifies the theme of *imitatio Christi*, and softens the distinction between
the martyrs and the angels in the visionary scenes. The medieval literary ap-
petite and manuscript record favored the *Acta minora* over the *Passio*: more
than sixty copies of the former survive, but only a handful of copies of the
latter are extant. The versions of the story differ widely: for example, the *Acta
minora* marginalizes the visions for which Perpetua is famed.

The *terminus ante quem* for the *Passion of Perpetua and Felicitas* is often
located in Tertullian, who refers to Perpetua around 207 CE. Tertullian's only
reference to the *Passio* comes in his treatise *On the Soul*.[30] In his discussion of
arguments about the soul's postmortem transition to heaven, Tertullian refers
to one of Perpetua's dream-visions: "How is it that the most heroic martyr
Perpetua on the day of her passion saw only her fellow-martyrs there, in the
revelation which she received of Paradise, if it were not that the sword which
guarded the entrance permitted none to go in thereat, except those who had
died in Christ and not in Adam?" (*De anim.* 55.4–5).[31] There are a number of
discrepancies between Tertullian's version of the vision and the account provided by the *Passio*. In the latter, the vision does not belong to Perpetua but
rather to her fellow martyr Saturus. The chronology of events is also slightly
problematic. Tertullian places the vision on the day of Perpetua's martyrdom,
yet in the redactor's chronology the vision occurs several days beforehand, for
after Saturus's vision there is a description of Felicitas giving birth two days
before the games (*Passio* 15.4). Tertullian and the redactor disagree, therefore,
on the identity of the visionary and the date of the vision. Many scholars have

attributed these mistakes to Tertullian himself, but it should be noted that he never refers to details supplied by the redactor and apparently even misremembers autobiographical material. It is possible, therefore, that Tertullian had in his possession a collection of undated visions (and perhaps a diary) attributed to Perpetua or, to put it another way, that he did not have access to the material supplied by the redactor. Tertullian's usefulness for dating the composition of the entire *Passio* is up for debate.

Moreover, there are a number of historical and legal incongruities in the account. Perpetua is described by the redactor as well educated, well married, and from a good family (*honesta nata*) (*Passio* 2). If this is the case, then why is her father publicly beaten? Why does she breast-feed her child instead of employing a wet nurse?[32] Why is she imprisoned and executed *ad bestias* with her nonaristocratic fellow Christians instead of being privately beheaded as befitted a woman of her status? Most importantly, why is her child not given to her husband's family as the law dictated for married women? Narratively, these incongruities serve a purpose. Her absent husband makes way for her union with Christ, and her execution with the other Christians solidifies her Christian family. There still remains the legal difficulty of her child. To be sure, the focus on Perpetua's family emphasizes the replacement of her biological family with her spiritual family, yet no satisfying explanation has been given for the fate of her child. These historical improbabilities raise doubts about the authenticity of the text. We are left with two possibilities: either the account is a theological reformulation from which historical events cannot be reconstructed with absolute certainty, or, as Kate Cooper has argued, the redactor has radically reworked the Perpetua story independently of the events themselves.[33] Cooper notes that, read independently, Perpetua's diary suggests that she is an unmarried concubine, an observation that makes sense of all of the historical and legal problems noted above. Even in this case, her diary is neither pristine nor intact. The repeated narrative claims that Perpetua herself wrote the diary are not conclusive (*Passio* 2.3; 14.1).[34] If anything, these details invite suspicion and comparison with other known forgeries that self-consciously refer to authorship, such as 2 Thess 3:17. Thus, despite the general air of authenticity that surrounds the text, we must admit that the editor has augmented Perpetua's diary and we should remain skeptical about the extent to which we have access to Perpetua herself.

Even if a complete version of the *Passion of Perpetua and Felicitas* was in existence by the end of the first decade of the third century CE, the traditions pertaining to Perpetua were continually shaped, adapted, and expanded into the medieval period. Nor is it clear that during this period the Latin *Passio* was the dominant version that served as the determinative subtext for later interpretations and development. A recently discovered manuscript of Augustine's sermons suggests that Augustine knew and cited both the *Acta minora* and the *Passio*.[35] The growing influence of Perpetua's story is further attested by a fourth-century catacomb from Spain that depicts Perpetua treading on the head of a dragon as she ascends a ladder to heaven. All of this goes to show that the legend of Perpetua and Felicitas was constantly expanding and continuously augmented. In discussing the character of the *Passio*, the earliest literary remnant of the martyrs' story, we are focusing on just one moment in the development of a legend. Our ability to see this moment clearly is compromised by the lateness of the manuscript evidence relative to the events themselves. Perpetua's voice is muffled by the layers of interpretation added by successive generations of editors, artists, and homilists.

THE CHARACTER OF THE *PASSION OF PERPETUA AND FELICITAS*

Even if the textual history of the account were smooth and featureless, the *Passion of Perpetua and Felicitas* would still be a composite document. The text claims to contain three distinct authorial hands: the diary, or prison memoir, of Perpetua written, we are told, by her own hand (*Passio* 3–10); the vision of Saturus, which he himself wrote down (*Passio* 11–13); and the editorial portion (*Passio* 1–2, 14–21). Perpetua's memoir recalls her exchanges with her father; her brief trial before Hilarianus;[36] the period of her imprisonment; her relationship with her other family members, including her infant son; and her visions. Saturus's portion is a single vision of heavenly matters in which the martyrs are invited to interject themselves into ecclesiastical affairs, but refuse to do so. The narrative, editorial portion includes the introductory preface, the description of the martyr Felicitas giving birth in prison, and the martyrs' final execution.

A lingering concern for readers of this text is the authenticity of the first-person diary section. Did Perpetua write the diary herself while she was imprisoned? An answer in the affirmative would make the *Passio* the first piece of Christian women's writing, not to mention one of the earliest examples of autobiography. Scholarly assessments of the authenticity of Perpetua's memoir are divided, with eminently reasonable arguments posited on both sides of the debate.[37] The self-consciously literary nature of the account—Perpetua invites others to finish her story, and the narrative insists that Perpetua herself wrote the visions—is unusual. Even if Perpetua did compose some form of prison memoir, only portions of that work have been included in the extant text, as is evident from the conclusion of Saturus's vision, where the redactor notes, "These are the more important visions of the blessed martyrs themselves, Saturus and Perpetua, which they themselves recorded" (*Passio*

14.1). We can infer from this statement that there were other, less important visions that were omitted and that editorial intervention determined which material was of greatest significance. At the very least then, the diary of Perpetua has been, in the words of Jan Bremmer, "discursively reshaped to make [it] as effective as possible."[38]

The account opens with a preface found only in the Montecassino manuscript that situates the events of the narrative within a history of heroic figures. The language of exemplarity (*vetera fidei exempla*) draws upon the conventions of Greek rhetoric and education in order to suggest that both the ancient examples and the martyrs described in the account are patterns worthy of imitation. Their function in the text, however, is edificatory (*Passio* 1.1). The preface accentuates the presence of the Spirit as actor in the life of the Church and in the visionary experiences of its members:

> But let that be the concern of those who judge the one power of the one Spirit according to epochs of the temporal world—though all more recent events ought for that very reason to be judged as greater, according to the superabundance of grace that has been decreed for the final stages of earthly time. For in the last days, saith God, I will pour out of my Spirit upon all flesh: and their sons and daughters shall prophesy; and on my servants and on my handmaidens I will pour out of my Spirit; and young men shall see visions, and old men shall dream dreams. And so we too, who both acknowledge and honor new visions in the same way that we do prophecies as being similarly and equally vouchsafed, and who count all the other workings of the Holy Spirit as serving the instruction of the Church (for which moreover this same Spirit was sent to administer all gifts among all people, according as the Lord hath distributed unto each), of necessity do we compile records of the new as well, and make them known through public reading for the glory of God, lest any weakness in our faith or loss of hope infer that the grace of divinity was to be found only among the ancients, whether in the gift of martyrs or of revelations; since God is always bringing to pass what he has promised, as proof for those who do not believe, and as a benefit for those who do.[39] (*Passio* 1.3–5)

The reference to the new visions and the Spirit, together with the citation from Acts 2:17/Joel 2:28–29, has led a number of scholars to argue that the redactor of the text and likely also Perpetua herself were adherents of the New Prophecy.[40] This reading is perhaps confirmed by the liturgically styled consumption of cheese (*caseus*) in one of Perpetua's visions of heaven (*Passio* 4.9). That Perpetua accepts the cheese with "joined hands" (*iunctis manibus*) may suggest a connection to Montanist eucharistic practices in which, according to the fourth-century heresiographer Epiphanius, the adherents consumed cheese.[41] That the account has a particular focus on female visionaries and that Tertullian, a Montanist in his later life, utilized one of the visions in his work adds further weight to their argument. On the other side, however, rests the tremendous reception that the *Passio* received among anti-Montanists. Augustine, for instance, used it in a number of homilies to exhort his congregation to a more virtuous conduct. Augustine clearly domesticates the behavior of the saints, but the fact that he is willing to use them as moral exemplars suggests that he viewed them as nonthreatening.[42] The *Passio* neither polemicizes against nor explicitly advocates for the New Prophecy, making the identification of its position vis-à-vis Montanism difficult. Even as the text labors to define what is Christian and what is not, the focus of this task is the coproduction of the terms "Christian" and "martyr." If communal boundaries are being policed in this text, they do not appear to be forcing a cleft between Montanists and non-Montanists. The ambiguity here may be more instructive than incidental: perhaps the boundary between Montanists and Catholics in the early church was more porous than later heresiologists would lead us to believe.

Whether or not the text can be identified with the New Prophecy, many scholars have treated the *Passio* as an example of apocalyptic literature.[43] This characterization has been so influential that scholars have seen the literary ideologies of apocalyptic works and martyrdom as essentially intertwined. In the words of David Frankfurter, "apocalyptic literature . . . provided a principal instrument of martyrological propaganda."[44] The interest in the *Passio* rises out of a renewed scholarly interest in the phenomenon of apocalypticism and the genre of apocalyptic literature. As a text with a highly eschatological perspective containing visions of the afterlife and imagery of Satanic interference in the world, the *Passio* shares many of the literary elements of this genre.[45] It is a text set under the awning of persecution that describes the heavens and the afterlife and deals with contrasting notions of judgment. The Christians of the *Passio* are removed from earthly affairs altogether. Perhaps a more productive question would be "How do the apocalyptic elements in the *Passio* function for the community utilizing this text?"

The visions in the work are most frequently identified with apocalyptic genres. Perpetua recounts four visions, two of which involve heavenly and eschatological themes. To these can be added Saturus's vision of ecclesiastical conflict at the gates of heaven. Perpetua's visions appear to be generated by incubation: she asks for a vision and then receives it. Perpetua casts herself as one who can talk with God (*fabulari cum Domino*), a statement that places her in a quasi-prophetic role. She asks for a *visio*, a technical term designating a specific prophetic experience. The language picks up on the citation from

Acts 2 in the opening preface and explicitly identifies Perpetua as one of the new examples for faith. After the Christians are imprisoned, and at the request of her brother, Perpetua asks for a vision to discern their fate. She records the following dream:

> I see a ladder made of bronze, huge, reaching all the way up to the sky—but narrow, so that people could only go up one at a time. There were iron weapons of all kinds stuck in the rails on both sides—swords, javelins, hooks, daggers, lances. If anyone climbed the ladder carelessly or without looking up, he would be torn up by these weapons, and pieces of his flesh would get caught in them. At the foot of the ladder there was a serpent lying there, huge, waiting in ambush for people who wanted to climb up and frightening them off from climbing up. But Saturus climbed up, and he went first. (Afterwards he turned himself in to save us, because he was the one who had instructed us in the faith; but he was not there when they arrested us.) When he got to the top of the ladder he turned around and said, "Perpetua, I am here for you. But careful! Don't let the serpent bite you!" "In the name of Jesus Christ," I said, "he will not hurt me." And down there at the foot of the ladder, as if he were afraid of me, the serpent stuck his head out slowly and I, as if stepping on the first rung of the ladder, stepped on his head. And so I started climbing.
>
> Then I saw a wide open space, a garden, and in the middle of it a grey-haired man sitting down. He was dressed like a shepherd, tall, milking some sheep. People dressed in white were standing around him, thousands and thousands of them. Raising his head, he looked over at me and said, "Welcome, child." And he called me over and gave me a mouthful or so of the cheese that he was milking. I cupped my hands and took and ate it. And the people standing around all said, "Amen." (*Passio* 4.3–9)

Perpetua's first vision of the heavens is a mosaic of scriptural and cultural imagery and intertexts. She takes her first step from the head of the now-domesticated dragon of Revelation and winds her way up Jacob's ladder out of the prison and earth to a parallel heavenly realm. In heaven the topography of the psalms is landscaped with Virgil's *Aeneid,* and she is greeted by the pastoral shepherd of the *Apocalypse of Peter.* Approaches to Perpetua's vision of the ladder have rested largely on scholars' oneiric theory and their appraisal of the authenticity of the account.[46] Many have interpreted the dream through the prism of Perpetua's status as catechumen. The liturgical elements of the vision—the eating of cheese and resounding "Amen"—can be read as allusions to baptism. The weapons that frame the ladder are a gesture to her fate as martyr. For those like Peter Dronke who view this as a "painstakingly truthful record of authentic dreams," explicitly theological interpretations of the vision should be avoided as they obscure the detail of the account.[47] As already noted, however, the visions are selected by the redactor for their importance not just to Perpetua, but for the wider Christian community. Perpetua's vision is solicited by the group for the significance that it holds for them all. In the world of the text, as well as in the mind of the redactor, Perpetua's vision is selected because it has communal significance.

The eschatological key to the work is raised in Perpetua's vision of the heavenly arena, where she moves from a prelapsarian garden to a gritty amphitheater:

> The day before our combat in the arena I see the following vision. The deacon Pomponius has come up to the entrance of the prison and is knocking loudly. So I went out and opened the door for him. He was wearing a loose white robe and had on a pair of elaborate sandals. He said, "We are waiting for you, Perpetua. Come!" And he took me by the hand and we started walking along some rough, winding paths. Finally we made it to the amphitheater—just barely, out of breath—and he brought me into the center of the arena and said: "Don't be afraid. I am here with you and suffering along with you." Then he left. Then I see a huge crowd, eagerly watching. But I knew that I had been sentenced to combat animals, so I was surprised that none were being let loose on me. Instead an Egyptian came out as my opponent, hideous to look at, along with his assistants. He was the one who was going to fight me. Some handsome young men came to my side as well, to assist and support me. And I was stripped down and became a man, and my assistants started rubbing me down with oil the way they do before an athletic contest. Over there I see him—the Egyptian—rolling around in the dust. Then a man came out, huge, towering over the top of the amphitheater, with a loose robe on—a purple tunic framed by two stripes in the middle of the chest—and elaborate sandals made of gold and silver. He was holding a staff like a gladiatorial trainer, as well as a green branch which had golden apples on it. He asked for silence and then said: "If the Egyptian beats her, he will kill her with a sword. If she beats him, she will be given this branch." Then he withdrew. We went up to each other and started throwing punches. He kept trying to grab me by the feet, and I kept kicking him in the face. Then I was floating in mid-air and started hitting him without really touching the ground. But when I saw that there was a lull, I put my hands together, interlaced my fingers, and grabbed his head. He fell down flat on his face and I stepped on his head. The crowd began to shout and my assistants to sing in joy. I went over to the trainer and took the branch. He kissed me and said, "Peace be with you, daughter." And I headed out in glory, towards the Gate of Life and Salvation. (*Passio* 10.10–13)

The vision is a prefiguration of Perpetua's martyrdom and serves for Perpetua as a kind of preparation for martyrdom; along with the martyrs' prison discussions of modes of execution (*Passio* 19.2), it steels the young confessor for what is to come. When she awakes, Perpetua recognizes that the dream is about her contest in the arena and that her battle will be not with wild beasts, but with the devil (*Passio* 10.14). The visions function as *ekphrasis;* they demonstrate the manner in which victory is achieved.[48] The fulfillment of the vision of execution with the execution itself creates a chain of templates for emulation. The visions are athletic training for Perpetua and the audience. The portrayal of the martyr as athlete is far from unique. Athletic imagery appears in the *Letter of the Churches of Vienne and Lyons* where it is adopted from Paul and the Maccabean literature.[49] Depiction of the martyr as a noble athlete explains the image of the martyr's crown and illustrates with delicate simplicity the extent to which earthly types (athleticism) imitate superior forms (combat and martyrdom). The encounter with the Egyptian (devil) in the imagined arena endows Perpetua's actions with a cosmic significance, provides a frame of reference for the audience, and prefigures her battle in the physical arena. The otherworldly battle sets the stage for and provides the interpretive framework for everything that follows; the vision is a martyrological map for the characters and audience to follow.

SPECTACULAR DEATH IN THE ARENA

According to the narrative of the *Passion of Perpetua and Felicitas,* the martyrs were executed in the amphitheater on a special day, the birthday of Caesar Geta, the younger son of the emperor Septimius Severus. Ancient Romans were accustomed to encountering death in their everyday lives; as classicists have noted, the amphitheater provided the opportunity to see the struggle for life on display.[50] Gladiatorial combat was a Roman preoccupation. The gladiator was celebrated for his bravery, his skills in combat, and, crucially, his ability to die well. Scenes of gladiatorial combat adorned wall paintings, mosaics, lamps, and graffiti; children rehearsed contests with wild animals, with ducks and housecats; and Tacitus complained that discussions of contests dominated dinner party conversations (*Dialogus* 29). During the Roman republic, gladiatorial shows were held to mark the funeral of an aristocrat. Initially, the number of gladiators participating was relatively small— three pairs of gladiators for the funeral of Junius Brutus Pera and his sons in 264 BCE; forty-four pairs as part of the funeral games for Marcus Aemilius Lepidus in 216 BCE—but the scale of such events swiftly increased.[51] These *munera* (gladiatorial contests) provided by aristocratic families to honor their deceased relatives raised the public profile and status of their family and played a role in the competition for public office. Under Augustus the number of *munera* and size of events began to be controlled. Certainly by the reign of

Tiberius *munera* were no longer associated exclusively with funerals and instead marked events in the lives of the imperial family such as birthdays, accessions, and triumphs.[52] Precisely this kind of event provides the backdrop for the *Passio*.

Death in the amphitheater was about more than the execution of individual gladiators. The stadium was the arena for displays of imperial power, for the subjugation of the empire's enemies, and for the degradation of the person. As Gillian Clark observes, these assaults on the bodies of criminals "acted out the rejection of the criminal from the human community, by his or her reduction to the level of a beast—a body without rationality—or of a corpse."[53] That this punishment was usually inflicted upon those of low social status made it all the more degrading for more privileged *honestiores* who were technically exempt from such degrading forms of execution. A criminal condemned to the arena was stripped of identity, publicly exposed, and reduced to a subhuman species.

The articulation of space within the amphitheater itself mirrored the differences between the status of the observers and that of the participants. The floor of the arena was lowered below ground level, thereby inscribing a higher/lower dichotomy. The performance of *fantasias* (scenes from myth and history) operated in two basic forms: those convicted were sometimes made helpless and were sometimes furnished with weapons. The execution of criminals in amphitheaters was a ritualized practice that attempted to impose a particular set of hierarchies upon the participants. The creation of a hierarchically ordered space that physically lowered the condemned to the level of animals and then required them to compete against animals for their survival enforced difference. Execution *ad bestias* was, as the Latin suggests, a practice that animalized and barbarized the participants, reducing them to animal status and forcing them to behave in an animal-like fashion. This differentiated the condemned criminals from their "civilized" audience.

In the *Passion of Perpetua and Felicitas* the process of denaturing was amplified by the attempts of the Romans to force the martyrs to dress as priests and priestesses of Saturn. Compelling condemned criminals to play mythical and historical roles in the arena is well attested in antiquity.[54] The deaths of the convicts were integrated into the drama as part of a scene from mythology, history, or their own criminal career. The introduction of role-playing and mythology into gladiatorial combat provided a narrative structure for the event and turned it into theater. As a result, those condemned were deprived of their identities in the final moments of their lives. Instead of a condemned criminal, Laureolus is hanged or Hercules burned (Martial, *De Spectaculis* 7). The criminal is effectively robbed of the opportunity to die well. It is no lon-

ger the criminal but instead the dramatic figure who is on display; tl
vidual has become no more than a persona. In the *Passio*, attempts to d
and subjugate the martyr are destabilized by the Christians' noncon
in the ritual. Perpetua refuses to allow herself to act the part of a priestess of
Saturn and insists that the group die as Christians (*Passio* 18.4–6). In the
arena she appears composed and dignified; her refined pose rejects the ritual's
attempts to contain and subjugate her. Rearranging her garments and pinning
up her hair are both acts of femininity, which recall Greek drama, and defiant
acts of civility that refuse the process of denaturing. The execution of Perpetua in the arena, however, is subordinate to her visionary struggle in the amphitheater with the Egyptian. The positioning of the vision before the actual
contest renders her sufferings in the arena communal and collegial. Her battle
in the otherworldly arena makes the result of the execution in the earthly arena
a foregone conclusion.

RESISTING AUTHORITY: ESSENTIAL CHRISTIANS

One of the more personal scenes in the *Passion of Perpetua and Felicitas* is Perpetua's dialogue with her father before her trial. He attempts to
dissuade her from making a public confession of Christian identity, but Perpetua is insistent. She gestures to a vase nearby and states that just as the
vase cannot be called by any other name, so she cannot be called other than
that which she is, a Christian (*Passio* 3.1).[55] The statement is performative; in
stating that she is Christian and can be nothing else, Perpetua makes it so.

At the same time, her protestation that she is a Christian and can be nothing other than what she is picks up on the language of the less-well-known
female Carthaginian martyr Secunda. One of three female martyrs in the *Acts
of the Scillitan Martyrs*, Secunda follows the statement by her sister-martyr
Vestia, "I am Christian" (*Christiana sum*), by saying "What I am, I wish to
be" (*Quod sum, ipsud uolo esse*) (*Ac. Scilli.* 1.9). The responses of the three
female martyrs can hardly be regarded as legal testimony; the proconsul does
not question them individually, and they speak almost in unison. As a result,
Vestia's declaration that she is Christian seems to be elaborated by Secunda's
statement. Perpetua's discussion of the connection between her Christian
identity and her essence is reminiscent of this scene from the *Acts of the Scillitan Martyrs*. Like Secunda, Perpetua can be nothing other than what she is,
a Christian.

Being and becoming Christian in these texts involves rejecting other identity markers and resisting the normal social structures and values that ordered Roman society. In the extant account, this process begins with Perpetua
rejecting her father's authority and continues as she sheds the privileges of

her status, imprisoned and executed with her fellow martyrs even though, being well-born, she should be beheaded. The handing over of her child and the mysterious absence of her husband assist in her transformation from respectable *matrona* to bride of Christ.

Arguably the most distinctive moment of identity elision in the text is in her vision of the battle with the Egyptian when she is stripped of her clothing and transformed into a man (*et expoliata sum, et facta sum masculus*). Much has been made of this detail in the dream.[56] Perpetua's body, upon which she invites us to ruminate, is masculinized, and this masculinization resists and subverts the readers' expectations: "expecting to see a female body humiliated by its exposure to the public eye, we see instead the shameless display of the oiled body of a male athlete."[57] Perpetua's transformation into a man is a performance of masculinity that exemplifies Christian discourse in which Christian and male become coterminous in the martyr. Perpetua's body is molded into the turgid, oily form of the ideal male, the athlete. But the vision does not have the last word on the matter, as in the physical arena Perpetua is feminized: as already noted, she tugs at the hem of her clothing to conceal herself, and she modestly fastens her hair (*Passio* 20.3–5). Felicitas and Perpetua face a mad heifer that is matched to their sex; it is an animal icon of hysterical woman and a sign that gender segregation was alive in the arena (*Passio* 20.1). In the arena the fragility and femininity of the two women's bodies are emphasized as the author forces the reader's gaze onto their bodies, onto Felicitas's breasts, dripping with milk, and onto their collective youth and beauty (*Passio* 20.2). To the very end the crowd and the audience cannot look away: after her final contest, Perpetua is returned to the arena for execution in full view of the crowd (*Passio* 21.7). In her last performance of Christianity, she guides the trembling gladiator's sword to her throat (*Passio* 21.9). Perpetua's neck is open to interpretation—she is at once in control (and thus masculine), executed in a womanly fashion, and yet oddly malleable. In the eyes of the reader, the form of her body never quite sets.

The depiction of Perpetua is multivalent and ambiguous. The sands of gender shift beneath the weight of her footsteps. She transitions from well-educated *matrona* to *nupta Christi*. Her depiction resists social expectations on multiple levels and expresses a distinctive sense of Christian identity. At the same time, this new Christian identity is projected in the heavenly arena of the visions. Even as Perpetua sheds her status and gender in the arena, she acquires recognition and community in her visions of the afterlife. As the martyrs near the moment of death, they interpret their execution as a form of baptism: Saturus describes himself as washed, saved by the blood he shed in the arena (*Passio* 21.2–3). The martyrs then exchange kisses, which allude to the ritual kisses of eucharistic liturgy.[58] The use of baptismal imagery for martyrdom is hardly unique to this text, but the culmination of the ritual in the community-binding kiss joins the martyrs somatically as well as symbolically (*Passio* 21.7). The performance of baptism at the moment of death drinks from the Pauline font and gestures to the afterlife that awaits. The actions in the arena are prefigured by the visions that serve as a template for the martyrs to follow. It is to the parallel heavenly world posited in the visions that the martyrs belong. The visions function as both preparation for the battle and confirmation of its outcome.

LITERARY TIES TO THE *ACTS OF PAUL AND THECLA*

The baptismal imagery that floods the final scene in the arena evokes memories of the Christian virgin Thecla, a disciple of Paul and controversial heroine of the *Acts of Paul and Thecla*. The similarities between Thecla and Perpetua are startling.[59] Both are well-born young women who come into conflict with prominent members of their family over their conversion to Christianity: Thecla abandons her fiancé and wars with her mother; Perpetua rejects her father's appeals that she deny that she is Christian. Both women are fearless outside as well as inside the *domus*. In the arena, Perpetua guides the hand of the gladiator to her throat, and Thecla confidently hoists herself onto the pyre.

The most distinctive parallel is their shared attitude toward those who had died without baptism. While imprisoned, Perpetua sees her deceased brother in a state of torment and attempting to reach an overflowing basin:

> I see Dinocrates coming out of a place of shadows, and many others were in there too. He is extremely hot and thirsty. He looks dirty and pale. There is a wound in his face—the one he had when he died. (Dinocrates had been my brother according to the flesh, seven years old, killed by a disease that had disfigured his face with sores, so that everyone was quite horrified by his death.) So I had been offering prayers for him; and now there was so wide a gap between us that neither of us could reach the other. And then, where Dinocrates was, I saw a basin full of water. Its rim was higher than the boy was tall and he kept standing on tiptoes, trying to get a drink. I felt dreadful. The basin had water in it but because its rim was so high up, he was never going to be able to drink from it. (*Passio* 7.4–8)

Perpetua prays and intercedes for her brother Dinocrates and receives a second vision in which he appears refreshed and healed (*Passio* 7–8). We can safely infer that she has successfully obtained for him some kind of postmortem baptism or salvation. Thecla, for her part, prayed for the daughter of Queen Tryphaena (*Acts of Paul and Thecla* 29).

The common concern for the unbaptized deceased is distinctive. Bremmer suggests that Perpetua, as an educated young woman, has perhaps read the *Acts of Paul and Thecla*.[60] If Perpetua is the author of this section, then this is certainly possible. Alternatively, the editor may have accentuated the parallels when editing the so-called diary portion or by developing the theme in the narrative. In the *Acts of Paul and Thecla*, Thecla remarks that even if she were not able to endure by herself, Paul would assist her. Paul, in this case, was the Lord in disguise. Thecla's observation is similar to Felicitas's statement that she would endure martyrdom more easily than childbirth because "what I am suffering now I suffer for myself, but then there will be another inside me who will suffer for me, just as I will be suffering for him" (*Passio* 15.6).

The probability that the *Passion of Perpetua and Felicitas* is dependent upon Thecla traditions is strengthened by the evidence for Thecla's popularity in North Africa around the time of its composition. Red-clay pottery from North Africa depicting scenes from the Thecla story demonstrates that the story circulated as late as the fourth and fifth centuries.[61] In addition to the opaque reference to books associated with Paul in the *Acts of the Scillitan Martyrs* already discussed, in *On Baptism* Tertullian dismisses a text associated with the Apostle Paul, which, he says, is misused by other Christians to support women's roles in baptism:[62] "But if certain Acts of Paul, which are falsely so named, claim the example of Thecla for allowing women to teach and to baptize, let men know that in Asia the presbyter who compiled that document, thinking to add of his own to Paul's reputation, was found out, and though he professed he had done it for love of Paul, was deposed from his position" (17.5).[63] The textual history of the passage is difficult, but it seems that Tertullian is discussing a work about Paul.[64] His consideration of the use of the *Acts of Paul* as support for baptismal practices illuminates our understanding of the *Passion of Perpetua and Felicitas*. Whereas to the modern eye the visions of Dinocrates raise the possibility of embryonic notions of purgatory and postmortem baptism, to the ancient reader the controversial element was the role of the female protagonist.[65] Perpetua's intercession for Dinocrates, a clear allusion to baptism, arises out of a social situation in which women were administering baptism and authorizes the continuation of this practice by connecting it with a Carthaginian, married version of Thecla.

It is noteworthy that both the *Acts of the Scillitan Martyrs* and the *Passion of Perpetua and Felicitas* may refer to the *Acts of Paul and Thecla*. This association would seem to suggest that those responsible for the composition of these two martyr texts were influenced by Thecla traditions. While the *Acts of Paul and Thecla* was likely composed in Asia Minor, this circumstance does not mean that martyrdom was imported to North Africa from Asia Minor. The image of Thecla is used to characterize Perpetua, but there are also notable differences between the two women: Thecla is praised and esteemed as a virgin; Perpetua is a wife and mother. Their contrasting statuses as virgin and *matrona* are not romantic incidentals; these identities elicit different responses and propose different models for the audience members. Whereas Thecla escapes unharmed from the arena, Perpetua's story climaxes with her death. More than just a narrative adaptation, the use of the *Acts of Paul and Thecla* in the *Passion of Perpetua and Felicitas* was a self-conscious device intended to support particular baptismal practices, not merely to promulgate martyrdom.

Conclusion

Martyrdom has often been categorized as a subset of apocalyptic literature. When this classification is proposed, North African martyrdom leaps to the forefront of the discussion; statements about the apocalyptic character of martyrdom rely largely, if not exclusively, on snippets of information from the *Passion of Perpetua and Felicitas*. Perpetua's dreams, her battle with the Egyptian, and her exclusive focus on suffering and death have contributed to the scholarly vision of martyrdom as the rallying cry of the beleaguered and oppressed. As we have seen in previous chapters, general characterizations of martyrdom have misrepresented the subtle and diverse constructions of martyrdom and the many functions of martyrdom literature. Even for the much-loved *Passio,* apocalyptic elements in the text should not be allowed to eclipse the richness of the account.

Upon reading these texts, one receives the overwhelming impression that North African Christianity was exclusively pro-martyrdom. Indeed, the author of the *Passio* wants to persuade his audience of the necessity of martyrdom as a facet of Christian identity. Yet these constructions of Christianity may also betray hints of opposition in the Christian community. In criticizing flight during times of persecution, Tertullian admits that there were those for whom flight seemed preferable (*Fug.* 5.1). That Tertullian condemns their behavior does not make those who fled non-Christians. Perhaps the same can be said of Perpetua's father, often assumed to be non-Christian although the text never specifies one way or the other. Perpetua's response to her father and appeal to her nature as Christian may suggest that he is a Christian who is opposed to martyrdom.[66] Her father is not a self-described member of a schismatic group but someone unconvinced of the necessity of death. While it is tempting to cast such individuals as moderates or cynics, to do so without importing an assumption about what makes for a true martyr is difficult. It is to ancient discussions of the nature of the true martyr and to the borders and limits of martyrdom that we now turn.

6

Alexandria:
Clement and the True Martyr

For many ancient Christians, as for ancient Romans, Greeks, and Jews, dying a noble death was something to be embraced, valued, and perhaps even coveted. Yet despite the general high regard in which martyrs and martyrdom were held, some Christians were more interested in avoiding untimely death. Amid the spectacular din of the confessions of martyrs, the roar of the crowd, and the clamor of the courtroom, there were quieter, hesitant voices. Many martyr acts present martyrdom as a sharp choice that cut to the core of Christian identity—life or death, salvation or damnation, Christ or apostasy—but things may not have been so cut and dried for everyone. In the history of ideas, distinctions have been drawn between those who were enthusiastically pro-martyrdom, those who were pro-martyrdom, and those who were anti-martyrdom. These categories are, in turn, aligned with doctrinal positions: the philosophical group known as the Gnostics are cast as anti-martyrdom; Montanists and Donatists as enthusiastic practitioners of voluntary martyrdom; and the orthodox as occupying a neutral, moderate, pro-martyrdom stand. The rhetorical formation of the true martyr in antiquity was decidedly more complicated and sophisticated than these categories lead us to believe. Not only are the designations "Montanist," "Gnostic," and "orthodox" homogenizing caricatures, but, as we will see, the categorization of these positions as for and against martyrdom fails to reflect the texture of ancient discourse.

The construction of the true martyr was as contested among early Christians as it is among modern scholars. Through a lens focused on Alexandria and on Clement of Alexandria's treatment of martyrdom, we examine the ways in which martyrdom was produced discursively in early Christianity. The approach is not comprehensive, but rather is strategically concentrated on two objectives: first, to deconstruct the idea that attitudes toward martyrdom can be delineated on doctrinal grounds, and second, to reveal how ancient authors constructed true martyrdom as distinct from other forms of martyrdom such as voluntary martyrdom or anti-martyrdom.

Clement of Alexandria

The delineation of different forms of martyrdom and the rhetorical formation of the true martyr began in earnest with the second-century Christian philosopher Clement of Alexandria (d. ca. 215 CE). Alexandria, the home of Clement until his flight from persecution in the early years of the third century, was a bustling city second in size only to Rome. It had an especially storied history of persecution, as religious unrest and friction had plagued the city since the Ptolemaic period. In the first century, Alexandria had been the setting of a series of religious riots between Jews and Greeks, and an uprising in 115–117 CE had led the emperor Hadrian to deport the majority of the Jewish population. It was not unusual, then, to find religious groups in conflict in Alexandria.

Unlike the other authors examined in this book, Clement of Alexandria wrote neither martyr acts nor apologies. His ideas about martyrdom appear mostly as part of larger discussions of virtue in his voluminous work the *Miscellanies*. If there were early accounts of the deaths of martyrs, such as the execution of Potamiaena and Basilides, who died in Alexandria around 205 CE, Clement does not appear familiar with them, nor does he supply much information about persecution in the region during this period.[1] His occasional references to martyrdom highlight the training and composure of the martyrs; it was, he says "fear that derives from the law" that "trained [the martyrs] to show piety even with their blood" (*Strom.* 2.125.2–3).[2] Clement's interest is not in the sources of persecution, but in the foundations of perseverance; his interpretation of historical instances of martyrdom tied that martyrdom to discipline, training, and the exercise of piety.

As one of the first theologians to discuss martyrdom at any length, Clement is often assumed to be innately pro-martyrdom, rather than cautiously supportive.[3] Where he differs from his proto-orthodox contemporaries, Clement is treated as offering merely a "reflective approach" on a common theme.[4]

Given the distinctiveness of Clement's thoughtfulness, attemp
made to locate the origins of his perspective in earlier traditions
of martyrdom has been figuratively rooted in the biblical fig
whom he regularly cites, the accounts of the deaths of the Mac
line epistles, the Gospels, the Shepherd of Hermas, Revelation, *1 Clem.*
self-controlled philosophy of the Stoics, and Platonic notions of perfection.[5]
That Clement interprets scripture and reflects on philosophical principles is
not disputed. He utilizes the same traditions as ostensibly pro-martyrdom figures such as Tertullian. His apparent lack of familiarity with contemporary
martyrdom literature is instructive; he cites neither texts from the Ignatius-
Polycarp tradition nor any account that could be categorized as a martyr act.
We cannot be sure that Clement is in fact familiar with the genre of the martyr
act. Even if he drank from the same bloody well as Ignatius and Tertullian,
Clement created a different vision of martyrdom. For our purposes, however,
it is more pressing to deal with how he constructs the true martyr than to hypothesize about possible influences on that construction.

For Clement, martyrdom is overlaid by the discourse of perfection (*Strom.*
4.1.1) and his ideal Christian—the gnostic.[6] Martyrdom is a practice that a
good Christian (or, in Clement's terms, a gnostic) might be expected to perform
and is associated with personal salvation, penance, and purification (*Strom.*
4.42.5; 74.3; 104.1; 143.1). These practices of *paideia,* and martyrdom's place
among them, drew upon cultural norms and philosophical ideals in order to
allow Clement to present Christianity both as contiguous with traditional philosophy and as the summit of the philosophical quest.[7] As Robin Darling Young
has demonstrated, both the execution of perfection and the performance of
martyrdom are results of philosophically styled training and spiritual exercises.[8] Clement "emphasized a kind of philosophical *paideia*" that was designed
to train Christians "to detach themselves from the body and sensible world and
to prepare them to offer their bodies in a certain state of calm."[9] There is considerable overlap between the attributes and exercises of the gnostic and those
of the martyr. If the perfect knowledge of Clement's gnostic is oriented toward
knowledge of God, this knowledge must be manifested in the exercise of virtue:
self-control, gospel-focused life, and temperance. These very same qualities were
components of martyrdom. The practices and virtues inculcated in the martyr
are ideologically and operatively identical to those required of the nondying
gnostic. Martyrdom, for Clement, is part of living a life in accordance with the
knowledge of God, but martyrdom is certainly neither essential to this life nor
qualitatively different from that life's other parts.

In comparison with other authors, Clement downplays the idea that postmortem rewards should motivate martyrdom and emphasizes that the good

should be pursued for its own sake (*Strom.* 4.14.1; 29.4; 135.3–4). Martyrdom is not functionally distinct from other aspects of good conduct; thus, if it is a sacrificial offering, it is sacrificial in the same way that prayer (*Strom.* 7.31.7), virtue (*Strom.* 7.14.1), abstinence from passion (*Strom.* 5.67.1), and care for the downtrodden (*Strom.* 7.49.5) are offerings to God.[10] Likewise, while persecution comes at the hands of demonic force, so too do all forms of temptation. When Clement utilizes martyrological topoi such as endurance or courage, he everywhere broadens their application. The contest for virtue is not only fought in the arena; it is won in the forum, the household, and the interior life. The rhetorical effect of this expanded use is to domesticate martyrdom. Martyrdom becomes in the hands of Clement one of many venues through which the gnostic is called to act in a specific manner. If gnostics find themselves in a situation in which martyrdom is expected, then they are required to accept it. Clement's basic position can be and often is summarized as one in which martyrdom was desirable but should not be sought out; he was "moderately supportive of the idea of martyrdom, but not at all exhortative."[11]

Even as Clement expands the forum in which virtue can be performed and right action is expected, he narrows the practice of true martyrdom. He discursively carves out an image of the true martyr that is distinct from the foolhardy self-exposure of those who rushed to death and from the reluctance of heretics to consider martyrdom. In articulating the landscape of martyrdom in this way, Clement positions himself as the via media between these two extremes:

> Now some of the heretics who have misunderstood the Lord, have at once an impious and cowardly love of life; saying that the true martyrdom is the knowledge of the only true God (which we also admit), and that the man is a self-murderer and a suicide who makes confession by death; and adducing other similar sophisms of cowardice. To these we shall reply at the proper time; for they differ with us in regard to first principles. Now we, too, say that those who have rushed on death (for there are some, not belonging to us, but sharing the name merely, who are in haste to give themselves up, the poor wretches dying through hatred to the Creator)—these, we say, banish themselves without being martyrs, even though they are punished publicly. For they do not preserve the characteristic mark of believing martyrdom, inasmuch as they have not known the only true God, but give themselves up to a vain death, as the Gymnosophists of the Indians to useless fire. (*Strom.* 4.16–17)

On one hand, Clement condemns those who have charged forward to martyrdom. He aligns these enthusiasts with exotic and antiquated practices (Gymnosophists) that had cultural value in Clement's day, but value that Clement rejects.[12] He rhetorically expels them from his community and debases and negates the significance of their offering.[13] They are not, he says, true martyrs; they are without witness (*amartyros*). Their practice is not only rendered barbaric and exotic, but is elsewhere interpreted by Clement as simplistic. In his exegesis of Matt 19:29, Clement distinguishes between simple martyrdom (death) and gnostic, true martyrdom. The latter, he writes, entails a life lived purely, in knowledge of God, without passion, and in obedience to God. This life involves perpetual witness to death, but that death can be either natural or unnatural. In this way, Clement subtly denigrates the accomplishments of simple bodily martyrdom. On the other hand, he also deplores the stance of the heretics who avoid martyrdom altogether out of impiety and cowardice. The description of this group as cowardly subtly feminizes its members and elides the rational basis for their position.

The distinctions between Clement's position and those of his interlocutors are hardly the radical breaks in thought that his rhetoric leads us to believe. In pushing the heretics to the margins, Clement acquires power. In creating and claiming the middle position, he also assumes the rhetorical high ground that the Aristotelian mean affords him. His own perspective, grounded as it is in a philosophy of love, emerges as a middle course and thus as the default position on martyrdom. Much has been made of the ways in which Clement is influenced by the positions of his opponents and takes a reasonable middle position between them.[14] Much more should be made, however, of the ways in which he creates this middle position and sets himself firmly on it. Scholars have tended to treat Clement's categories of true martyrdom, enthusiasm, and anti-martyrdom as an adequate description of the various positions on martyrdom in his day, yet perhaps he is more constructive than descriptive. Unclear, for instance, is the extent to which ancient Christians before Clement saw rushing forward to martyrdom as a practice distinct from other forms of martyrdom. We should look beyond Clement's rhetoric to the ways in which the true martyr was shaped in the early church. This will set Clement in context by considering the extent to which other early Christians shared his distinctions, distinctions that have cast long shadows over scholarly histories of martyrdom.

VOLUNTARY MARTYRDOM

In accounts of martyrdom, the practice of offering oneself for martyrdom has been isolated from normative martyrdom.[15] This practice, variously termed "voluntary martyrdom" or "provoked martyrdom," is broadly defined as bringing about martyrdom either by presenting oneself to authorities or by

licited disclosure of one's Christian identity.[16] The specifics of this defi-
..ition are debated and the character of individual executions is contested,
but there is some general agreement that voluntary or provoked martyrdom
existed as a discrete phenomenon. Since Clement, ecclesiastical and scholarly
analyses of this subject have maintained that during the pre-Decian period it
was adherents of the New Prophecy who incorrectly and foolishly sought to
become voluntary martyrs. Some histories have even argued that voluntary
martyrdom was so essential to the New Prophecy that it was the defining
feature that distinguished adherents of the New Prophecy from other Christians.[17]

The assumption that adherents of the New Prophecy were enthusiastic
supporters of voluntary martyrdom has shaped the way in which martyrdom
and Christian history are narrated. As William Tabbernee notes, some early
Christian martyrs—the lawyer Vettius Epagathus, for example, whom we encountered in chapter 4 (*Lyons* 5.1.10)—have been identified as Montanists
merely because their conduct is deemed by a modern reader to be in some way
antagonistic, or provoking the judge.[18] Implicit in this categorization is not
only the assumption that Montanists were voluntary martyrs, but also the assumption that Catholics (that is, those who are distinguished and distinguished
themselves as non-Montanists) were *not* voluntary martyrs. Not only has voluntary martyrdom become an essential feature of the New Prophecy, the New
Prophecy has become the sole proprietor of voluntary martyrdom. In a succession of important publications, however, Tabbernee deftly demonstrated
that adherents to the New Prophecy were no more prone to voluntary martyrdom than orthodox Christians.[19] Tabbernee has been instrumental in exposing
the extent to which the New Prophecy movement has been mischaracterized
and how notions of orthodoxy and heresy have been bound up in characterizations of martyrdom. His analysis has brought to the fore the extent to
which the alignment of orthodoxy and heresy with specific forms of martyrdom is a rhetorical construction. Implicit in Tabbernee's work, however, as in
other scholarship, is the assumption that voluntary martyrdom existed as a
separate, identifiable category and practice in the ancient world before the
time of Clement.

There was no technical Greek or Latin term for a voluntary martyr in the
first and second centuries.[20] When Christians were executed, whatever their
communal affiliation or the role they played in their own arrest, they were
memorialized as martyrs. The lack of terminology is interesting, not because
technical terms are a prerequisite for something's existence (they are not), but
because, as we saw in the introduction, the use of the term *martys* has played
such an instrumental role in scholarly discussions of the emergence of martyr-

dom. Yet where there are no linguistic terms to serve as guides, scholars feel free to work with assumptions and highly individual taxonomies about what makes a martyrdom provoked or voluntary. It is worth stepping back and asking whether or not volunteerism *was* singled out as distinct from other martyrological practices in ancient discourse. Would an ancient reader prior to or unfamiliar with Clement have necessarily viewed self-offering or voluntary martyrdom as something different from martyrdom? Instead of looking at instances of execution that we might judge voluntary or provocative, we should consider how early Christian authors distinguished between different kinds of martyrdom.[21] Yet contemporary assumptions about the nature of martyrdom have set the terms for scholarly analysis of ancient discursive practices. As seen in the introduction, commitments to a particular definition and characterization of martyrdom undergird the discussion of martyrdom itself. Concerns about the refinement and purity of the martyr's intents and actions saturate martyrological historiography. Therefore, in attempting to parse the creation of ancient categories, we must be mindful of the refraction of ancient practices through the lens of our own system of values.

The category of the voluntary martyr has spiraled out of scholarly discussions about the emergence of the category "martyr" in the ancient church. Voluntary martyrdom appeared as a category in the English language in the seventeenth century and passed from sermons into scholarship with Edward Gibbon's *History of the Decline and Fall of the Roman Empire*.[22] Gibbon's negative appraisal of the phenomenon set the tone for subsequent discussion, but it was in the nineteenth century, and under pressure from scientific inquiry, that classical scholars began to distill the category into its elemental form. In an essay on the idol-destroying voluntary martyr Polyeuctus, French epigrapher and hagiographer Edmond Le Blant contrasts the views of church leaders with those of the laity, writing, "in the Christian camp . . . the crowd had its passions, and sometimes too easily hailed as martyrs those whom the Church itself refused to include among its saints."[23] For Le Blant, the acclamation of Polyeuctus as a saint was the fault of the passionate, thoughtless crowd. Le Blant also writes that "according to the strict rules and requirements in ancient times, Polyeuctus would not be a martyr; the very act of violence which made his memory famous would exclude him from all right to this title"; his assumption is that ecclesiastical rules were enforced in ancient times but were somehow overturned by the unruly, passionate rabble.[24] Voluntary martyrdom is situated within a certain social sphere. The people condone this behavior; the laity, in Le Blant's summary, is a hapless bystander. Conceptually, Le Blant's narrative pushes voluntary martyrdom outside of orthodoxy. There is a certain irony here. The crowd that in the martyr acts was often responsible for getting Christians martyred is in Le Blant's narrative now responsible for making Christians martyrs. The apposition of an (as yet nonexistent) thinking and well-regulated *Église* and an unruly, passionate crowd invokes the binary of the educated elite and the unthinking populace. That there were no such strict regulations in antiquity demonstrates the extent to which "the church" here is a cipher for Le Blant's own well-ordered perspective. The distinction between true and false martyrdoms is grounded in social status. Le Blant may not have the vocabulary to discard certain forms of martyrdom as voluntary, but he has the ideals.

The wish to distinguish between voluntary martyrdom and true martyrdom is common in secondary literature after the nineteenth century. In his influential essay "Why Were the Early Christians Persecuted?" G. E. M. De Ste. Croix takes a genealogical approach. He suggests, with reservations, that voluntary martyrdom was not an exclusively Montanist practice and argues that it was likely to have begun much earlier, in the Maccabean period.[25] He still insists on a genealogical thread, though, and traces voluntary martyrdom from the Maccabees to the "abnormal mentality" of Ignatius of Antioch.[26] This genealogy seeks to essentialize voluntary martyrdom, to constrain it as a distinct and—to De Ste. Croix—abhorrent form of martyrdom, and to account for its popularity during the third and fourth centuries. "If the Church was prepared to forgive, and even applaud, all such infractions of discipline," he writes, "why did it condemn them without qualification beforehand? Why did it not merely issue a warning against the dangers of volunteering for martyrdom, both to the individuals concerned and to their church? The answer, surely, is that in practically all cases of voluntary martyrdom the mass of simple believers forced the hand of their more intelligent and worldly-wise leaders and insisted on having the volunteers venerated just like other martyrs."[27] De Ste. Croix's statement betrays two commitments: to a notion of a stable, uniform, definitive church that acted decisively and with conviction, and to a polarization of "simple believers" and "intelligent," "worldly-wise leaders." Even though he is prepared—in a footnote—to describe the tension between martyrs and nonmartyrs more ambiguously as a "contradiction between theory and practice," his dichotomy reinforces Le Blant's classism and stereotypes.[28]

De Ste. Croix's picture of ancient martyrdom is more complex than a mere binary of true martyrs and voluntary martyrs. In his typology of martyrdom he includes both "voluntary martyrs" and "quasi-volunteers," and also—somewhat separately—"religious suicide." The first rather more familiar category he populates with those who "(a) explicitly demanded the privilege of martyrdom; or (b) came forward of their own accord in times of persecution and made a public confession of Christianity which was bound to lead to instant execution; or (c) by some deliberate act—destroying images, for example, or assaulting a provincial governor while he was sacrificing—clearly invited arrest and execution."[29] Between the poles of these volunteers and "the ordinary martyrs," De Ste. Croix slips in a middle group of "quasi-volunteers":

> I. Those in whom we cannot demonstrate a conscious desire for martyrdom for its own sake, but who were rigorists of one kind or another, going beyond the general practice of the Church in their opposition to some aspects of pagan society—for example, Christian pacifists who refused military service; II. those who without, as far as we know, actually demanding or inviting martyrdom, deliberately and unnecessarily attracted attention to themselves, for example by ministering openly to arrested confessors, and hence brought about their own arrest; III. martyrs who are not recorded to have been directly responsible for their own arrest, but who after being arrested behaved with deliberate contumacy at their trial.[30]

De Ste. Croix's neatly and carefully delineated taxonomy runs into problems as he begins to amass his evidence. He cites the martyrdom of the virgin Potamiaena as an instance of quasi-voluntary martyrdom, type III, because when threatened with rape, the emboldened maiden "made some abusive reply, for which she was immediately put to death."[31] This categorization, however, is colored by De Ste. Croix's understanding of what forms of behavior are unreasonable, rigorous, or provocative. Potamiaena's desire to avoid sexual violation even at the expense of her life is not out of keeping with that of her non-Christian contemporaries. As we saw in the example of Lucretia, Roman women were implicitly encouraged to commit suicide rather than risk their chastity. For this kind of death they were explicitly praised.[32]

For a classicist, De Ste. Croix has a remarkably modern way of evaluating what values are worth dying for. His classification system speaks more about his own cultural context than that in which ancient authors found themselves. It should go without saying that the category of quasi-voluntary martyr did not exist in the ancient world; rather, the classification is grounded in De Ste. Croix's assessment of the good death. Even in the writings of self-consciously prosuicide scholars who come closest to a reappraisal of the evidence, there has been a tendency to import modern conceptions of agency and suicide into ancient depictions of martyrdom. Arthur Droge's innovative study of voluntary martyrdom muddies the waters by showing how "orthodox" martyrs "provoked" their deaths, but he continues to use modern constructions of provocation and suicide.[33]

Within second-century and early-third-century Christianity, we need to look hard for a text that delineates different forms of martyrdom. Methodologically, the task is problematic. Evidence for voluntary martyrdom can be amassed only from texts that distinguish between specific forms of or attitudes toward martyrdom, and these distinctions are never neutral. After Clement, the earliest evidence for distinct forms of martyrdom comes in the third-century *Martyrdom of Polycarp*.[34] The author counterposes the conduct of Polycarp and that of Quintus: whereas Polycarp sought refuge outside of the city, Quintus offered himself for execution, only to recant at the last moment (*Mart. Pol.* 4). Polycarp's reticence is described in biblical terms, as a martyrdom "according to gospel" (*Mart. Pol.* 1.1; 22.1). His prudent self-withdrawal, cast as patience, serves an exemplary function, for "just as the Lord did, he too waited that he might be given up" (*Mart. Pol.* 1.2). The scripturally and mimetically framed contrast between the two figures nudges the reader toward the example set by Polycarp and away from Quintus's rash and ultimately unsuccessful attempt to seek martyrdom. Certainly we can see here a denunciation of voluntary martyrdom.

Further evidence for the emergence of voluntary martyrdom as a discrete practice is found in the translation and editing of the Greek *Martyrdom of Papylus, Carpus, and Agathonike* (ca. 250 CE). In the original Greek account, Agathonike is a bystander from Pergamum who immolates herself on the pyre of the two primary martyrs (*Mart. Carp.* A 44). Although she has been adjudged a Montanist, more recent scholarship has tended to suggest that she was merely influenced by Montanism.[35] There is no evidence, however, to identify her as anything other than Christian. Working some time after the events, most likely during the Decian period, the Latin translator alters the account so that Agathonike is arrested with the other martyrs (*Mart. Carp.* B 1.1).[36] The emendation of the text suggests that her death was problematic for the translator of the Latin version, who balks at the notion of a martyr throwing herself into the flames by her own volition; by explicitly noting her arrest, the translator renders her death acceptable to an audience that would not have been comfortable with this kind of martyrdom. In other words, we can assume on the part of the translator a crystallized dislike of volunteerism. The date for the earlier Greek version of the account is unclear. We must assume that Agathonike's self-immolation was unproblematic for the Greek author but that during the period between the original composition and the editing of the work in the middle of the third century, a rejection of voluntary martyrdom had begun.

The earliest evidence for the creation of voluntary martyrdom as a practice distinct from true martyrdom is found in the early third century with Clement; whether his Christian predecessors or contemporaries shared his distinction is not clear.[37] We can, however, note the reworking of attitudes toward flight during times of persecution in his contemporaries. For Tertullian, the line distinguishing forms of martyrdom also cuts between those who flee from persecution and those who are martyred; he utilizes the discourse of honor and shame to make this distinction. Although sometimes willing to accept flight from persecution in preference to apostasy (*To His Wife* 1.3.4), Tertullian is generally disapproving of the practice, which he occasionally views as apostasy itself (*Fug.* 5.1). That the Spirit "encourages martyrdom rather than flight" (*Fug.* 9.4) creates a dichotomy between the two possibilities, but there is no discernible difference in his writings between voluntary martyrdom and martyrdom—voluntary martyrdom is martyrdom. By contrast, for Clement, who fled the Severan persecution in Alexandria in 202 CE (Eusebius, *Hist. eccl.* 6.11.6; 6.14.9), and for the author of the *Martyrdom of Polycarp,* who justifies Polycarp's flight to the countryside, the condemnation of voluntary martyrdom as a distinct phenomenon serves to explain initial flight from persecution. Unlike Cyprian of Carthage, Clement never returns to face death.[38] It would be reasonable to suppose that for Clement the point at which martyrdom becomes necessary is the point at which one is forced to confess or deny Christ. The discursive production and condemnation of voluntary martyrdom shapes flight from persecution as patience. Where voluntary martyrdom is parsed as passionate foolishness and excluded from true martyrdom, initial flight followed by execution is presented as true martyrdom or martyrdom "according to gospel." Martyrdom and flight define one another. Clement's strategy is remarkably effective, for the terms of the debate have shifted from the defense of flight in times of persecution to an attack on enthusiasm.

AVOIDANCE OF MARTYRDOM

As for enthusiasm, there is a slight methodological difficulty in identifying those individuals who were hesitant to embrace martyrdom or were intellectually opposed to it. Other than Clement and Cyprian, the bishop of Carthage in the middle of the third century, evidence for Christians exiling themselves or lapsing by offering sacrifice comes from those who polemicize against these practices. Only with Clement and Cyprian do we begin to see exegetical and rational foundations for self-exile. In the hands of critics such as Tertullian, flight could become synonymous with cowardice and apostasy. In *On Flight in Persecution,* Tertullian condemns exile in time of persecution. Interpreters of Tertullian have tended to read these instructions as largely homiletical and exhortatory: Tertullian, they say, is not disagreeing with some intellectual faction that advocated flight during persecution; he was instead combating human weaknesses and cowardice that might lead a person to go into exile rather than face execution. Certainly, Tertullian's writings equate flight with cowardice, but this does not mean that there were not parties in Carthage who, like Clement, had an intellectual basis for their avoidance of unrest. The rhetorical construction of flight as either cowardice or prudent self-withdrawal makes it impossible to reach beyond our extant sources to the historical events themselves.

Clement is critical of those volunteering themselves for martyrdom, but he also rounds on intellectual opponents who discourage or ridicule the practice. These heretics are, at various junctures in Clement's writings, identified with certain individuals and groups who have been historically labeled Gnostics. One of Clement's first targets is Heracleon, a follower of Valentinus (*Strom.* 4.70–73), but not a "Gnostic." According to Clement, Heracleon did not reject martyrdom in toto but distinguished between, on one hand, a simple verbal confession and, on the other, a lived confession that occurs throughout the course of a person's life. The verbal confession is made by those who acknowledge their beliefs only in the courtroom and is valid only if supported by a life lived with good conduct and faith. Heracleon does not see the martyrological equivalent of the deathbed confession as something to be highly regarded. Clement largely agrees with Heracleon; they differ only in that Clement acknowledges the accomplishment of martyrs who endure to death, even if they have not lived spotless lives.

Clement splits hairs with Basilides in a similar fashion (*Strom.* 4.12.83–85). Basilides apparently had argued that bodily suffering was divine punishment and that the tortures endured by a confessor were the result of previous sins. Utilizing the topos that Christians were persecuted for the name alone, not for their sins, Clement replies that Basilides's line of reasoning vindicates persecutors and makes good conduct unnecessary. After all, he argues, if divine providence governs all, then what sense does it make to be virtuous? Both Clement and Basilides share a concern that providence not be linked to injustice, and both consider martyrdom to be good; it is in the conclusions they draw from this common stock that they differ.

Clement's views on Valentinus are similarly condemnatory. He cites the portion of Valentinus commonly known as fragment 4 as part of a larger section describing heretical opposition to martyrdom: "You are immortal from the beginning, and you are children of eternal life. You wanted that death will be bestowed upon you in order that you use it up and waste it, so that death would die in you and through you. For when you, on the one hand, nullify the world, but on the other, will not be dissolved, you rule over creation and the entire corruption" (*Strom.* 4.89.4). Clement claims that Valentinus described a "race saved by nature" that had come from above to destroy death, from which he infers that Valentinus attributed death to an inferior creator deity.[39] The attribution of these views to Valentinus is not certain, but Jens Holzhausen uses them to argue that "Valentinus criticizes a theology that promises man that he will overcome death through suffering martyrdom."[40] He concludes that Valentinus here rebuts the notion that martyrdom serves as payment for eternal life and positions him as rejecting martyrdom altogether. The truth may have been less cut and dried than Clement would have us believe. A number of Valentinian accounts describe suffering in positive, even redemptive terms.[41]

In scholarly commentary, Clement's arguments have marshaled support for a rather sharp divide between orthodox Christians, who practiced martyrdom, and Gnostics, who avoided it. Elaborations of this binary have drawn in contrasting concerns about the body, resurrection, and creation as ways to flesh out these different positions. Clement is not the only church father through whom Gnostic views of martyrdom have been reassembled; as is the case for other heresiological stereotypes, Gnostic attitudes to martyrdom have been extracted from Irenaeus.[42] In *Against the Heresies,* Irenaeus describes Basilides as arguing that salvation belongs only to the soul and not the body. "For this reason, persons of such a persuasion are also ready to recant [their opinions], yes, rather, it is impossible that they should suffer on account of a mere name, since they are like to all" (*Haer.* 1.24.6; cf. Clement, *Strom.* 4.81; Tertullian, *Adversus Valentinianos* 30). Like Justin before him, Irenaeus seems unwilling to admit the existence of Gnostic martyrs, allowing only for the possibility of the occasional, accidental martyr (*Haer.* 4.33.9). In describing the Christian encounter with heresy, Irenaeus not only uses the fact of martyrdom as a means of distinguishing between the two groups, but also employs martyrological and gladiatorial imagery to force the two apart. Utilizing the language of the arena, Irenaeus casts himself as the martyr and the heretics as wild beasts and dumb animals (*Haer.* 4.31.4). The violence of the heresiological contest is striking: Irenaeus hopes to inflict the heretics with wounds and trample them underfoot (*Haer.* 4.31.4). Such imagery emulates the discourse of martyrdom in Gaul: battle with heresy functions like conflict with the animals, which in turn encapsulates the cosmic battle with Satan. In an ironic act of narrative violence, Irenaeus drags the Gnostics to the arena in order to force them to play the persecutor.

The contention that Gnostics disregarded both the body and martyrdom has been largely adopted by martyrdom scholars, most notably Frend, who has argued that the Gnostics were opposed to martyrdom on principle.[43] This recapitulation of Clement's Gnostic/orthodox binary both obscures the thickly braided discourse of martyrdom in antiquity and advances an agenda that reifies and denigrates the Gnostics. The contributions of Gnosticism or Gnostic texts to the discourse of martyrdom in the early church are ripe for reconsideration.

The Nag Hammadi Codices, the Tchacos Codex, and Valentinian and "Gnostic" Ideologies of Martyrdom

The discovery of the Nag Hammadi hoard and the Tchacos Codex have revolutionized the ways in which scholars conceptualize not only Gnosticism, but also Gnostic attitudes to martyrdom. Their careful examination has been instrumental in drawing attention to the differences between various Christian groups and the philosophical and theological foundations of their positions. With respect to martyrdom, Elaine Pagels describes the perspectives on martyrdom in the Nag Hammadi codices as "surprisingly diverse," noting that while some accounts affirm martyrdom, other texts denounce it, and still others accept it in certain circumstances. She identifies, however, one commonality: "in every case, the interpretation of Christ's passion corresponds to the attitude to martyrdom."[44] If Pagels is even only partially correct about the formal connection between the passion and martyrdom, then in this respect Gnostic and non-Gnostic attitudes to martyrdom are structurally no different. Pagels may generalize here, and there certainly are views of martyrdom that are not explicitly connected to the passion, but her observation about diversity reopens a discussion about the discourse of martyrdom in the numerous texts traditionally but inadequately labeled as Gnostic.

A preliminary difficulty when it comes to any discussion of "Gnostic ideologies of martyrdom" is that the Gnostics as constructed by Irenaeus, Clement, and Frend do not appear to have existed. Whereas early-twentieth-century scholarship on the subject was content to operate with broad amorphous definitions about the nature of Gnosticism and to be led through a deserted wasteland of concrete evidence by the eager grasp of Irenaeus, recent generations of scholars have questioned the existence of the category altogether. Even if we sidestep the scholarly quagmire into which the term "Gnostic" inevitably leads, the difficulty still remains of how we construct the relationship of various groups and individuals (Gnostics, Valentinians, Basilides, and Sethians) to one another. Our purpose here is not to make a definitive statement about Gnostic ideologies of martyrdom or even to suggest that there is such a thing as a characteristically Gnostic ideology of martyrdom. Instead, we use the questionable, troublesome designation "Gnostic" in order to demonstrate the redundancy and inaccuracy of the caricature of Gnostic views of martyrdom. The purpose of this analysis is to expose the shared values and common terms of "orthodox" and "Gnostic" constructions of martyrdom.

Wary of treating the plethora of material too superficially, we focus on two texts—the (most likely) Valentinian text the *First Apocalypse of James* and the Gnostic *Gospel of Judas*—and the ideologies of martyrdom contained in them. Although there is some debate about the character of these two texts and their respective views on martyrdom, the fact that they are both preserved in the Tchacos Codex means that there was at least one social location in which they were read in concert.[45] Our purpose is to deconstruct the notions that Gnostics were fundamentally opposed to martyrdom and united in their characterization of martyrdom and that they developed their arguments in splendid isolation from more mainstream martyrdom literature.

FIRST APOCALYPSE OF JAMES

The *First Apocalypse of James* appears among the pages of the Nag Hammadi cache and as a part of the newly discovered Tchacos Codex. Before the discovery of the Tchacos manuscript, few modern interpreters had emphasized the martyrological character of the *First Apocalypse of James,* but with the translation of this codex, which preserves the final lines of James's martyrdom, the *First Apocalypse of James* has been reassessed as an example of martyrdom literature. Observing that all three extant texts of the Tchacos Codex (*Gospel of Judas, First Apocalypse of James, Letter of Peter to Philip*) are concerned with violence and the meaning of suffering, Karen King has suggested that not only the *First Apocalypse of James* but also the codex as a whole functions as preparation for martyrdom. The reasons for the compilation of this codex may therefore offer an alternative interpretation of suffering and death.[46]

The text of the *First Apocalypse of James* tracks the progress of the apostle as he advances in knowledge toward martyrdom. As the stones strike his body at the end of the account, James calls out, "Forgive them, for they do not know what they are doing" (cf. Luke 23:34).[47] The James encountered by the reader at the beginning of the account has improved markedly. The weeping, feminine figure who upon learning of his impending martyrdom needed to sit down has been transformed into a manly *imitator Christi*.[48] That the structure of the account moves from the death of Jesus to the death of James only rearticulates the mimetic connection between James and Jesus.[49] The entire text forms a mimetic chain—the audience imitates James imitating

Jesus—and in this respect is functionally similar to other martyrdom literature, both Gnostic and non-Gnostic.[50]

Narratively, through a series of dialogues between Jesus and James, the
account prepares James and, by extension, the reader for martyrdom.[51]
In modern terms, the *First Apocalypse of James* is a story of personal growth
and development in which martyrdom has a tentatively salvific purpose. In
the Tchacos Codex text, Jesus consoles James, saying, "When they arrest
you and stone you, you will be saved" (*1 Apoc. Jas.* TC 11.20–23). Just as
for Jesus, so too for James; his own death will be his salvation. Even if martyrdom is purposeful, though, suffering is not. The task that awaits James is
to overcome fear.[52] Jesus maintains that he did not die; he was delivered
(*1 Apoc. Jas.* TC 11.14–15). The confident interpretation of martyrdom as
deliverance may sound much like other martyrological reconstructions of
death as salvation but in fact invokes strikingly different anthropological
and cosmological structures. Suffering is not the path to salvation that it is
in other martyrdom accounts we have seen.[53] Rather, suffering should be
accepted should the situation arise. In the words of King, "it comes with the
territory."[54]

The knowledge in which James and the audience are instructed is that they
themselves will not suffer—not because they will escape martyrdom, but
because their nature is spiritual, not fleshly, and therefore they cannot be
harmed by the powers that seek to do them ill. The weak flesh, says Jesus, will
die, but not James himself (*1 Apoc. Jas.* TC 19.13–16). Suffering should, however, be accepted as a necessary by-product of living in a world ruled by ignorant and malicious rulers. There is not much for James and the audience to be
concerned about. James's task is to overcome both the passions of the flesh,
through the exercise of manly self-control, and the rulers.[55]

The careful reader will note functional, structural, and thematic similarities
between the *First Apocalypse of James* and other martyrdom literature sur-
veyed in this book. Exhortations to imitate Christ and earlier generations of
martyrs are a commonplace in Christian martyrdom literature, which does not
render these accounts ideologically identical but rather suggests a common
rhetorical vocabulary and martyrological grammar. The authors may disagree
on the intrinsic value of suffering, but they utilize the same rhetorical tools and
hold some values in common. Ironically, the position of the author of the *First
Apocalypse* on the question of whether one should be willing to be martyred
does not seem radically different from that of Clement of Alexandria. Both
authors agree that it is necessary to accept martyrdom as a hazard of existence
and an opportunity to display virtue, even if they would disagree on other points
such as the reality of Christ's death.

GOSPEL OF JUDAS

The *Gospel of Judas,* the much-discussed *codex célèbre,* is found, like the *First Apocalypse of James,* bundled together in the Tchacos manuscript. Its notorious protagonist aside, the account is also well known due to its virulently anti-martyrdom position.[56] Although the text may have been composed within a context of the persecution of Christians, the author has written an angry, highly polemical narrative of Jesus's death that sets contemporary Christians, rather than Roman authorities, in its sights.[57] The text reconfigures the death of Jesus in order to denounce the sacrificial theology and eucharistic practices found in the Ignatian corpus and the *Martyrdom of Polycarp.* Pagels and King have proposed that this antisacrificial rhetoric is also aimed at martyrdom.[58] For the author of the *Gospel of Judas,* by encouraging people to sacrifice themselves as martyrs, "the twelve" (presumably the apostles and their successors) had led the multitude of Christians astray (*Gospel of Judas* 5.17). Judas maintains that martyrdom styled as self-sacrifice only perpetuates the idolatrous worship of God and, still worse, is a form of human sacrifice. The language and rhetoric of Judas's denouncement are startling, for they forcefully compare the martyrdom of Christians to pagan idolatry and human sacrifice.[59]

The strongly antisacrificial bent to the *Gospel of Judas* and the ire of the narrator toward other Christians is acute. This can be contrasted with the *First Apocalypse of James,* in which the rejection of the fleshly body sits comfortably with an allegorical reading of Jesus's role as priest (*1 Apoc. Jas.* 28.8–18). The author of the *Gospel of Judas* positions himself in opposition to those who delight in sacrificing themselves to God. The polemic against martyrdom as sacrifice is distinctive but may not be as far removed from orthodox views of martyrdom as some have assumed.[60] The interpretation of the martyr's death as sacrifice was by no means ubiquitous.[61] In chapter 4, we saw the author of the description of the execution of Alexander and Attalus in the *Letter of the Churches of Vienne and Lyons* reject sacrificial interpretations of the martyrs' deaths. The executioners are displayed as cannibalistic animals whose enjoyment of the burning flesh of the martyrs indicts them both before God and on their own terms. If we wish to imagine how texts worked in dialogue with one another, then it would be worth hypothesizing about how the antisacrificial discourses of the *Gospel of Judas* and the *Letter* intersect and overlap. Antisacrificial approaches to martyrdom were no more the exclusive domain of Gnostic literature than martyrdom was the possession of the orthodox.

Conclusion

The intellectual and ideological foundations of reluctance and enthusiasm are rarely documented and are instead constantly elided by ancient record. If these practices can be historically associated with schismatic or heretical groups, then they are rhetorically stabilized by Clement and attributed to the nonorthodox. Clement's self-positioning as the moderate, temperate bastion of orthodoxy is rhetorically powerful, reproducing an Aristotelian cultural investment in moderation as a means of self-elevation. Martyrdom that occurs outside of this construction is either the nonrational product of excessive passion, like the voluntary martyrs, or the result of womanly cowardice, as in the case of the Gnostics. The association of volunteerism and reluctance with the ugly feminizing vices of excessive passion and cowardice sets up a contrast with the manliness of Clement's prudent orthodox martyr. The rhetorical effect of this construction is twofold: on one hand, heretical groups are associated with these passionate, nonrational forms of self-governance; on the other, there is no orthodox intellectual basis for these practices.

Clement's construction of the true martyr as the true gnostic Christian has had far-reaching effects. Traditionally, overviews of ancient Christian martyrdom have tended to plot three points on a sliding scale: the hot enthusiasm of the New Prophecy, the frigid apostasy of the Gnostics, and, in between, the measured position of the orthodox, who got it just right. Yet, when used in a survey of the ancient Christian ideological terrain, this model produces results that are flatly two-dimensional. Under the slightest pressure, Clement's model breaks down. Adherents of the New Prophecy were perhaps no more enthusiastic about martyrdom than any other group, and some Gnostic authors wrote approvingly about martyrdom. There was no homogenous, moderate, orthodox position on the performance and significance of martyrdom. Views of martyrdom were constantly re-shaped and re-produced. In a study of the first and second centuries, it is ill-advised, indeed impossible, to line up doctrinal categories with martyrological praxis. Later generations of early Christian authors such as Clement will reify martyrdom and bind its forms to specific socio-ecclesiological groups. Martyrdom was put to work, set to police the borders of orthodoxy even as the self-styled sentries of the church evaluated the quality of martyrdom.

Conclusion

In the historiography of martyrdom, the singular, binding character of martyrdom is everywhere asserted. Celebrated Protestant hagiographer John Foxe boldly addresses his best-selling *Actes and Monuments* to the true and universal church and describes his martyrs more than one hundred times as witnesses to truth.[1] Foxe's statement exemplifies the Christian belief that in martyrdom the truth of individual Christian beliefs, practices, and doctrines is made known. Foxe sees the courage of the martyrs and their willingness to give up that which is assumed to be most valuable—their lives—as a testimony to the truth of the Christian church, or rather his Christian church. By connecting his persecuted sixteenth-century contemporaries with a bloody list of early church saints, Foxe asserts and legitimizes the divine mission of the Protestant reformers. His genealogy of martyrs spanning the course of history makes reformers blood brothers of apostles. Foxe is in good company; the connection between doctrinal correctness, divine authentication, and martyrdom is made by Catholics, Anabaptists, Latter-day Saints, and Mennonites, to say nothing of Muslims, Jews, Hindus, and Sikhs. Suffering is the process by which moral and doctrinal superiority can be established.

The claim that martyrdom authenticates mission is an established rhetorical move that relies on two assumptions: first, that an individual prizes his or her life above everything else; and second, that the practice of martyrdom is peculiar only to the position that the author of the claim supports. For Foxe, therefore, there can be no Muslim or Catholic martyrs because their existence would bankrupt his exclusive claim to truth. Foxe's response is to turn earlier martyrs into Protestants, to read earlier generations of saints as martyrs for a Protestant Jesus. The same rhetorical move was made a millennium earlier by Justin Martyr, who claimed Socrates as a "Christian before Christ," and centuries after by Joseph Smith, the founder of the Church of Jesus Christ of Latter-day Saints, who claimed Foxe's martyrs as "honest, devoted followers of Christ."[2]

The discourse of singularity reproduces itself in histories of martyrdom. Here, genealogy and pathology wind their way through historiography, ancient and modern. Scholarly efforts to narrate the history of martyrdom, constructed as both "genuine martyrdom" and exceptional voluntary martyrdom, anchor themselves in the assumption that martyrdom literature and the amorphous concept of martyrdom can both be traced to an ancestral source. Closer inspection reveals that the categories and assumptions used to construct the history of martyrdom are extracted from either Roman responses to Christianity or the narratives of later Christian historiographers. Both the pathological model for the spread of martyrdom and the characterization of certain Christians as enthusiastically seeking out and volunteering for martyrdom are found in the writings of Pliny. Yet outside of such ideologically weighted assessments, there is no reason, literary or historical, to suppose that these authors are drawing on some common source.

As we have seen, beneath this discourse of singularity and homogeneity lies striking diversity. There is no unifying feature to these texts; language, imagery, and values differ from region to region, group to group, and text to text. Even the practices their authors seek to cultivate vary widely; some texts encourage fortitude, others resistance, still others domesticity. One might argue that these different ideologies of martyrdom are not so distinct at all but are, instead, merely different examples of a universal conviction that suffering and martyrdom are good. Yet even this statement, with all its lack of specificity, would be too bold. In the *First Apocalypse of James*, martyrdom is accepted as a feature of life properly ordered toward knowledge of God, but suffering is constantly denied. There was no universal consensus. Various groups and authors labored to define and restrict the good death to their own heroes and their own communities.

There is no historical reason to suppose that martyrdom is more singular and monolithic than other contested values and ideas. For instance, the figure of Christ might reasonably be called a divine savior in the various forms of ancient Christianity. But this would be a woefully inadequate description of early Christian Christologies, riding roughshod over the manifold articulations of who Christ was—his nature, person, essence, and work. Such diversity is hardly an insignificant variation on a theme. So it is with martyrdom, and to say otherwise is either to be seduced by the rhetoric of martyrdom as truth or to characterize martyrdom as uniformly abnormal and thus abnormally uniform.

Where authors utilize similar scriptural texts, cultural icons, and societal values, it is not necessary to view these connections as literary dependence or ideological uniformity, even if there are ties between these groups. No single element or theme is readily apparent in every instance of martyrdom. Many early Christians struggled to wield the rhetorical power of suffering for Christ, while others such as Clement or the author of the *First Apocalypse of James* attempted to shift from lauding suffering to valuing long lives lived with quiet continence. The rhetoric of martyrdom and conflict could be harnessed in polemics: Irenaeus casts his heretical opponents as wild beasts, while the *Letter of the Churches of Vienne and Lyons* and the *Gospel of Judas* portray the figurative opponents as practicing human sacrifice. The malleability and utility of the discourse of martyrdom reached far beyond the amphitheater. If there is unity here, it is in the ways that ideologies of martyrdom function, not in the values they construct. Where fissures appear, they do not, as Clement would have it, break down upon lines of orthodoxy and heresy, or even into tidy geographically bounded models. These texts intersect with one another to make, unmake, and remake early Christianity.

It is clear that the singularity of martyrdom, a concept deeply embedded in histories of martyrdom, should be discarded. But the question still remains of how we envision the origins of martyrdom and think about martyrdom's relationship to human nature. In his important study of violence in late antiquity, Thomas Sizgorich suggests that all narratives of martyrdom follow similar patterns of "primordialist discourse"—a kind of mythology—that itself fed into Muslim notions of jihad.[3] Sizgorich's suggestion, rooted as it is in social-scientific methodologies, offers an alternative, nongenealogical explanation for the appearance of martyrdom. The approach of this book has been to ask how suspending the question "why martyrdom?" and the assumption this question makes about the unnaturalness of martyrdom affects the way we narrate the history of martyrdom. Ancient Christian sources would seem to put the question differently and ask, "Why not martyrdom?" It is the contention of this book that we must take the disjuncture between modern and ancient first principles seriously, and that, even as we listen carefully for the muffled voices of (potentially many) dissenters, we resist the temptation to psychoanalyze or pathologize martyrdom itself. It is thus with deliberation that I have avoided the question of how these communal dramas of violence fostered a real willingness to embrace martyrdom.[4] The evidence suggests that there were diverse theologies and practices of martyrdom, ideologies nurtured by various intellectual, scriptural, and cultural traditions. It is, perhaps, a cultural script that glorifies comfort and the pursuit of long life at any cost that reads martyrdom as unintelligible.

This survey of martyrological discourse in the ancient world reveals some uncertainty in the dating of early martyr acts. Few, if any, of the texts examined in this book can be firmly nailed down in the second century; in many cases there are compelling reasons for locating a text in the third century. Losing chronological footholds is unsettling, and it is difficult to narrate a history of anything without solid dates and confidence in our sources. But the threat of uncertainty is not in and of itself a reason to maintain the authenticity of these accounts and the traditional dating for their composition. Even if the dearth of evidence binds the historian's hands, it is necessary to consider the possibility that the majority of extant martyr acts date from the Decian period and beyond. These revised dates demonstrate that the work performed by ideologies of martyrdom is not yoked to any historically verifiable persecution. In the centuries that followed the period on which this book is focused, ideologies of martyrdom continued to feed into late antique theories of violence. It was the self-positioning of Christians as an afflicted community that cemented the conceptual foundations of Christian religious violence.[5]

Even as this book is a history of the ideologies of martyrdom in the first and second centuries, we should not be content to give up the notion that these ideologies shaped actual bodies. While a correlation between ideals, ideologies, and theology cannot be directly mapped onto events and did not control individuals, the recognition that we do not have access to historical martyrs should not render our analysis of martyrdom literature abstract and hypothetical. Even if very few Christians were actually arrested, imprisoned, tortured, and executed, the audiences of these accounts, those composing and listening to these narratives, were and still are embodied subjects presented with constructions of the body. Just as exhortations to or regulations of any kind of bodily practice necessarily affect the construction of the body and the sense of what it means to be embodied, ideologies of martyrdom shaped not only community self-definition and Christian identity, but also the construction of the body itself.[6] The depiction of the martyr's body created a frame of reference for bodily experiences such as pain, hunger, fasting, grief, and joy. In moving past the dichotomy between historical reality and construction, it is not necessary to give up either. The relationship between historical and constructed bodies is the reciprocal relationship between the martyr's body, as constructed in the text and by the readers, and the social, physical, and political bodies of the readers, as constructed by the text and by their own sense of embodiedness.[7] Whether ancient Christians suffered prolonged agonies in the arena or long lives bearing the burdens of self-restraint, their bodies were shaped by these ideologies of martyrdom.

Notes

Introduction

1. For admiration see Droge and Tabor, *Noble Death;* for disdain see Riddle, *Martyrs* and Keller, *God and Power.*

2. Bremmer, "Motivation"; Castelli, *Martyrdom,* 197–203; Perkins, "Rhetoric"; Middleton, *Radical Martyrdom,* 1.

3. Brox, *Zeuge.* Brox's study, although methodologically flawed, orchestrated a profound shift in the study of martyrdom. Before his work the consensus maintained that martyrdom began at least with *1 Clem* 5, if not before (so Lightfoot, *Apostolic Fathers,* 1.26–27; Delehaye, *Sanctus,* 76–80; Von Campenhausen, *Idee,* 27–29, 51–55). For an appreciative assessment of Brox, see Barnes, *Hagiography,* 13 n.29.

4. Bowersock writes, "In these early years of the second century . . . the concept of martyrdom as we know it gradually took shape. With it soon came the word 'martyrdom' among the Christians in its modern sense" (*Martyrdom,* 17).

5. As Boyarin delicately illustrated, if one were to walk from Paris to Florence, stopping at every town along the way to converse with its inhabitants, one would notice a gradual, slight, and continuous change from Italian to French as one walked. The change of the guard at the border between the two countries does not bear out linguistically; there is "no border on the ground" (*Dying,* 9).

6. For a discussion of the importance of manliness in early Christian martyrdom, see Cobb, *Dying,* 7–17.

7. In her pilgrimage diary Egeria relays how she attended the "martyr shrine of Saint Thecla" (*Itinerarium* 22.2) in Hagia Thekla. Similarly, the expanded version of the *Acts*

of *Paul and Thecla* (*ATh*sel) describes how Thecla vanished into a rock and concludes by calling her "the first female martyr" (Lipsius, ed., *Acta Apostolorum Apocrypha*, 272). Gregory of Nazianzus includes Thecla among the apostolic martyrs Paul, James, Stephen, Luke, and Andrew (*Oration* 4.69 [Against Julian 1]). These examples and their interpretation are taken from Davis, *Cult*, 5, 40, 44–47. It is important to note that *ATh*sel uses the conventions of the martyr act (the would-be rapists are described as being like lions, for instance) in order to bolster the claim that Thecla is a martyr. See the discussion in Davis, *Cult*, 45.

8. Van Henten, *Maccabean Martyrs*. The identification of the Maccabees as the "original martyrs" is a critical component of Frend's magisterial *Martyrdom and Persecution in the Early Church*, in which the Maccabees form the opening chapter.

9. For a discussion of the gradual development of the genre, see Delehaye, *Passions*; Bisbee, *Pre-Decian Acts*; Bremmer, "Perpetua," 78–80; and Barnes, *Hagiography*, 47.

10. The idea of "dying for one's religious beliefs" is expansive precisely because ancient definitions of religion cannot be mapped concretely onto our own. The methodological difficulties in *defining* religion, not to mention the presence of religion in all aspects of ancient life, make this a larger question than has previously been considered. Given that all aspects of ancient society—politics, cuisine, education, warfare, and ritual—can be subsumed under the idea of religion, we may find ourselves including instances of martyrdom that, by modern standards, seem political. The use of the term "belief" certainly privileges Christianity, but even with respect to ancient Christianity, the situation is not much clearer. It is precisely within the martyr acts that the identity of the Christian is formed and solidified.

11. A functional definition of martyrdom is proposed by van Henten and Avemarie in *Martyrdom and Noble Death*, 3.

12. Castelli, *Martyrdom*, 173.

13. Riddle, *Martyrs*. Riddle's negative construction of martyrdom as the end result of "social control" may be less a criticism of martyrdom than a commentary on the rhetoric of social control so prevalent in the New Deal and 1930s America. See, for example, statistician Stuart A. Rice's optimistic statement that the New Deal and its aftermath were "the era of social control" ("Statistical Opportunities," 2). Given the popularity of the idea of social control, especially at the University of Illinois–Chicago, where Riddle worked, his seemingly aggressive attack on martyrdom may serve as a nuanced criticism of the effects and dangers of social control. I am grateful to my colleague Tom Stapleford for introducing me to early-twentieth-century social reform.

14. De Ste. Croix, "Early Christians," 133. This example and the next are taken from Perkins, *Suffering Self*, 33. The description of Ignatius's longing for death as "pathological" is cited and adopted by Bowersock in *Martyrdom*, 6–7. To be fair to De Ste. Croix, he states that Ignatius's desire for death has "often been called pathological," without explicitly stating that he shares this view.

15. Frend, *Martyrdom*, 197.

16. Gibbon remarks of Sigismund's epithets saint and martyr, "A martyr! How strangely that word has been distorted from its original sense of a common witness" (*Decline and Fall*, 4:121; cited in Bowersock, *Martyrdom*, 6).

17. The presumption that death can be escaped and the assumption that it should be avoided are shaped, in modern medical societies, using the rhetoric of "the natural." It is natural to want to live, to avoid pain, and to defer death, just as it is unnatural—even crazy—to seek death out. Death is framed as the antithesis to life, personified as shadowy, faceless, violent, and evil. The idea of death as a practice, instrument, or art form is barely represented in modern language. Within scholarship on martyrdom, a particularly sharp rebuttal of the vilification of death is found in Droge and Tabor, *Noble Death*.

18. See the synthesizing of Frend, *Martyrdom*; and Bowersock, *Martyrdom*.

19. A more positive understanding of the mechanics of martyrdom's spread can be detected in the work of scholars such as Delehaye. For Delehaye, the simple homogony of martyrdom can be juxtaposed with the complexity he sees in the cult of the saints, of which, ironically, martyrdom comes to form a part. He writes that to compile a history of the cult of a saint is a "nearly superhuman" task, but that martyrdom is a simpler affair ("Loca sanctorum"). Delehaye's singular martyrological tradition is not, for him, evidence of the martyr's insanity but, rather, of that martyr's witness to the truth. For Delehaye, martyrdom is singular because it bears witness to religious truth and religious truth is, naturally, singular. I am grateful to David Eastman for drawing my attention to Delehaye's views on the complexity of the cult of the saints.

20. See also Suetonius, *Nero* 16.2. For a discussion of the valence of *superstitio* among ancient Romans, see Janssen, "Bedeutungsentwicklung"; Janssen, "Superstitio." For a discussion of the rhetorical use of accusations of *superstitio* or *desidaimonia* and the construction of Christianity as *superstitio*, see Martin, *Inventing Superstition*, 18–20.

21. A classic example is the historical construction of homosexuality as mental disease in the United States. For a discussion of this phenomenon, see Terry, *American Obsession*.

22. Perkins, *Suffering Self*, 193.

23. The displacement of biological norms (i.e., the natural) by cultural norms may sound like a dissolution into cultural relativity. This is not necessarily the case, and it would be a mistake to treat cultural constructions as more stable entities than "nature."

24. I allude here to Castelli's remark that "regardless of the historicity of the martyr's story, it is a story that can both make an ethical demand and lend legitimacy to other forms of power claims" (*Martyrdom*, 32).

25. Melito of Sardis is the first Christian author to have asserted that "bad emperors" persecute where "good emperors" protect the Christians. See Eusebius, *Hist. eccl.* 4.26.9–10; and Tertullian, *Apol.* 5.

26. Arguably the most important of these is Mommsen, *Römisches Strafrecht*, 340–1, 346–51.

27. De Ste. Croix, "Early Christians," 106–7.

28. For recent overviews of this subject, see Ameling, "Pliny"; and Cook, *Roman Attitudes*, 138–240.

29. The replies to Pliny are formulated as if all composed by Trajan, but it seems unlikely that he crafted every response himself. Trajan employed a secretary, the *ab epistulis*,

whose primary responsibility was to read and respond to the considerable amount of correspondence the emperor received. It is likely that the *ab epistulis* composed many of the letters in Trajan's name. For a discussion of the *ab epistulis,* see Millar, *Emperor,* 83–110, 224–28. Considerable scholarly effort has been dedicated to distinguishing between the work of the *ab epistulis* and of Trajan.

30. Sherwin-White, "Early Christians."

31. De Ste. Croix, "Early Christians—A Rejoinder."

32. On this De Ste. Croix and Sherwin-White agree. See De Ste. Croix, "Early Christians," 106–7; and Sherwin-White, "Early Christians." Barnes's exhaustive appraisal of the evidence has only reaffirmed this proposal; see Barnes, "Legislation."

33. See Harrill, "Servile Functionaries"; Ebbeler, "Letters"; Ebbeler, "Tradition."

34. Ludolph, *Epistolographie*; Gunderson, "Catullus"; Marchesi, *Art,* 1–11.

35. Ebbeler, "Tradition," 272.

36. Noreña, "Social Economy," 239.

37. Van Dam, *Families,* 132.

38. Garnsey and Saller, *Roman Empire,* 32–40. The problem is helpfully summarized in Harrill, *Slaves,* 9–11.

39. On Roman provincial administration in general, see Kunkel, *Introduction;* Cary and Scullard, *History;* Richardson, *Roman Provincial Administration;* Lintott, *Imperium Romanum,* 22–32.

40. On Pliny's letters (and Tacitus) serving as a literary source for, e.g., Tertullian, see Birley, "Persecutors," 41–42.

41. See Rives, "Decree," who argues that the decree of Decius was intended to unify geographically diverse and principally local religious practices in a specific religio-political practice.

42. See the statement of MacMullen that "brutal routines of law in action were no doubt stored away in the memory of every citizen" ("Judicial Savagery," 152).

43. A more comparative approach is proposed and presented in Rhee, *Early Christian Literature,* 1–8. Rhee perceptively identifies scholarly commitments to the "historical" character of the apologies against the "literary" character of the apocryphal acts and martyr acts as one reason for the generic distinction. I would augment Rhee's theory by suggesting that the supposedly more historical character of the *acta* has contributed to the separation of apocryphal acts from martyr acts.

44. For a discussion of the dialogical relationship between scripture and martyrological portraits, see Moss, *Other Christs,* 56.

45. Farkasfalvy and Farmer, *Formation.*

46. For a summary of the evidence for official persecution during the period of 1 Peter's composition, see Achtemeier, *1 Peter,* 29–36. For the view that the members of the community that produced Revelation perceived themselves to be more persecuted than they actually were, see Collins, *Crisis,* 165–66.

47. Lipsius, *Apokryphen Apostlegeschichten,* 1:7–8.

48. This "astonishing" pattern is noted by Klauck, *Apocryphal Acts,* 256.

49. For an overview of scholarship on the dating of these accounts, see Klauck, *Apocryphal Acts.*

50. Bremmer, "Five Major Apocryphal Acts," 164.

51. Rosweyde, *Fasti sanctorum.*

52. Ruinart, *Acta primorum martyrum*; Gebhardt, *Acta martyrum selecta*; Delehaye, *Legendes*; and Delehaye, *Passions.*

53. Von Harnack, "Das ursprüngliche Motiv," 116, translated and cited in Bisbee, *Pre-Decian Acts,* 12–13.

54. Von Harnack, *Chronologie,* 2:463–82. The quest for authentic historical *acta* is a guiding principle for and undergirding interest in the collections of Ruinart and Rudolf Knopf, and even for more modern collections such as Musurillo, Lanata, and Bastiaensen et al. For a summary and recent list of early (rather than merely authentic) accounts, see Barnes, *Hagiography,* 343–49.

55. Delehaye, *Legendes,* 106–9.

56. Bisbee, *Pre-Decian Acts,* 33–64, 81–94.

57. Grant, "Eusebius," 131.

58. Castelli, *Martyrdom;* Lieu, *Image;* Grig, *Making Martyrs;* Cobb, *Dying;* Leemans, *Memory.*

59. Asad, *Formations,* 85–91. Asad takes his leave from Perkins's *Suffering Self.* He notes that when Perkins discusses the function of martyrdom, she focuses on the symbolic and political work that martyrdom texts do, and on the way they challenge the dominant societal values of the ruling classes in the Roman empire.

60. Asad, *Formations,* 87

61. Asad, *Formations,* 91.

62. At certain points, for instance in his description of Sunni martyrs (*Formations,* 90–91), Asad notes the distinction between pain and suffering. Here though he distinguishes these examples from Christian martyrdom.

63. Lane Fox, *Pagans,* 436.

64. This tendency is particularly evident in the writings of American scholars influenced by the cultural turn. Continental scholarship continues to examine the evidence for historical events and the dating of texts.

65. Barnes, "Pre-Decian *Acta Martyrum,*" and Barnes, *Early Christian Hagiography,* 54–95. In his more recent study Barnes includes a number of additional texts, the provenances of which are less certain (*Martyrdom of Fructuosus, Martyrdom of Pionius, Martyrdom of Montanus and Lucius*). Given that even the most conservative and optimistic dating places these texts outside of the scope of this work, it is not necessary to deal with their dating here.

66. The importance of regionalism on ancient constructions of religion has been noted by Lane Fox, *Pagans,* 33; Rives, *Religion,* Cancik and Rüpke, eds., *Römische Reichsreligion;* Frankfurter, *Religion;* and Kaizer, *Religious Life.*

67. The importance of social networks in early Christianity has been highlighted by Alexander, "Mapping"; White, *Social Networks;* and Harland, "Connections."

68. For a discussion of the relationship between Romans and "barbarians" at the frontiers of the empire, see Brown, *Rise,* 35–92.

69. The term "micro-Christianities" is borrowed from Brown's magnificent work *The Rise of Western Christendom,* 355–82.

70. The notion that history progresses uniformly at a transgeographical steady rate is, to some extent, implicit in Brown's study on the transformation of the Roman empire

(*The Rise of Western Christendom*). The attachment to continuity or transformation has been recently called into question with respect to the dissolution of the Roman empire by Wickham, *Inheritance*.

71. Burrus, *Saving Shame*; Rhee, *Early Christian Literature*.

72. Shaw, "Body/Power/Identity."

Chapter 1. Cultural Contexts

1. See discussion of "Difficult Definitions" in the introduction.

2. Baumeister, *Anfänge;* van Henten labels those who see martyrdom as originating with Christianity as "simply wrong" (*Maccabean Martyrs,* 4).

3. Von Campenhausen, *Idee;* Bowersock, *Martyrdom,* 8.

4. Bowersock, *Martyrdom,* 5.

5. Bowersock, *Martyrdom,* 7. Cf. Perkins, *Suffering Self,* 15–40. Perkins's view was anticipated by Dodds's statement that "in these centuries a good many persons were consciously or unconsciously in love with death" (*Pagans,* 135).

6. On the use of "tradition," see Tanner, *Theories,* 163.

7. So Engberg-Pedersen, "Paul's Necessity," in which he argues that Paul's ideas were formulated in specific situations and by a complex of "necessities." Although I agree with Engberg-Pedersen's argument, it is not necessary to see conceptual change as the product of necessities. Intellectual production is a complex process.

8. For a critique of the traditional model of reception, see Brakke, Jacobsen, and Ulrich, *Beyond Reception,* 9, where they write that reception is frequently understood as "taking something from one block of religion and culture and bringing it into another."

9. For a discussion of the reception of Socrates throughout the Hellenistic period and in early Christian literature, see Wilson, *Death,* 89–141.

10. For a discussion of martyrs outside of orthodoxy, see MacMullen, *Christianizing the Roman Empire,* 134 n.13; and Hilhorst, "Christian Martyrs."

11. For discussion of the noble tradition, see Eigler, "Exitus." For the relationship between the noble death tradition and the literature of the Jesus movement, see Seeley, *Noble Death,* 83–141; Collins, "Genre"; Collins, "Noble Death"; and Sterling, "*Mors philosophi.*"

12. For example, Epictetus, *Discourses* 1.9.13–15; Marcus Aurelius, *Meditations* 11.3.

13. Herodotus, *Histories* 1.86 (trans. De Sélincourt), 40.

14. The idea of battle securing a "good death" is found in Homer, *Iliad* 15.496; Tyrtaeus, 10.13–14; Euripides, *Trojan Women* 386–87; Thucydides, *History of the Peloponnesian War* 2.43. The sentiment crosses into Roman thought and is found in Virgil, *Aeneid* 2.317; Silius Italicus, *On the Punic Wars* 10.66; and Horace, *Odes* 3.2.13.

15. Thucydides, *History* 2.43 (trans. T. E. Wick), 112.

16. Musonius Rufus's position is preserved in Plutarch's *On Controlling Anger*. See discussion in Harris, *Restraining Rage,* 119.

17. Williams, *Roman Homosexuality,* 139.

18. See, for example, Plato, *Phaed.* 114E (63).

19. For the construction of masculinity in the Roman empire, see Gleason, *Making Men.* On the ways in which various cultures construct "real" as against biological manhood, see Gilmore, *Manhood,* 11.

20. Edwards, *Death,* 179.

21. A great deal has been written about sacrificial death in Euripides. For an overview of the literature, see Bremmer, "Sacrificing."

22. For the argument that virginity was a measure of innocence and youth, see Mossman, *Wild Justice,* 142–63. For Polyxena more generally, see Bremmer, "Myth and Ritual." To these well-known examples of female fortitude can be added the lesser-known self-sacrificing maidens Makaria and the daughters of Erechtheus, lesser-known in the case of the Makaria because she is unnamed in the *Heraclids,* and in the case of the maidens of *Erechtheus* (ca. 420 BCE) because their story proved unpopular with the theatergoing public.

23. Other versions of this story are found in Dionysius of Halicarnassus, *Antiquitates Romanae* 4.64–82; Ovid, *Festivals* 2.721–852; and Plutarch, *On the Virtue of Women* 14.

24. On the cultural resonance of weaving, see Johnston, "New Web."

25. Lucius Brutus, who avenges Lucretia in Livy's version, construes her death as a sacrifice. On the political ramifications of her death, see Edwards, *Death,* 180–82.

26. The *lex Iulia de adulteriis coercendis* was part of a program of Julian laws (*Leges Juliae*) promulgated by Augustus and intended to promote the role of the family in Roman society. It made adultery both a private and a public crime punishable by banishment and, under certain circumstances, by death.

27. See Loraux, *Tragic Ways,* 49–56, who notes that the abdomen is the usual site for male deaths whereas the throat, and hanging in particular, is the locus for female death.

28. Bronfen, *Over Her Dead Body,* xi.

29. See the discussion of Perpetua in chapter 4 and, particularly, Perkins, *Suffering Self,* 15–76; Cobb, *Dying,* 102–22; Cooper, *Virgin,* 45–67; and Harrill, *Slaves,* 157–65.

30. That the martyrs are masculinized is noted by all; see, for example, Burrus, "Torture," 56; and Streete, *Redeemed Bodies,* 31.

31. Streete, *Redeemed Bodies,* 41.

32. See Frilingos, "Sexing the Lamb," 313. Cobb writes, "The stories of these female martyrs show that in addition to masculinizing their Christian women subjects, authors also feminized them" (*Dying,* 121).

33. The association of femininity and death that has been articulated with respect to ancient Greek mythology has been a principle in anthropological studies. See Turner, "Death," with criticisms in Bynum, "Women's Stories."

34. Smith, *Fools,* 23.

35. For attempts to distinguish history from hearsay, see Chroust, *Socrates;* Navia, *Socrates;* and Brickhouse and Smith, *Plato's Socrates.*

36. Derrida, *Post Card.* I am borrowing this example from Wilson, *Death,* 89.

37. For the view that Socrates's trial was politically motivated, see Stone, *Trial,* 138–39. For the perspective that the trial was motivated by religious concerns, see Brickhouse and Smith, *Plato's Socrates,* 137–75. For a recent, accessible reappraisal, see Waterfield,

Why Socrates Died. According to some historians, Socrates was never meant to have stood trial. The legal accusations were a political move designed to force him into exile. See Chroust, *Socrates,* 24; and Montuori, *Socrates,* 197.

38. So Smith, *Fools,* 38.

39. Stone, *Trial,* 230.

40. Hackforth, *Plato's Phaedo,* 180.

41. Epictetus, *Discourses* 4.1.165. Cf. *Discourses* 1.9.25, where Epictetus encourages his audience to wait for a sign from God.

42. Most recently Roskam, "Figure."

43. See Plato, *Phaed.* 61–64 and *Laws* 873d; Aristotle, *Nicomachean Ethics* 1138a–b, 1116a12–14. Diogenes Laertius preserves a number of Cynic sayings that imply that Cynics may have recommended certain kinds of self-killing (*Lives* 6.76–77, 94–95, 100). For a survey of philosophical views of self-killing, see Droge and Tabor, *Noble Death,* 17–47. Droge and Tabor identify four philosophical views on self-killing: (1) the argument of the Pythagoreans, who condemned voluntary death outright; (2) the argument of Plato and Aristotle that self-killing was a rebellion against the state but might be justified in situations in which one was ordered to do so by the state itself; (3) the Epicurean and Stoic view that voluntary death was permissible in the event that endurance was impossible; and (4) the Neoplatonic view that self-killing could never be rational because it was the inevitable result of succumbing to passion. For a discussion of suicide in antiquity, see Hirzel, "Selbstmord"; and Van Hoof, "Voluntary Death." For a bibliography on suicide in ancient Rome, see Grisé, *Suicide,* 299–308.

44. For a list of suicides in Greek and Roman literature, see Mair, "Suicide." Stoic philosophies of death may have been particularly influential on early Christian articulations of martyrdom. For the influence of Stoicism on early Christian martyrdom in general, see Aune, "Mastery"; Straw, "Special Death"; and Denzey, "Facing the Beast."

45. In Pindar's version, Ajax's death was born out of anger and brought "blame upon all the Greeks who went to Troy" (*Isthmian Ode* 4.35). This portrayal of Ajax's death is noticeably different from that by Sophocles. Given that Pindar writes that Homer "set the record right" concerning the reputation of Ajax, it could be that Pindar is reacting to a version of the myth similar to that of Sophocles.

46. For a survey of *devotio* in the Roman period, see Versnel, "Two Types"; and Versnel, "Self-Sacrifice," 171–79.

47. Josephus is not the first to posit (albeit as a feature of comparison) a relationship between Spartans and Jews. For a survey and discussion of this material, see Bremmer, "Spartans and Jews."

48. For the notion of cultural transgression in apposition to subversion, I am indebted to the work of Harrill, "Paul."

49. For the generic designation of these accounts as court tales, see Collins, *Daniel,* 42–47.

50. For a catalog of examples from Asia Minor and Egypt, see Davis, *Cult,* 225–38. For Thecla's cult in Syria, see Burris and Van Rompay, "Thecla"; and Burris and Van Rompay, "Further Notes."

51. The importance of such devotional items in the dissemination of the cult of the saints is highlighted in Brown, *Cult,* 88–89.

52. See Stevenson, *Catacombs,* 80. On the history of the catacombs, see Pergola, *Catacombe,* 130–37, 196–203.

53. Castelli, *Martyrdom,* 164.

54. See a fourth-century casket from Pannonia that depicts Daniel flanked by lions and palm trees in Malbon, *Iconography,* 429–30, fig. 387. The association of palm branches with martyrdom begins with Origen, *Commentary on John* 31, where palms are identified as a symbol of the martyr's victory in war. Palm trees also represent heaven and allude to Daniel's existence there.

55. Bousset and Gressmann, *Religion,* 394.

56. Bowersock, *Martyrdom,* 9.

57. Frend, "Martyrdom"; van Henten, *Maccabean Martyrs.* On the influence of the Maccabees in Christian literature, see Young, "Woman"; Ziadé, "Martyrs"; and Joslyn-Siemiatkoski, *Christian Memories.*

58. Neither Josephus (*Jewish War* 1.42–44) nor Adinolfi (*Questioni,* 103–22) sees Eleazar's death as noble. It certainly does not have the efficacy of the deaths of the martyrs in 2 Macc 6–7 or of Razis in 2 Macc 14.

59. The traditional scholarly date for 2 Macc places it sometime after 125 BCE with a date perhaps as late as the first century (for discussion, see van Henten, *Maccabean Martyrs,* 50–56). But see now Schwartz, *2 Maccabees,* 11–15, who argues that the work was composed close to the events themselves. With respect to 4 Macc, van Henten suggests a date around 100 CE but concedes that it could have been written between 80 and 120 CE (*Maccabean Martyrs,* 78).

60. This pattern is identified and nuanced by van Henten, *Maccabean Martyrs,* 26–27.

61. For the view that the practices for which the martyrs die are not ancestral customs being defended but rather a new identity being created, see Nongbri, "Motivations."

62. Rajak, "Dying."

63. On this topos, see Harrill, "Cannibalistic Language."

64. Van Henten, *Maccabean Martyrs.*

65. For discussion, see van Henten, *Maccabean Martyrs,* 116–24, 144–51.

66. Van Henten writes that Razis suffered a heroic suicide (*Maccabean Martyrs,* 5). The distinction between Razis and the other martyrs centers on the manner in which Razis dies. Although this has been an important feature in modern discourse, which distinguishes martyrdom from suicide, it is not at all clear that contemporary readers of 2 and 4 Macc had a similar focus (*pace* van Henten, 7). For a discussion about the role of self-killing in relation to heroic Jewish figures, see Zerubavel, *Recovered Roots,* 203–7.

67. On the use of the body as an act of resistance with respect to Maccabean literature in general, see Shaw, "Body/Power/Identity," 276–80.

68. Following van Henten, Schwartz, *2 Maccabees,* 65, 489–90.

69. Moore and Anderson, "Taking It," 253.

70. See Young, "4 Maccabees," 330.

71. Cooper, *Fall,* 224.

72. Van Henten, *Maccabean Martyrs,* 10–14.

73. The importance in Judaism of dying for the law is noted by van Henten, *Maccabean Martyrs,* 130; Rajak, "Dying," 63; Boyarin, *Dying,* 127–28; and Boyarin, *Border*

Lines, 72–73. None of these scholars considers the ways in which Christian identity and discourse of martyrdom "for law" respond to and are shaped by this particular element of Jewish tradition.

74. Boyarin, *Dying,* 96.

75. How genres are formed and defined are prevailing and oppressive questions. Within the study of ancient religion, genre debate has coagulated around the study of gospel and apocalyptic genres. See Doty, "Concept," 418; Hellholm, "Problem"; Aune, "Apocalypse"; Mazzaferri, *Genre,* 59–84; and Duff, *Modern Genre Theory.* On the importance of context as a dynamic environment with which genre interacts, see Bakhtin, *Speech Genres.* For the purposes of this discussion I assume that people cannot help but think with genre categories and expectations. Even if these expectations are subverted or frustrated, they nonetheless exist in the minds of the audience.

76. The name of this subgenre is derived from Pliny's characterization of Titinius Capito's collection of death accounts (*Ep.* 8.12.4). For the classic treatments of the subject, see Ronconi, "Exitus illustrium"; and Marx, "Tacitus." See also Döring, *Exemplum Socratis;* Eigler, "Exitus"; Morford, "Tacitus' Historical Methods"; Neyrey, "'Noble Shepherd'"; and Seeley, *Noble Death.*

77. For the collection of Greek romances, see Reardon, *Collected Ancient Greek Novels.* For the importance of the genre of the romance in the study of martyrdom, see Perkins, *Suffering Self,* 41–76; and Cooper, *Virgin,* 20–44.

78. Pervo, "Early Christian Fiction."

79. Perkins, *Suffering Self,* 75.

80. Cameron, *Christianity,* 116.

81. Since the first comprehensive study of the subject, Wilcken's *Zum alexandrinischen Antisemitismus,* many fragments have continued to appear, only adding to the enigma that surrounds the composition of the *Acta Alexandrinorum.*

82. The *Acts of Appianus* are compiled from two papyri: *P. Yale Inv.* 1536 (Yale papyrus collection) and P. Oxy. 33. Our text here follows P. Oxy. 33. Translations here follow van Henten and Avemarie, *Martyrdom,* 39–40.

83. Trans. van Henten and Avemarie, *Martyrdom,* 39.

Chapter 2. Asia Minor

1. The phrase "local and sporadic" has been a commonplace in scholarly histories of early Christian martyrdom, but see now Holloway, *Coping,* 36.

2. Traditional datings have placed the execution of Ignatius before the death of Trajan in 117 CE (Eusebius, *Hist. eccl.* 3.21–22; and Jerome, *Chronicle* 194–95), but see now Barnes, "Date," 123–26; and Barnes, *Hagiography,* 15. Barnes argues that allusions to Valentinian teachings in Ignatius's letters mean that he could have died no earlier than 140 CE. This assumes, of course, that Barnes's identification of allusions is correct. He argues, for example, that the use of a rare Greek term for touch in both Valentinus and Ptolemaeus (as reported by Irenaeus) indicates that the two authors are in dialogue with one another ("Date," 124–25). The force of this argument is undercut by the presence of the same term in the Gospel of Luke. Perhaps both Ignatius and Val-

entinus are interpreting Luke. One might further argue that the concept is more common in Christian circles than in Greek literature in general.

3. For a recent critique of the dating of Ignatius's letters, see Barnes, "Date of Ignatius," who places Ignatius's letters in the mid-second century.

4. Unless otherwise noted, translations from the *Ecclesiastical History* both here and elsewhere follow those of the *Nicene and Post-Nicene Fathers*.

5. For lists of the texts available in each recension, see the table in Lightfoot, *Apostolic Fathers*, 1:222. A stemma for the transmission of manuscript tradition is provided in Koester, *History*, 2:57.

6. Koester, *History*, 2:58; Ehrman, *Apostolic Fathers*, 1:212.

7. The Latin, first published in 1498, contains all of the supplementary letters, whereas the Greek, published in 1558, lacks Mary of Cassobola's response to Ignatius.

8. Ussher, *Polycarpi*; Voss, *Epistulae*; Ruinart, *Acta*.

9. Also included with the Ignatian epistles were *The Asceticon of Father Pachomius, A Narrative Concerning an Aged Coenobite, Whose Name Was Malcus, Questions and Answers of the Egyptian Fathers, The Epistles of Evagrius to Melania*, and *The Epistle of My Lord Ignatius, the Bishop* [Ign., *To Polycarp*]. And, in a second volume bound with the first, Ascetic Works of Evagrius, of the Monk Marcus; Lives of the Egyptian Fathers, Letter from St. Basil to St. Gregory of Nazianzus; and the Peshitta Version of the Prophecy of Isaiah. See Cureton, *Corpus Ignatianum*, xxviii.

10. For a summary of the discussion and repudiation of Cureton's theory, see Lightfoot, *Apostolic Fathers*, 1:272–314.

11. See Brent, *Ignatius of Antioch*, 1–13.

12. Lake, *Apostolic Fathers*, 1:168.

13. So Bisbee, *Pre-Decian Acts*, 133–62.

14. Weijenborg, *Lettres*; Joly, *Dossier*; Rius-Camps, *Four Authentic Letters*; Lechner, *Ignatius*. These works should be read with Schoedel, "Letters of Ignatius."

15. This conclusion is reached largely on the basis of Polycarp, *To the Philippians* 13.2.

16. For Ignatius's dependence on Paul, see the classic article by Bultmann, "Ignatius and Paul"; Koester, *History*, 2:283–91; Schoedel, *Ignatius*, 9–10; Holmes, *Apostolic Fathers*, 174.

17. See "Pathologies of *Passio*," in the introduction.

18. Cave, *Doctrine*, 190.

19. Johanny, "Ignatius of Antioch," 64. For a comparison with contemporary views of suicide, see Tanner, "Martyrdom."

20. Unless otherwise noted, translations of Ignatius and *Mart. Pol.* are taken from Holmes, *Apostolic Fathers*.

21. For a discussion of *devotio*, see chapter 1. The allusion is identified by Heyman, *Power*, 184.

22. On this point, see Goguel, *L'Eucharistie*, 249.

23. Frend argued that the sacrificial language and ideology of martyrdom in Ignatius were derived from Maccabean and other Jewish literature (*Martyrdom*, 199). I follow Heyman in viewing this imagery as an interaction with Roman imperial cult. See Heyman, *Power*, 184–85.

24. Brent, *Imperial Cult,* 210–50.

25. Heyman, *Power,* 185.

26. Brent, *Imperial Cult,* 226–28; and Heyman, *Power,* 184.

27. For *Mart. Pol.* as a turning point in the history of ideas, see Bowersock, *Martyrdom,* 17. For *Mart. Pol.* as the first example of the use of the term *martys* to denote someone who suffers and dies, see the classic study by Brox, *Zeuge;* Strathmann, "Martus"; Baumeister, *Anfänge,* 239–45; and Buschmann, *Martyrium des Polycarp,* 98–107.

28. See, for example, Helen Rhee's statement that two of *Mart. Pol.*'s themes (*imitatio Christi* and athletic heroism) "govern not only this piece but also all the subsequent Martyr Acts" (Rhee, *Early Christian Literature,* 40). See similar statements in Dehandschutter, "Martyrium Polycarpi" and "Martyre de Polycarpe."

29. This analysis is based on a suggestion I made in Moss, *Other Christs,* 196–98, and further developed in Moss, "Dating." I here revise my position on the dates of the tenure of L. Statius Quadratus and the high priest Philip. For an overview of the traditional position on the date of the text, see Hartog, *Polycarp,* 61–73.

30. The textual history of the account cannot be parsed here fully. For a rich discussion of the textual variants, see the section on "Text and Textual Criticism" in Dehandschutter, *Polycarpiana,* 3–42.

31. Von Campenhausen, "Bearbeitungen," 253–301.

32. Barnard, "Defence"; Musurillo, *Acts,* xiv; Barnes, "Pre-Decian *Acta Martyrum,*" 510–11.

33. So Dehandschutter, *Martyrium Polycarpi,* 182–84.

34. Frend, Review of "Bearbeitungen" and *Martyrdom,* 216; Koester, *History,* 2:345–47; Bisbee, *Pre-Decian Acts of Martyrs,* 123. The greatest champion of von Campenhausen's work has been his compatriot Hans Conzelmann, who refined the theory and distilled it down to a single observation: *Mart. Pol.* is a highly redacted text. Conzelmann focuses on the account's opening in which twelve martyrs are mentioned. The disappearance of these companions leads Conzelmann to argue that in its original form the account was a story about twelve Smyrnean martyrs, but that before the fourth century and Eusebius, the text was heavily redacted in order to focus the reader's attention on the illustrious bishop Polycarp.

35. For criticisms of von Campenhausen's use of Eusebius in his interpolation theory, see Barnes, "Pre-Decian *Acta Martyrum*"; Barnard, "Defence"; and Dehandschutter, *Martyrium Polycarpi,* 144–50, 214–15. For a discussion of Eusebius as historian and theologian, see Grant, *Eusebius,* 114–25. While many scholars, Barnard and Dehandschutter especially, have pointed to the theological character of Eusebius's *Hist. eccl.* and the resulting problem for scholars treating him as a church historian, few have approached *Mart. Pol.* with the same degree of skepticism. If Eusebius is suspect for presenting events in light of his own theology, the same dim view should surely be taken of the authors of the martyr acts.

36. So Dehandschutter, *Martyrium Polycarpi,* 175–87; Baumeister, *Anfänge,* 294–95.

37. In the nineteenth century, radical critics Lipsius, Holtzmann, and Keim attempted to dislodge *Mart. Pol.* from its scholarly pedestal but without much success. See Lipsius, "Märtyrertod Polykarps," 200; Holtzmann, "Verhältnis," 187–214; and Keim, *Urchris-*

tentum, 90. The authenticity of the account was first defended by Lightfoot, *Apostolic Fathers,* 1:604–45. He is followed by Barnard, "Defence"; Musurillo, *Acts,* xiii–xv; Holmes, *Apostolic Fathers,* 298; Bowersock, *Martyrdom,* 13; and Ehrman, *Apostolic Fathers,* 1:361.

38. The obscurity of Philomelium in the second century forms part of the basis for Ronchey's later dating in the third century. See Ronchey, *Indagine.* There is an early-third-century inscription that can be assigned to the church in Philomelium. See Ramsay, "Cities," and discussion in Mitchell, *Anatolia,* 2:41. Mitchell cites *Mart. Pol.* as his only other source for the Christian community at Philomelium (*Anatolia,* 2:37).

39. Barnes seems to understate the extraordinary character of the events when he states that this "may be significant" (*Hagiography,* 61). Barnes explains the improbabilities in the trial by arguing that the account is based on an eyewitness account rather than official court documents. This is a reasonable argument that accounts for how courtlike information is contained in a text that does not follow the conventions of an official court report. It does not, however, account for the historical improbabilities and incongruities in the narrative.

40. In the past an additional technical problem for the dating of *Mart. Pol.* was found in the confusion surrounding the terms of office of the high priest and proconsul. According to the appendix to the account (*Mart. Pol.* 21), Philip the Asiarch was the high priest at the time of Polycarp's trial and execution (*Mart. Pol.* 12.2), and L. Statius Quadratus was the proconsul responsible for the trial. In an important publication Barnes argued that the tenures of these figures were fundamentally irreconcilable: Philip the Asiarch served as high priest in 149/150 while "no conceivable argument will put the proconsulate of Statius Quadratus before 153/4" (Barnes, "Note," 436). In his most recent work and on the basis of new evidence, however, Barnes has revised this argument and suggested that Polycarp was martyred on 23 February 157. Barnes, *Hagiography,* 368–73.

41. For literary allusion in martyrdom literature, see Moss, *Other Christs,* 3–17.

42. For lists of parallels, see the critical editions of Bastiaensen and Chiarini, *Atti,* 601–5; and Bihlmeyer, *Apostolischen Väter,* 162. For a discussion of the use of the New Testament in *Mart. Pol.,* see Dehandschutter, "New Testament." For a discussion of the relationship between *Mart. Pol.* and the passion narratives, see Steitz, "Charakter"; Guillaumin, "Marge"; Dehandschutter, *Martyrium Polycarpi,* 241–54; and Moss, *Other Christs,* 56–59. A more thematic analysis is given in Saxer, *Bible,* 27–33. For a less positive take on imitation in the martyrdom accounts, see Lieu, *Image,* 59–63; and Holmes, "Martyrdom," who suggests (correctly) that it is difficult to identify intertexts with precision.

43. Once a basic parallelism is established, other elements of the Polycarp story can be viewed through the mimetic lens. The curious trial and execution of Polycarp in the stadium parallel the very public proclamation of Pilate to the crowd and the unjust and illegal nature of his trial. The proconsul's desire to know Polycarp, his attempts to intimidate and persuade (*Mart. Pol.* 10.1; 11.1–2; Luke 23:20 and John 19:12), and his amazement at Polycarp's attitude (*Mart. Pol.* 12.1; Matt 27:14) all gesture toward the passion narratives. Polycarp's three-part refusal to sacrifice parallels the three separate occasions upon which Jesus is "tried" in gospel narratives. The dove that emerges from

the side of Polycarp can likewise be cast as a mirror image of the baptism of Jesus (see Matt 3:16 and John 1:32).

44. Lightfoot, *Apostolic Fathers,* 1:612–13. He cites a number of examples from Eusebius (*Hist. eccl.* 2.23, 3.32; *On the Martyrs of Palestine* 7), Augustine, *Sermons* 309; and Irenaeus, *Haer.* 3.18.5. Many more such examples could be amassed; see Moss, *Other Christs,* 59–73.

45. Lightfoot, *Apostolic Fathers,* 1:614. Emphasis original.

46. Lightfoot is followed by Barnard, "Defence," 195, and Lake, who remarks of the parallels, "The coincidences are remarkable, but none are in themselves at all improbable" (*Apostolic Fathers,* 2:319).

47. The similarities between Socrates and Polycarp were first noted by Geffcken, "Christlichen Martyrien." These similarities include their age (*Apology* 17D; *Crito* 52E; *Mart. Pol.* 9.3) and nobility (*Phaed.* 58D; *Mart. Pol.* 2.1; 2.2; 2.3; 3.1; 3.2); their refusal to flee to escape prosecution (*Phaed.* 98E–99A; *Mart. Pol.* 7.1); that they were both charged with atheism (*Euthyphro* 3B; *Mart. Pol.* 3.2; 12.2) and refused to persuade others of the veracity of their claims (*Apology* 35D; *Mart. Pol.* 10.2); their prayers before death (*Phaed.* 117C; *Mart. Pol.* 14.1–3); the use of sacrificial terminology to describe their deaths (*Phaed.* 118A; *Mart. Pol.* 14.1); and the exemplary function of their deaths (*Phaed.* 115C; *Mart. Pol.* 1.2; 19.1). For a recent study, see Butterweck, "*Martyriumssucht,*" 8–22. There may well have been an early Christian tradition of assimilating its heroes (Jesus included) to Socrates. See Sterling, "*Mors philosophi.*"

48. For examples of similar remarks in the Nag Hammadi codices, see NHC VI 65:8–14.

49. Epiphanius (*Panarion* 50.1.7–8) attributes the *Acts of Pilate* to the Quartodecimans.

50. See discussion in Maraval, *Lieux saints,* 41–47. The classic example of relic invention is found in Lucian's *Revelatio Sancti Stephani.* Lucian discovers the body of Stephen after being visited three times in a dream by Rabbi Gamaliel, a teacher of the Apostle Paul (Acts 22).

51. Schaff, *History,* 2:82; Lane Fox, *Pagans,* 446; Chiovaro, "Relics," 50. In scholarship on martyrdom, relics often stand as ciphers for the cult of the saints, references to relics being understood as references to the cult of the martyr. In this way, many interpret *Mart. Pol.* 17–18 as the earliest reference to the cult of the saints. See Corbett, "Relics"; Louth, "Hagiography," 358.

52. See Corbett, "Relics," which cites 2 Kgs 2:14, 13:21; Matt 9:20; Acts 5:15, 19:12. The majority of these examples are healing stories in which possession of the remains of a powerful figure brings about the healing of a secondary character. While these examples resonate strongly with the cult of the saints and may certainly be viewed as providing the scriptural foundations for later Christian practices, they should not be treated as if part of the history of relics in the church. That there were instances in which human remains were used for medical purposes before the advent of the Christian era does not mean that Christians always venerated relics.

53. See Réville, *Polycarpus Smyrnae.* In defense of the relics, Saxer argued that the cult of the saints was brought to North Africa from Asia Minor and that the reference to the *dies natales* of the martyrs in *Ac. Scilli.* can be used to date *Mart. Pol.* to earlier than 180 CE, the date assigned to *Ac. Scilli.* Saxer's argument rests on a number of as-

sumptions about the spread and nature of martyrdom. First, his proposed connection between North Africa and Asia Minor is supported by the opening chapter of the *Passio*. In addition to this passage that alludes only to Montanism, not to Asia Minor, there is no discernible link to Asia Minor other than the reasonable (but by no means certain) assumption that Montanists came to Carthage from Asia Minor. We should not conflate the cult of the saints with Montanism. Even if we follow Saxer in thinking that the ideology of martyrdom was exported to Carthage from Asia Minor, why must we assume that this ideology includes the veneration of relics? Can we not view the specific interest in the celebration of the saints evident in Tertullian and the *Passio* as developing in North Africa? There is insufficient evidence to suggest that the cult of the saints moved to Roman North Africa via Asia Minor. Saxer, "L'Authenticité," 992–99.

54. For a discussion of the relics of Thomas in Edessa, see Segal, *Edessa,* 174–76, 250. According to tradition the relics of Thomas were whisked from India to Edessa in the second century by a merchant and subsequently moved from a small church outside the city to the basilica in 394 CE. The story of the translocation of the leg bone may well have been created in the fourth century in order to establish a narrative for the relic's arrival in Edessa. For the date of the *Acts of Thomas,* see Bremmer, *Apocryphal Acts.*

55. Moss, *Other Christs,* 149–72.

56. It is also possible that *Mart. Pol.* 17–18 is a later redaction and the text as a whole is earlier. If this is the case, then it is critical that scholars desist from treating the account as the earliest example of the cult of the saints.

57. Keim, *Urchristentum,* 115.

58. Musurillo, *Acts,* 14; Holmes, *Apostolic Fathers,* 324; Ehrman, *Apostolic Fathers,* 2:390.

59. Lightfoot discards the phrase but writes, "If this reading be retained, the Catholic church in Smyrna is tacitly contrasted with heretical communities in the same city" (*Apostolic Fathers,* 1:622). He insists that even if the phrase is original, this does not mean that the account is directed against Montanists, and he cites a number of "heretical" groups to which the account can be tied.

60. Hübner, "Überlegung," 31–79.

61. A similar argument is made by Dehandschutter, who argues on the basis of scant comments in Irenaeus, *Ap. John,* and the *Testament of Truth* that the "Gnostics" were anti-martyrdom and that consequently, in presenting a view of martyrdom as following God, the author of *Mart. Pol.* is criticizing the Gnostics ("Martyre de Polycarpe," 102–4). He cites Irenaeus, *Haer.* 4.33; *Testament of Truth* 9.3; and the *Apocryphon of John* in general.

62. See, for example, Mark 8:34–36. On martyrdom as a means of following Jesus, see Moss, *Other Christs,* 19–44. For Clement of Alexandria, *Strom.* 4, see discussion in chapter 6.

63. For a critique of these stereotypes, see the discussion in chapter 5 and Brakke, *Gnostics,* 1–27.

64. Holmes, "Martyrdom," 421.

65. For the polemical function of the concept of martyrdom "according to gospel," see Buschmann, *Martyrium Polycarpi,* 321–27; and Buschmann, *Martyrium,* 51.

66. "Voluntary martyrdom" as a scholarly term is fraught with difficulties. For a discussion of its development in secondary literature and the ancient discourse that it is used to represent, see chapter 6.

67. If, as many have argued, *Mart. Pol.* was written in 150–165 CE, Quintus is correctly cited as the first voluntary martyr and *Mart. Pol.*'s disapproval of Quintus as the first condemnation of voluntary martyrdom in the early church; cf. De Ste. Croix, "Voluntary Martyrdom," 157–58. According to De Ste. Croix, the chronological successors to *Mart. Pol.*'s antivoluntary martyrdom position are Clement of Alexandria, *Strom.* 4.4.17.1–3; 4.10.76.1–77.3; 7.11.66.3–67.2; Tertullian, *On the Military Crown* 1.4.4– 5; and Origen, *Commentary on John* 28.23.

68. Calder, "Philadelphia"; Calder, "New Jerusalem"; Grégoire and Orgels, "La veritable date"; von Campenhausen, "Bearbeitungen"; Simonetti, "Alcune osservazioni"; Ronchey, *Indagine*, chaps. 2 and 4.

69. Schwegler, *Montanismus*, 65; Bonwetsch, *Geschichte*, 108; Ermoni, "Crise," 84; Labriolle, *Crise*, 52–54; Kraft, "Altkirchliche Prophetie," 269–70; Frend, *Martyrdom*, 291–92, 361; Barnes, *Tertullian*, 177–78; Cohn, *Pursuit*, 25–27; Knox, *Enthusiasm*, 49; Birley, "Persecutors," 47.

70. In responding to Ronchey's work, a number of scholars have highlighted the disparity between the caricature of Montanists as enthusiastic martyrs present in *Mart. Pol.* and the actual practices and perspectives of the so-called Montanists. This objection is noted by Trout, Review.

71. Tabbernee, "Christian Inscriptions"; Tabbernee, "Early Montanism"; Tabbernee, *Montanist Inscriptions*, 146–50; and Tabbernee, *Fake Prophecy*, 201–42.

72. The word group is used in both Maccabean literature and also in Rev 2:3, but philological historians have seen the use of the term in these texts as primarily legal.

73. See den Boeft and Bremmer, "Notiunculae Martyrologicae IV," 108. Barnes raises the possibility that the phrase is an interpolation into *Mart. Pol.* (*Hagiography*, 377).

74. So Musurillo, *Acts*, xxviii–xxix; Bastiaensen and Chiarini, *Atti*, 150, 154; Dehandschutter, *Martyrium Polycarpi*, 64; and Ameling, "Christian Lapsi."

75. Von Campenhausen, *Idee*, 82–85. The more general scholarly observation that Polycarp, like other martyrs, imitates Christ and other biblical figures was first noted by Egli, *Altchristliche Studien*, 72–74. Victor Saxer follows suit, viewing the perfection of Polycarp's martyrdom according to gospel as part of the redactor's theological program; see his *Bible*, 27–35.

76. According to Holmes, "a gospel-shaped martyrdom is not one that merely recapitulates or imitates events of the passion of Jesus, but rather one that (regardless of whether it parallels any of the events of the passion) reflects a particular approach to (one might even say a theology of) martyrdom: one that reacts rather than initiates (thus permitting the divine will to be accomplished), one that demonstrates the concern for others exemplified by Jesus, and one that is characterized by endurance in the face of trials" ("Martyrdom of Polycarp," 421).

77. The difficulty of ascertaining the precise intertexts for the binding in *Mart. Pol.* poses a challenge for discussions of intertextuality in general and, more specifically, for the artificial differentiation of cultural and textual appropriation. The ambiguity in the

Polycarp story directs us to the blurry line between culture and text. Literary intertexts are no more fixed and solid than cultural intertexts. This blurred line is exposed in the tendency of scholars, myself included, to argue that intertexts and influences were "in the air" rather than held in the hand. Impossible to prove or disprove, the recourse to atmospheric culture is perceived to be a stronger rhetorical posture than literary dependence. This rhetorical slight of hand skims over the diverging commitments to authorial intent and audience response embedded in notions of influence and intertext, respectively. What the recourse to atmospheric intertexts reveals is the impossibility of identifying one intertext to the exclusion of all others.

78. That mutual intertextuality alters the perception of Jesus was an idea I first raised with respect to Stephen in Acts 7 in *Other Christs,* 56.

Chapter 3. Rome

1. Irenaeus, *Haer.* 3.3.2; Minucius Felix, *Octavius* 31.7; Hermas, *Visions* 3, and *Similitudes* 9. For a discussion of Roman Christianity's origins, see Lampe, *From Paul,* 7–11.

2. Acts 23:13–15.

3. So Lampe, who infers from Tacitus, *Ann.* 15.40, that Trastevere was one of the four quarters of Rome spared in the fire (*From Paul,* 47). Lampe goes on to suggest, on the basis of *1 Clem* 5.2, that the "jealousy and envy" of the Jews may have contributed to the mistreatment of Christians. This seems unlikely. There are some methodological problems with using Tacitus as a source for the fire of Rome. The *Annals* date to around 115–120 CE, and the report about the Christians doubtless reflects views of Christians in Tacitus's own period.

4. For a recent study of the interactions between Romans and Christians with respect to Nero, see Cook, *Roman Attitudes,* 105–10.

5. See the section "Socrates" in chapter 1.

6. Young, *In Procession,* 11.

7. Young, *In Procession,* 59.

8. Kelley, "Philosophy."

9. The polarization of apocalypticism and philosophy is largely grounded in their presumed social locations. Following the pioneering work of a cadre of scholars associated with Collins, *Apocalypse,* apocalyptic literature is treated as a product of persecution. The same assumption was made of martyrdom literature until recent studies detached martyrdom from persecution. On the association of martyrdom and apocalyptic literature, see Moss, *Other Christs,* 99–103. The setting of apocalyptic literature within the experience of persecution contrasts with the elite, ethereal intellectual contexts within which philosophy was produced. It is interesting to reflect on how the polarization of apocalyptic literature and philosophy implicitly reproduces the traditional binaries of passion and reason, a binary that is itself derived from Aristotle.

10. See Droge and Tabor, *Noble Death,* 17–52.

11. For centuries Justin enjoyed the double accolade of "martyr and philosopher." From the sixteenth century onward, however, he suffered under a veritable backlash

from scholars who attacked his philosophical pedigree and intellectual capabilities. See, for example, Middleton, *Free Inquiry,* 38. Since the eighteenth century scholars have rehearsed this debate about the quality of Justin's philosophy, and Justin's reputation as philosopher has never fully recovered: the sobriquet "Justin, Martyr and Philosopher" that adorns his tomb in San Lorenzo Fuori Le Mura in Rome has been abbreviated in common parlance to just "Justin Martyr."

12. For a discussion of "popular" or "missionary" philosophy, see Hadot, *Ancient Philosophy,* 38, 177.

13. The information provided by Justin in *Dial.* may not be historically accurate. In presenting himself to his audience, Justin works within the literary conventions of the biography of the philosopher.

14. Nock, *Conversion,* 254–71.

15. The manuscript evidence for Justin's *Apologies* is derived from three texts: *Parsinus graecus* 450, *Phillipicus* 3081, and *Ottobianus graecus* 274. Except where noted, citations of the Greek text and translations of the *Apologies* follow the judgment of Minns and Parvis, *Justin.*

16. For a discussion of the rhetorical program of the apologists and its function in boundary-making, see Edwards et al., eds., *Apologetics;* and Setzer, *Resurrection.*

17. For self-definition in the work of Justin with respect to his self-conceived relationship to both Hellenism and Judaism, see the work of Horner, *"Listening";* Dunn, *Parting;* and Lieu, *Neither Jew nor Greek?* A neat summary of recent research on Justin is provided in Slusser, "Justin Scholarship."

18. It would be an overstatement to say that Justin's use of the "name" topos is purely rhetorical, but we should bear in mind that he is not blandly informative. His contrasting presentation of these two groups of Christians served a valuable rhetorical function. It seems likely that this other group are those heresies he wishes to discard, the disjointed, schismatic clumps he lists in *1 Apol.* 26.

19. De Ste. Croix, "Early Christians," 110.

20. Ando, *Imperial Ideology,* 406–13.

21. So, Lieu, "Constructing."

22. By polarizing these groups of named Christians, Justin sets up a type and an antitype for his Christian audience. The general principle that martyrs served as examples for members of the early church is here made highly specific—their exemplary function is offset against those who profess the name, but profess it incorrectly and superficially. This situation is notably different from that envisioned in *Mart. Pol.* 4, where Quintus the Phrygian recants his beliefs and offers sacrifice. Justin addresses superficiality and ethical conduct directly, but only hints at apostasy.

23. For an assessment of these views, see discussion in Lieu, *Neither Jew nor Greek?,* 135–37.

24. This is not to say that ancient Romans were unaware of the problems associated with false confessions. See Quintilian, *Inst.* 5.4.1; and Crook, *Law,* 274–75.

25. Matthews, *Perfect Martyr,* 100.

26. Parvis, "Justin, Philosopher." For a summary of the various arguments about the composition, genre, and purpose of the *Apologies,* see Minns and Parvis, *Justin,* 25–31.

27. Von Harnack, *Analecta*, 3–5. Grant ("Woman") has gone so far as explicitly to identify not only the Christian teacher as the known Valentinian Ptolemy, but also the woman as Flora. Paul Parvis comments that "one of the somber manifestations of the tendency of scholarship to abhor a vacuum is the assumption that there cannot be two people in the same place at the same time with the same name—even a place as large as Rome" ("Justin," 32). Von Harnack's position still has some support in Lüdemann, *Heretics,* 247 n.107.

28. A number of early Christian narratives, for example the *Acts of Paul and Thecla*, describe how a young woman, having rejected a suitor, is betrayed by her former admirer to the authorities. This theme may be related to a broader theme in ancient novels.

29. See, for example, the summary of Chrysippus's position in Diogenus Laertius: "For our natures are parts of the nature of the universe. Therefore, the goal becomes 'to live consistently with nature,' i.e., according to one's own nature and that of the universe, doing nothing which is forbidden by the common law, which is right reason, penetrating all things, being the same as Zeus who is the leader of the administration of things" (*Lives* 7.88). The only instance in which the law of nature and the law of the nations are in conflict is slavery. Roman jurisprudence maintained that slavery was not according to nature but according to (Stoic notions of) fate. See Harrill, *Slaves,* 21.

30. Minns and Parvis, *Justin,* 277 n.5.

31. Tatian was familiar with the writings of Justin and utilized them in *Against the Greeks*. For Justin's influence on apologetics in general, see Parvis, "Justin Martyr."

32. The separation of the manuscript evidence of *Ac. Justin* into three recensions is discussed in de' Cavalieri, "Atti"; Burkitt, "Oldest Manuscript"; Lazzati, "Atti"; Lazzati, *Sviluppi;* Bisbee, "Acts"; and Bisbee, *Pre-Decian Acts*. The precise relationships of the three recensions, and in particular of recensions A and B, are particularly complex, as there are few theological clues to aid their dating. Employing the traditional text-critical premise that brevity indicates priority, Lazzati concludes that their relative chronology follows the expected A-B-C pattern. The absolute dating of the texts is more difficult. Lazzati dates recension A to a period of peace before the end of the persecution of Christians under Roman rule; recension B he views as a fourth-century reworking of A; and recension C he deems considerably later, perhaps even fifth century (*Sviluppi,* 119). In his collection of Christian martyrdoms, Musurillo is unwilling to commit to a particular view of the relationship between recensions A and B but nevertheless concludes that "it would seem more likely that the middle version does indeed derive from the tradition of the shorter one" (*Acts,* xviii). A central part of the debate concerning this relationship between recensions A and B is the presupposed connection to the *commentarius* of the trial of Justin. There is ample evidence to indicate that *commentarii* were available in various forms to the broader public in the Roman period, so it is plausible that these documents were preserved in early Christian communities as part of a cult of martyrs. For the classic analysis of the availability and use of *commentarii*, see Coles, *Reports*. To this evidence can be added the preservation, in recension A, of a seemingly authentic "judgment," or *krisis*. Rusticus sentences the Christians saying, "Let those who have refused to sacrifice to the gods be scourged and beheaded [ἀπαχθήτωσαν] in accordance with the laws." According to Barnes, the Greek term used

here, ἀπαχθήτωσαν, is a literal translation of the Latin term *ducantur,* which denoted being led out for execution (cf. Pliny, *Ep.* 10.96.3; Barnes, *Early Christian Hagiography,* 63–64). Presumably, a helpful Roman Christian had translated *ducantur* from a copy of the official court documents for his or her Greek-speaking audience. It is important to note the verbal parallel to the sentencing of Ptolemaeus at 2 *Apol.* 2.15 (κελεύσαντος αὐτὸν ἀπαχθῆναι), for the use of the same term in both accounts may suggest that one text is emulating the other. We should not automatically conclude that *Ac. Justin* is based on a court document. While *Ac. Justin* does follow the general framework of the *commentarii* (*caput, oratio recta,* and *krisis*), there are numerous specific details that are not included in the text (Bisbee, *Pre-Decian Acts,* 95–117). The recensions of *Ac. Justin* lack the rigid formal characteristics that appear so consistently within the *commentarii* form, so it is preferable to view even the two earliest recensions as texts that utilized *commentarii,* rather than as *commentarii* in themselves. Bisbee has tentatively alluded to the possibility that B used a prototypical *commentarius* rather than A (*Pre-Decian Acts,* 117). As he acknowledges, though, unless an earlier date can be ascribed to one of B's readings, we must consider B to be a reworking of A. That B refers to an imperial edict which specifies sacrifice to the gods (B 5.8) may suggest that it was composed after 250 CE and the emperor Decius's edict that all members of the empire sacrifice before the magistrate.

33. Codex Parisinus graecus 1470 (ca. 890 CE).

34. Codex Cantabrigiensis add. 4489 (eighth/ninth century), codex Hierosolymitanus sancti Sepulchri 6 (ninth/tenth century), codex Vaticanus graecus 1667 (tenth century) and its copy Vaticanus graecus 655 (sixteenth century).

35. Codex Hierosolymitanus sancti Sepulchri 17 (twelfth century), codex Vaticanus graecus 1991 (thirteenth century).

36. Marcus Aurelius, *Med.* 1.15 (trans. George Long).

37. Bisbee's analysis of the form of the creedal statements in A and B and the prologues of the texts leads him to conclude that both recensions reached their final form in the mid to late third century (*Pre-Decian Acts,* 117).

38. Emphasis my own.

39. In the Hellenistic-Roman period popular conceptions of piety referred primarily to the worship of the gods but still carried undertones of the proper respect for the established orders or political and social spheres. Thus *pietas,* the Roman equivalent of εὐσέβεια, was used to denote the proper respect for ancestors, women for men, slaves for masters, and perhaps even the legions for the emperor himself. The centrality of *pietas* to imperial ideology can be seen on the coinage of Augustus and his successors, which bears the legend PIETAS referring to the pietas of the emperor. During this period *pietas* was located most firmly within religious spheres but was still based on the familial model contained in the image of Aeneas bearing his father on his shoulders from Troy.

40. Frend, *Martyrdom,* 255. See also Lieu, *Neither Jew nor Greek,* 64; Rhee, *Early Christian Literature,* 88–89; and Gruen, "Greek Pistis." For the standard discussion of the *mos maiorum,* see Wilken, *Christians,* 48–67.

41. We should note that in recension B the language of εὐσέβεια comes into play only with reference to the question of sacrifice to idols. In B 1.1 it is not the Romans them-

selves who are called "impious" but their decrees. Likewise, in B 2.1–2 Rusticus equates impiety with the refusal to sacrifice, and in B 5.4 Justin himself draws the same analogy by likening sacrifice to idols as a turn from piety to impiety. The Romans are implicated in these denunciations and called wicked champions of idolatry, but their wickedness is linked to their defense of idolatry, not a Satanic influence, *pace* Bisbee, who argues that the magistrate is "Satan's puppet" (*Pre-Decian Acts,* 105). Satan is only introduced in recension C where there is a sharp escalation in anti-Roman language and thought. Bisbee's argument that the magistrate is an instrument of Satan is undermined by the reading of the text in the epitome in the Cambridge codex. The epitome does not mention Satan despite the epitomist's obvious interest in demonic activity (cf. the epitome to the account of Theophanes and Pansemne, which begins by linking impiety with Satan). For the text of the epitome, see Burkitt, "Oldest Manuscript," 64.

42. Frend, *Martyrdom,* 254–56.

43. See Diogenes Laertius, *Lives* 9.26–28, 58–59. This understanding of Justin is clearly reinforced in the epitome of the Cambridge codex where he is portrayed at his trial as an aged philosopher (see Burkitt, "Oldest Manuscript," 64). This interpretation of Justin, however, could have been gleaned from other sources such as Eusebius.

44. Bisbee, *Pre-Decian Acts,* 105.

45. See, for example, *Acta minora* 5.9: "Proconsul ad Perpetuam dixit: 'Quid dicis, Perpetua? Sacrificas?' Perpetua respondit: 'Christiana sum, et nominis mei sequor auctoritatem, ut sim perpetua.'" *Acta minora* in *Passio Sanctarum Perpetuae et Felicitatis* (ed. C. I. M. I. Van Beek), 66.

46. Brown, *Making,* 56.

47. Musurillo, *Acts,* 47.

48. A textual variant in the Cambridge codex and Vatican manuscript reads ἐκπληρώσεως. See Burkitt, "Oldest Manuscript," 65.

49. Apocalyptic scenes of destruction and renewal appear in 1 Thess 1:10; 4:13–5:10; Rom 8:18–25; Mark 13:24–31; 2 Pet 3:5–7; and Rev 6:13–14. For an overview of the arguments for Stoic backgrounds to 2 Peter, see Harrill's survey of the diverse Stoic views of the conflagration, "Stoic Conflagration Physics."

50. Harrill, "Stoic Conflagration Physics."

51. On Paul as martyr, see Tajra, *Martyrdom,* 166–97.

52. See discussion in Moss, *Other Christs,* 39–40.

53. For a discussion of the date of *Mart. Paul,* see Klauck, *Apocryphal Apostles,* 48–50; and Snyder, "Remembering," 60–64.

54. Another interpretation might suggest that Paul is otherworldly. The comical tree people in Lucian are described as (among other things) bald and sweating milk (Lucian, *A True Story* 23–24).

55. While martyrdom accounts in the apocryphal acts are often inappropriately excluded from discussions of martyrdom, *Mart. Paul* has been the subject of a number of recent studies seeking to position Paul among the other early Christian martyrs. See Eastman, *Paul,* 1–70; and Snyder, "Remembering."

56. In describing the death of Jesus in Luke as philosophical, I follow here Sterling, "*Mors philosophi.*" The assessment of Jesus's death as that of a "martyr," first espoused by Dibelius, seems to me to be a retrospective assessment that uses a modern notion of

martyrdom that presumes the existence of the category before the advent of Christianity. For the latter view, see Ehrman, *New Testament,* 133–34.

57. Parvis, "Justin Martyr."

Chapter 4. Gaul

1. *CIL* 13.1942; 13.1945. Lyons was also connected to Italy by the military road.

2. Frend cites an inscription from Marseilles that refers to the possible martyrdom of Volusianus, son of Eutyches (*Martyrdom,* 5). See also Fliche, "Origines chrétiennes," 166.

3. Leclercq, "Lyon."

4. So Frend, *Martyrdom,* 422 n.3.

5. See discussion in Eastman, *Paul,* 124–28.

6. For a discussion of the Phrygian presence in Gaul, see Wuilleumier, *Lyon,* 50–55. Inscriptional evidence suggesting ties between Asia Minor and Gaul includes *CIL* 13.2005; 13.2022; 13.2448. For a summary of the evidence for Phrygian Christians in Gaul, see Tabbernee, *Fake Prophecy,* 29; and Trevett, *Montanism,* 26–27. For a discussion of trade routes in Gaul, see Charlesworth, *Trade-Routes,* 201–2; Hackett, *Roman Gaul,* 120–60; and Chevallier, "Gallia Lugundumensis," 912–39. For the importance of shipping routes in the spread of Christianity to Gaul, see Milner and Milner, *History,* 3:195; Turcan, *Religions,* 90; and Frend, *Martyrdom,* 4–5. For a critique of this general theory, see Pietri, "Origines."

7. Simpson, *Epitome,* 73.

8. So Keresztes, "Massacre," 78–79; and Griffe, *Gaule chrétienne,* 1:19–27.

9. Phipps, "Persecution," 182–83.

10. See Frend, *Martyrdom,* 2–4. The full list of martyrs' names is given only in the early fifth-century *Martyrology of Jerome* and the later ninth-century *Martyrology of Ado.* It is noteworthy that this particular list does not survive in a precise form in texts from Gaul itself.

11. Although it is tempting to refer to this kind of community as an ecclesiastical diocese, the application of such formal terminology would be anachronistic in a period for which there is little evidence. The absence of individual bishops from the records says more about the lack of evidence for Christianity in Gaul than about the nature of central organization.

12. For the essentially Asiatic character of Christianity in Gaul, see Bauer, *Orthodoxy,* 208; and Koester, *History,* 2:10.

13. For the date, see Grant, "Eusebius"; and Barnes, *Hagiography,* 61. Barnes notes that there is no reason to assume that Eusebius knows the precise year for the date and that the events may have taken place even after the death of Marcus Aurelius in 180 CE.

14. Correspondence in the name of groups is itself unusual. Although there are letters addressed to and received from voluntary associations—Greco-Roman social groups frequently compared to early Christian churches—this correspondence is normally composed by the founders or patrons of the group; see *P. Enteuxeis* 20; 21; *P. Karanis* 575; and *P. Rainer* V 23. For a comparison of the literary production of early Christians and voluntary associations, see Ascough, *Paul's Macedonian Associations,* 108–9. The

use of this particular epistolary form begins with *1 Clement* and *Mart. Pol.* The epistolary shaping of *Lyons* in this way, however, does not indicate literary dependence on *Mart. Pol.* as the similarities may be accentuated by Eusebius. *Pace* Buschmann, *Martyrium*, 73–76; and Dehandschutter, *Martyrium*, 157–75.

15. For a discussion of Eusebius's use of sources, see Barnes, "Eusebius," 139.

16. PG 119, 536C–D.

17. Nautin, *Lettres*, 54–61, 93–95; Rousseau, *Irénée de Lyon*, 1:258–61. Nautin has been followed by Steenberg, *Irenaeus*, 10 n.24. It is a notable feature of scholarship on *Lyons* that those scholars whose primary focus is on Irenaeus argue for Irenaean authorship while those whose interests lie with martyrs and Eusebius tend to argue for independence and (sometimes) redaction. For the latter position, see Deferrari, *Eusebius*, 273 n.3.

18. That Vienne ranks before the more important Lyons, the capital of Gaul, has led some to suggest that Vienne was the location for the composition of the letter, an interpretation that avoids attributing any symbolic or theological importance to ranking. As we will see, though, throughout the account those individuals of lower social status are elevated above their social superiors. The positioning of Vienne ahead of Lyons likewise reflects the letter's thematic interest in the reversal of social roles.

19. For a discussion of the specific points of contact, see Nautin, *Lettres*, 56–59.

20. Barnes, for instance, argues that Irenaeus brought a copy of *Mart. Pol.* with him from Asia Minor (*Hagiography*, 62). For the lack of evidence for a literary relationship between *Lyons* and *Mart. Pol.*, see Moss, "Polycarphilia."

21. Eusebius writes: "Why should we transcribe the catalogue of the witnesses given in the letter already mentioned, of whom some were beheaded, others cast to the wild beasts, and others fell asleep in prison, or give the number of confessors still surviving at that time? For whoever desires can readily find the full account by consulting the letter itself, which, as I have said, is recorded in our Collection of Martyrdoms. Such were the events which happened under Antoninus" (*Hist. eccl.* 5.4.3).

22. *Pace* Dehandschutter, "Community," 6. The discussion of the martyrs and confessors, in particular, suggests a third-century setting. See discussion in Ruysschaert, "'Martyrs.'" For the hypothesis that 5.2–3 were written or interpolated in the third century, see Thompson, "Alleged Persecution," who argues that the entire text was composed in the third century; Drobner, who places 5.2.1–8 during the Confessors Controversy (*Lehrbuch*, 139); and Löhr, whose seminal argument on redaction in the letter emphasizes the interpolation of secondary additions into the account ("Brief," 139–40).

23. On anti-Montanist attitudes in this account, see Löhr, "Brief"; and Carriker, *Library*, 255.

24. It is likely, as Winrich Löhr has argued, that the *Letter* is a redacted account that was composed in multiple stages ("Brief"). Löhr's treatment offers the best source critical analysis of the account, but he is sometimes (understandably) reluctant to come down firmly on whether certain passages (e.g., 5.3) are secondary additions. A less convincing objection to a second-century dating emerges out of the letter's description of the church as "virgin mother." As the martyrs awaited their fate in prison, they apparently used their time to encourage their fellow Christians, both faithful and apostate: "But the intervening time was not wasted nor fruitless to them; for by their patience the

measureless compassion of Christ was manifested. For through their continued life the dead were made alive, and the witnesses showed favor to those who had failed to witness. And the virgin mother had much joy in receiving alive those whom she had brought forth as dead" (*Lyons* 5.1.45). Musurillo has put forward the argument that the image of the church as virgin mother was adopted from the late-third-century Methodius of Olympus's *Symposium* 3.8 (*Méthode,* 69–71). This image is not restricted to this verse and is well integrated into the account; it is not, therefore, an interpolation. Maternal imagery and notions of confession as birth and rebirth permeate the account of martyrs, lapsed Christians, and the heroic Blandina. The relationship between the *Letter* and Methodius is somewhat unclear. Methodius may be expanding upon and systematizing a concept nascent in the earlier martyrdom account. If, though, as Musurillo has argued, the image of the virgin mother is borrowed from Methodius, then we need to consider the possibility that the account as a whole dates to considerably later than the events it purports to have witnessed.

25. A number of theories have been advanced to explain the sudden outbreak of violence described in the letter. Oliver and Palmer ("Minutes") argued that the issuing of the *senatus consultum* (ca. 177), which allowed the provinces to obtain gladiators at little cost, and the granting of extra privileges to the Tres Galliae, which enabled local authorities to acquire condemned criminals for use as gladiators, prompted the outbreak at Lyons. They have been followed by Keresztes, "Massacre"; and Keresztes, "Marcus Aurelius," 337. The primary difficulty with this theory is that it does not fit well with the letter's depiction of events, according to which the Christians are arrested as the result of a popular uprising. To suggest that at the root of the persecution was the potential economic benefit of using condemned Christians posits great foresight and fiscal pragmatism on the part of the unruly mob.

26. Frend's contention that the *legatus* was acting against Trajan's directive to Pliny is ill-posed. The Pliny-Trajan correspondence was not binding, and the *legatus* acted out of his *cognitio extra ordinem* (*Martyrdom,* 6–9).

27. Wagemakers, "Incest."

28. For accusations of human sacrifice and cannibalism being used to discredit an enemy, see McGowan, "Eating People"; and Rives, "Accusations."

29. On spectacle in early Christian literature, see Frilingos, *Spectacles,* who provides a wonderful entrée into spectacles in the ancient world and the function of ekphrastic scenes in Revelation. On spectacle in ancient art see Bergmann and Kondoleon, *Art.*

30. Burrus, "Torture"; Cooper, "Voice," 152–53; duBois, *Torture,* 35–38, 47–68; Grig, "Torture and Truth"; and Harrill, "Domestic Enemy," 248.

31. In her influential study of pain, Scarry demonstrates that for the tortured, all that exists is pain; pain is reality (*Body,* 142–43).

32. So Cooper, "Voice," 153, who notes that in the Roman legal system, torture and truth were associated with one another by the theory of *basanos.*

33. For analogies between martyrdom and illness, see Augustine, *Sermons* 328.8 (PLS 2.801).

34. A similar phenomenon is at work in the *Passio,* in which Felicitas states that when she suffers in the arena, Christ will suffer with her (*Passio* 15.6). Both accounts may rely on Pauline understandings of Christ inhabiting the bodies of Christians.

35. The subtle distinction between pain and suffering is overlooked by Perkins in *Suffering Self*. In modern theological discourse, in which positive views of suffering are eyed with suspicion, there is occasionally a demarcation between suffering and pain that seeks to retrieve the latter as something of value. In a groundbreaking essay the poet Audre Lorde writes: "There is a distinction I am beginning to make in my living between pain and suffering. Pain is an event, an experience that must be recognized, named, and then used in some way in order for the experience to change, to be transformed into something else, strength or knowledge or action. Suffering, on the other hand, is the nightmare reliving of unscrutinized and unmetabolized pain. When I live through pain without recognizing it, self-consciously, I rob myself of the power that can come from using that pain, the power to fuel some movement beyond it. I condemn myself to reliving that pain over and over and over whenever something close triggers it. And that is suffering, a seemingly inescapable cycle" ("Eye to Eye," 159).

36. On bodily resistance, see Brown, *Body*, 12; and Shaw, "Body/Power/Identity," 273.

37. For a discussion of biblical echoes in this account, see Dehandschutter, "Community," 16–18; Moss, *Other Christs*, 62.

38. The points of contact between Maccabean literature and the *Letter* were first discussed at length by Perler, "Vierte Makkabäerbuch."

39. See Moss, "Blood Ties."

40. For discussion of Blandina, see Perkins, *Suffering Self*, 113–15; Burrus, *Saving Shame*, 23–28; Cobb, *Dying*, 113–17; and Streete, *Redeemed Bodies*, 15–16.

41. Harrill, "Domestic Enemy," 250. See Harrill, *Slaves*, 159–63.

42. So Bremmer, "Magic," 49 n.48.

43. Moss, *Other Christs*, 62.

44. An example of this general involvement is the statement that "the jailers [were] aroused and filled with the Devil" (*Lyons* 5.1.27).

45. The same idea of paradigmatic conduct is used in 1 Tim 1:16 and 2 Tim 1:13. Here pseudo-Paul proposes the apostle as a pattern for those seeking eternal life. In this instance, however, the virtues are patience, faith, and love. The idea of fearlessness in the love of the Father is more reminiscent of the argument of John 16:33, where courage and Christ's triumph are similarly linked, particularly in light of the frequent allusions to John throughout the *Letter*.

46. See discussion in Burrus, *Saving Shame*, 23–28; Cobb, *Dying*, 114; and Moss, *Other Christs*, 92.

47. For a comprehensive discussion of this text, see Lallemand, "Parfum." For a survey of scent in martyrdom literature in general, see Evans, "Scent."

48. Harvey, *Scenting Salvation*, 46–48.

49. The notion that scent is exhaled is present in antiquity (see the breathing trees in 1 Enoch 29:2).

50. That the letter uses *presbuteros* and not *episkopos* is not a guarantee of either the text's early date or its authenticity. Later in *Hist. eccl.* Eusebius again uses *presbuteros* to refer to Irenaeus (5.8.1).

51. Given the paucity of evidence for Ignatius's *Epistle to the Romans*, this should not be considered a clear-cut reference to Ignatius's letter.

52. That Irenaeus was born in Asia Minor and was influenced by his upbringing and education there cannot be contested, but this does not mean that he was not influenced by his experiences in Rome or Gaul or that he did not develop his own interpretations. The notion of a homogenous form of Christianity called Asiatic Christianity is highly problematic. The designation of Irenaeus as the "heir" of Johannine Asian Christianity exemplifies the implicit model of genealogy and inheritance (so Farrer, *Rebirth,* 30) and is even more difficult as it utilizes biological models of inheritance and purity to make its claim.

53. For an excellent and unique survey of the material relating to Stephen, see Bovon, "Dossier." Bovon's survey tends to focus on explicit citations rather than allusions. To his survey, with respect to the committal of the spirit (Luke 23:46; Acts 7:59–60) in the third and fourth centuries, we can add a handful of Latin martyrdom accounts: *Acts of Carpus* Latin 4.6; *Acts of Julius* 4.4; and *Martyrdom of Montanus and Lucius* 14.9.

54. Von Winterfeld, "Revelatio sancti Stephani," cited in Bovon, "Dossier," 282.

55. So Bovon, "Dossier," 288.

Chapter 5. Roman North Africa

1. For histories and studies of provincial Africa, see Birot and Dresch, *La Méditerranée;* Decret and Fantar, *L'Afrique du nord;* Despois and Raynal, *Géographie;* Février, *Approches;* Julien, *Histoire;* Charles-Picard, *Civilisation;* and Romanelli, *Storia.* For a bibliography of works on ancient Africa, see the most recent edition of the *Bibliographie analytique de l'Afrique antique.*

2. The history of North African Christianity as a specialized subject goes back to Münter's *Religion der Karthager,* which posited Roman origins for the church. He argued that fugitives of Nero's persecution brought Christianity to Carthage in the 60s CE. Von Harnack subsequently presented a speculative argument for the Jewish origins of the church in North Africa, against which Monceaux and Leclercq argued that disciples of the apostles had come from North Africa and that there was no knowledge of an early Italian mission from Rome. Important contributions on the Jewish origins of Christianity in Carthage include Delattre, *Gamart,* and Monceaux, "Colonies."

3. See Champlin, *Fronto and Antonine Rome,* 64–66.

4. It is by no means certain that the baker's wife is a Christian; she could be a Jewish proselyte. There is nothing distinctively Christian about the beliefs ascribed to her. See Benko, "Pagan Criticism," 1090–92. For the traditional view, see Schmidt, "Reaktionen."

5. *Pace* Decret, *Early Christianity,* who uses this evidence to suggest that there was probably a church in Carthage before the end of the first century (11). We can sympathize with his intentions, but it is impossible to assert a specific date merely on the basis that it makes sense for Christianity to have arrived in Carthage and spread south. There was a church before 150 CE, but we cannot assert a specific date with any certainty.

6. See Salisbury, *Perpetua's Passion,* 49–57.

7. On the archaeological evidence, see Stager and Wolff, "Child Sacrifice."

8. Diodorus Siculus, *Library* 20.14. See discussion of sources in Salisbury, *Perpetua's Passion,* 49–57.

9. Raven, *Rome,* 154; Bomgardner, *Story,* 142.

10. Newman, *Callista*, 150.

11. Wilhite, *Tertullian*, 1–37.

12. For the ways in which child sacrifice has been reified, imagined, and theorized by scholars of religion, see Frankfurter, *Evil Incarnate*, 123–24.

13. It is tempting to designate the setting of the trial as private, as if the martyrs were tried in secret away from the eyes of the ubiquitous and amorphous "people," who sometimes appear as the audience in the acts of the martyrs. This categorization projects, however, modern notions of public/private onto ancient space. For a discussion of visibility in the construction of Roman houses and the importance of delineating ancient Roman social spaces correctly, see Cooper, "Closely Watched Households."

14. Musurillo, *Acts*, xxii–xxiii.

15. Bastiaensen and Chiarini's extended commentary on the *Acts of the Scillitan Martyrs* is an exception to this rule (*Atti*, 405–9).

16. The phrase could equally be rendered as "books, that is, letters of Paul." My translation follows Gamble, *Books*, 150–51, in which he compares this passage to 2 *Clement* 14.2. An alternative translation, suggested by Bastiaensen and Chiarini, reads "books of epistles" of Paul (*Atti*, 140).

17. See, for example, discussion in Metzger, *Canon*, 156–57.

18. Von Harnack, "Alter," 337. Bonner argues that the books are gospels ("Scillitan Saints," 144–45). For the argument that the *libri* must be scrolls because they are held in a *capsa* (usually translated as a scroll container), see Gamble, *Books*, 81, 150–51. For the suggestion that the *capsa* is a scroll satchel, see Knust, "Latin Versions." Statistical evidence for the use of scrolls and codices during the late second century suggests that *libri* were more likely to be codices. See Roberts and Skeat, *Birth*, 38–44. Scholarship on the transition to the use of the codex is vast and has not produced a general consensus. See also Gamble, "Pauline Corpus"; Harris, "Codex"; Resnick, "Codex"; Haines-Eitzen, *Guardians*; and the recent reappraisal of the statistical evidence for the spread of the codex in Bagnall, *Early Christian Books*, 70–90.

19. Baronius's edition reads: "Quatuor Euangelia Domini nostri Iesu Christi et Epistolas sancti Pauli apostoli et omnem divinitus inspiratam Scripturam" (*Ex Annalibus Ecclesiasticis Baronii*, Ad annum 202). Bastiaensen and Chiarini have argued that the Latin of the short edition should be understood as *libri epistularum* ("books of the epistles") (*Atti*, 410). This reading lacks convincing manuscript support and seems to overlook the textual rub this phrase presented for later readers.

20. Eastman, *Paul*. Eastman follows Bastiaensen and Chiarini's reading; I have altered the chiasmus to reflect my own judgment.

21. Musurillo's translation here has been emended to follow the suggestion of Den Boeft and Bremmer, "Notiunculae Martyrologicae," 46–47.

22. Von Harnack takes this passage as the foundation of his assertion that Christianity prospered "by the power of its simplicity" (*Mission and Expansion*, 1:85). The simplicity seems to me to be at once a rhetorical claim and a reference to baptism, not a commentary on the ontological character of simplicity.

23. So Den Boeft and Bremmer, "Notiunculae Martyrologicae," 45–46, who follow Hiltbrunner, *Latina Graeca*, 15–105. This interest in simplicity is mirrored in Tertullian, *To the Nations* 2.2.5; *Apol.* 23.7, 47.4.

24. See Dominik, *Roman Eloquence.* For a discussion of Roman criticisms of superstition, see Martin, *Inventing Superstition,* 128–29. The connection of superstition with excess is implicit in Pliny's *Natural History* where the burning of expensive incense is condemned as *superstitio* (22.56.118).

25. The observation that martyrs go directly to heaven at their death was first made by Edward Gibbon in his monumental *History of the Decline and Fall of the Roman Empire* where he cited the postmortem expectations of the martyred death as one of the reasons for Christianity's success (chapter 15). Gibbon has been followed by many. For a recent discussion of the afterlife in North African martyrdom literature, see Bremmer, "Contextualizing Heaven." For the afterlife in general, see Segal, *Life After Death.*

26. See the discussion of postmortem judgment in Moss, *Other Christs,* 142–45.

27. Textually, there are a number of solutions. Musurillo argues that the list in *Ac. Scilli.* 1, which gives the names only of the main six martyrs, has been accidentally abridged (*Acts,* 87).

28. On the date of the martyrdom, see van Beek, *Passio sanctarum,* 162–66. The Greek version of the *Passio* and the *Acta minora* both state that the martyrs were arrested in Thurburbo Minus, a city roughly thirty-six miles to the west of Carthage, a reading favored by van Beek, *Passio sanctarum,* 3–4; Salisbury, *Perpetua's Passion,* 44–45; and Amat, *Passion,* 22–23. Scholars who reject the tradition include Robinson, *Passion,* 22–26; and Delehaye, *Passions,* 53. The salient point is that there are two separate literary traditions that are no doubt connected to local cultic interest in these saints. The conflicting literary traditions represent competing claims to ownership of and access to the saints. On the social status of the group, see Amat, *Passion,* 34–37; and den Boeft and Bremmer, "Notiunculae Martyrologicae VI," 52–55.

29. Following the discovery of a Latin manuscript of *Ac. Scilli.* in the British Museum (BM 11880) by Robinson, the majority of scholars have asserted the priority of the Latin version. For a discussion of the manuscripts and the various arguments for Latin priority, see the summary in Robinson, *Passion,* 106–11. The priority of the Latin version was established (to my mind concretely) by de' Cavalieri, *Scritti agiografici,* 1:41–155. Latin priority is assumed by most scholars, with the exception of Robert, "Visione." See also Fridh, *Problème;* Bastiaensen and Chiarini, "Perpetua"; and Amat, *Passion,* 51–66. For an excellent overview of the textual issues, see Bremmer and Formisano, "Perpetua's Passions."

30. *De anim.* itself is preserved only in one extant manuscript, the ninth-century codex Agobardinus (Parinius Latinus 1622), a collection of Tertullian's works. The text is assumed to be a sequel to the lost *De censu animae,* but the table of contents where the missing text is noted may simply be inaccurate.

31. Latin text: Quomodo Perpetua, fortissima martyr, sub die passionis in reuelatione paradisi solos illic martyras uidit, nisi quia nullis romphaea paradisi ianitrix cedit nisi qui in Christo decesserint, non in Adam?

32. See Joshel, "Nurturing"; Bradley, "Wet-Nursing"; and Bradley, "Social Role."

33. Cooper, "A Father, a Daughter and a Procurator." I am grateful to Kate for generously allowing me to read and cite her paper.

34. To this, Heffernan has added the argument that Augustine himself doubted the authenticity of the *Passion* ("Philology"). This argument has been largely refuted by

Dolbeau, *Revue*, 312–13. Dolbeau is followed by den Boeft and Bremmer, "Notiunculae Martyrologicae VI," 56–57, who note that nothing in *Passio* 2.3 warrants the conclusion that Augustine doubts the authenticity of the diary.

35. See discussion in Bremmer and Formisano, "Perpetua's Passions."

36. On the background and piety of Hilarianus, see Rives, "Piety."

37. See Dodds, *Pagans*, 47–52; Amat, "L'Authenticité"; and Barnes, *Tertullian*, 263.

38. Bremmer, "Perpetua." For discussion of the way in which women's stories in particular evaporate from early Christian history, see Clark, "Lady"; and Clark, "Women."
Even if we were to be convinced that Perpetua's diary was truly written by her own
hand, we would still do well to be mindful of Miles's observation (*Image*) that religious
symbols used by historical women were not created by women themselves.

39. Translations of the *Passio* are adapted from Farell and Williams, "Passion."

40. Wypustek, "Magic"; Butler, "*New Prophecy.*"

41. Epiphanius, *Panarion/Adversus Haeresis* 49.1.1. It is worth noting that no other
document linked cheese and Montanism until Epiphanius. At the same time, the fact
that the *Acts of Perpetua* altered *caseo* (cheese) to *fructu lactis* (fruit of milk) suggests
that the term "cheese" may have had negative connotations and that the redactor altered the text to eliminate any possible association with Montanism. See discussion in
Butler, "*New Prophecy,*" 94–95.

42. Steinhauser ("Augustine's Reading") has argued that Augustine was aware that
the *Passio* has a Montanist flavor, an intriguing suggestion because it implies that Augustine was unperturbed by this distinction and instead focused his energies on what he
perceived as the more threatening ecclesiastical elements.

43. See, for example, Balling, "Martyrdom"; Frankfurter, "Legacy," 137–38.

44. Frankfurter, "Early Christian Apocalypticism," 436. In this particular survey of
apocalyptic literature, Frankfurter uses the *Passio* to generalize about martyrdom literature.

45. Collins describes the apocalypse as "a genre of revelatory literature with a narrative framework, in which a revelation is mediated by an otherworldly being to a human
recipient, disclosing a transcendent reality which is both temporal, insofar as it envis-
ages eschatological salvation, and spatial insofar as it involves another, supernatural
world" (*Apocalyptic Imagination*, 4–5). *Semeia* 14, which Collins edited, lists a number
of thematic interests, including cosmogony, primordial events, recollection of the past,
ex eventu prophecy, persecution, other eschatological upheavals, judgment/destruction
of the wicked, judgment/destruction of the world, judgment/destruction of otherworldly
beings, cosmic transformation, resurrection, and other forms of afterlife. See Collins,
Apocalypse, 28.

46. For an analysis of the visionary material, see Miller, *Dreams*, 152–83; and Bremmer, "Perpetua and Her Diary." Tertullian treated the dream as evidence that only martyrs go to heaven (*De anim.* 55.5), while Augustine noted the motif of heavenly ascent
(*Sermons* 280–82). Perpetua's visions rehearse the cosmic battle of Revelation and ancient near eastern mythology. On the roots of apocalyptic literature in ancient near
eastern myth, see Clifford, "Roots."

47. Dronke, *Women Writers*, 6–7, cited in Miller, *Dreams*, 154.

48. On the function of *ekphrasis* in antiquity, see *Classical Philology* 102.3 (2007).

49. Pfitzner, *Paul,* 92–93; Rhee, *Early Christian Literature,* 92–93; Seesengood, *Competing Identities.* Seesengood argues that before the application of athletic imagery to Perpetua, the figure of the athlete was already a hybrid one.

50. For recent studies of the amphitheater and gladiatorial combat, see Welch, *Roman Amphitheatre;* Edwards, *Death;* Edmondson, "Dynamic Arenas"; Gunderson, "Flavian Amphitheatre"; Gunderson, "Ideology"; Köhne and Ewigleben, eds., *Gladiators;* Barton, *Sorrows;* Barton, "Scandal"; Futrell, *Blood;* Brown, "Death"; Kyle, *Spectacles;* and Barton, "Savage Miracles."

51. Val. Max. 2.4.7, Livy 23.20.

52. Augustus notes the number of celebrations held in honor of his own household in *Res gestae* 22.1. The decline in the offering of *munera* is discussed by Ville, *Gladiature,* 99–106, 116–21, 129–55.

53. Clark, "Bodies," 102.

54. On these staged executions, see Coleman, "Fatal Charades."

55. *Sic et ego aliud me dicere non possum nisi quod sum, Christiana.*

56. Burrus, *Saving Shame,* 30–32.

57. Burrus, *Saving Shame,* 31. For a discussion of the voyeuristic gaze in the *Passio,* see now Frankfurter, "Prurient Gaze."

58. For the importance of kissing as a form of community binding, see Penn, *Kissing Christians,* 1–10.

59. For discussions of various aspects of the parallels, see Rordorf, *Liturgie,* 445–55; Le Goff, *Naissance,* 76; and Bremmer, "Magic," 43–44.

60. Bremmer, "Magic," 44.

61. Van den Hoek and Herrmann, "Thecla." For discussion and critique of the evidence, see Davis, "Thecla." Davis argues that while these images may be of Thecla herself, it is also possible that they were representations of North African namesakes, a phenomenon for which there is documentation in the Egyptian context. I am grateful to Steve Davis for these references and for allowing me to read his forthcoming article.

62. On the dating and translation of Tertullian, see Evans, *Tertulliani Opera,* 291–92; Hilhorst, "Tertullian," 150–53; and Rordorf, "Tertullien."

63. Trans. Evans, *Septimii Florentis Tertulliani,* 36.

64. I have quoted here the twelfth-century *codex Trecensis,* but the Latin is still, in the words of Hilhorst, stammering ("Tertullian," 153). Gelenius's edition, published in 1550, clarifies some of the ambiguities. The importance of this text is raised by Hilhorst, who credits Rordorf for the suggestion. For a substantial and eloquent discussion of this textual variant, see Hilhorst, "Tertullian," 154–55.

65. On purgatory and postmortem baptism, see Trumbower, *Rescue,* 76–90.

66. So Cooper, "A Father, a Daughter and a Procurator."

Chapter 6. Alexandria

1. The *Martyrdom of Potamiaena and Basilides* is relayed in Eusebius, *Hist. eccl.* 6.5 and Palladius, *Lausiac History* 3. The date of the account is contested. Eusebius places the events during the prefectship of Aquila (ca. 205–210), in which case, Clement may have left Alexandria before their occurrence. Although scholars assume that Clement

deliberately avoids referring to or utilizing this literature, we need to consider the possibility that he was simply unfamiliar with it.

2. The specifics of the persecution in Alexandria are largely unknown. It may have been the result of heightened violence under Septimius Severus who, Eusebius tells us, stirred up violence everywhere (*Hist. eccl.* 6.1).

3. So Bowersock, who argues that Clement's use of the term "martyr" returns it to its original meaning: "Clement's analysis of martyrdom returned prudently to the original sense of the word," and elsewhere: "He is trying to turn the very word back into its original sense of 'bearing witness'" (*Martyrdom*, 67, 69). Bowersock is captive to Clement's rhetoric. The notion that there is some true meaning embedded in the characters that make up the word removes Clement from his historical context. Boyarin correctly notes his exceptionality and rightly describes him as "ambivalent" (*Dying*, 62).

4. This term is borrowed from van den Hoek, "Clement," 327. Many scholars have been charmed by the quiet moderation of Clement's approach. The intellectualism of moderation is a pervasive theme both in Clement's rhetoric and in modern commentary on moderate approaches to martyrdom. Van den Hoek further differentiates Clement's approach from the martyr acts and argues, on the basis of Baumeister's work, that it can be traced back to Daniel.

5. For a discussion of these potential sources, see van den Hoek, "Clement," 327–28. For a discussion of Clement and Plato, see Young, *In Procession*, 11.

6. The terminology here is somewhat confusing. Clement, like the group of Christians labeled by orthodox Christians and scholars "the Gnostics," uses the term "gnostic" to describe the ideal Christian. Even though Clement positions himself as an opponent to the Gnostics, they share key terminology.

7. So Buell, *Making Christians*, 120.

8. Young, *In Procession*, 38–39.

9. Young, *In Procession*, 11.

10. Van den Hoek, "Clement," 340–41. While acknowledging the fundamentally mimetic nature of martyrdom, Clement avoids the idea that these deaths are salvifically valuable in the way that the passion of Jesus was (*Strom.* 4.42.5; 43.2) and, despite quoting Hebrews frequently, never interprets martyrdom as reward or sacrifice. On sacrifice in Clement, see Heyman, *Power*, 203–5.

11. Van den Hoek, "Clement," 340; see also Droge and Tabor, *Noble Death*, 130–52; and Kelley, "Philosophy," 727. *Pace* Heyman, *Power*, 168 n.18.

12. Discussions of the gymnosophists in antiquity refer to them with great respect (Plutarch, *Life of Alexander* 64; Diogenes Laertius, *Lives* 9.61, 63). Philo describes them as virtuous philosophers (*Every Good Man Is Free*, 74, 92–93). Clement himself describes them as philosophers in *Strom.* 1.15.71.

13. Pamela Mullins Reaves, whose dissertation is under way at the University of North Carolina–Chapel Hill, has suggested in work kindly shared with me that Clement rejects this practice because, in his view, it despises the body (*Strom.* 4.17.4). It does not seem to me necessarily to divorce the doctrinal explanation (that they despised the body) from the practice (rushing to death) and the social group (perhaps Montanists). The point is that these identities are being coproduced.

14. For a discussion of Gnostic texts in Clement, see Völker, *Quellen,* 59; Bolgiani, "Polemica"; and van den Hoek, "Clement," 329–35.

15. This section draws upon Moss, "Discourse." For positivist studies of voluntary martyrdom, see De Ste. Croix, "Voluntary Martyrdom"; Dearn, "Voluntary Martyrdom"; Birley, "Voluntary Martyrs"; Voisin, "Prosopographie"; and Butterweck, *"Martyriumssucht."*

16. Some scholars are uncomfortable with the use of the term "voluntary martyrdom." In his delicate discussion of rabbinic martyrological discourse, for instance, Boyarin notes, "'provoked martyrdom' is a better term in my opinion, than 'voluntary martyrdom'—if martyrdom is not voluntary it is not martyrdom" (*Dying,* 121). We should note here that Boyarin assumes, as most do, a particular definition of martyrdom itself, which in turn shapes his definition of provoked martyrdom. Given that neither term existed in the ancient world and that the distinction between them is based on a modern definition of martyrdom, I will continue to use the term voluntary martyrdom here.

17. See, for example, Barnes, *Tertullian,* 177–78; Knox, *Enthusiasm,* 49; Birley, "Persecutors," 47; and discussion in Tabbernee, *Fake Prophecy,* 201.

18. On the martyrs of Lyons as adherents of the New Prophecy, see Tabbernee, *Fake Prophecy,* 219–24.

19. Tabbernee's work in this area cannot be highly enough recommended. See, particularly, "Christian Inscriptions"; "Early Montanism"; and *Fake Prophecy,* 201–42.

20. For the various terms used to describe voluntary martyrdom, see Droge and Tabor, *Noble Death,* 6–7; and Heyman, *Power,* 173 n.31

21. For lists and discussions of events that scholars have designated as voluntary or provoked martyrdom, see De Ste. Croix, "Voluntary Martyrdom"; Droge, "Crown"; and Tabbernee, *Fake Prophecy,* 201–42.

22. One charming early modern condemnation of voluntary martyrdom comes from Billingsley, *Brachy-Martyrologia:* "Obey young men; if I enforce a fact / Not good, 'tis not your voluntary act / You do not sin; be prudent then, I say, / Not actively but passively obey" (11). Whether or not the act is voluntary is debated in this account.

23. Le Blant, "Polyeucte," 337: "Dans le camp des chrétiens . . . la foule avait ses entraînements, et, trop facilement parfois, saluait comme des martyres des personages que l'Église se refusait à inscrire au nombre de ses saints." Translated in De Ste. Croix, "Voluntary Martyrs," 156.

24. Le Blant, "Polyeucte," 335: "Selon les rigoureuses lois de la discipline des anciens âges, Polyeucte ne serait pas un martyr; l'acte même de violence qui a illustré sa mémoire l'exclurait de tout droit à ce titre." Translated in De Ste. Croix, "Voluntary Martyrs," 156 n.4.

25. De Ste. Croix, "Early Christians," 132.

26. De Ste. Croix, "Early Christians," 133.

27. De Ste. Croix, "Voluntary Martyrdom," 157.

28. De Ste. Croix, "Voluntary Martyrdom," 157.

29. De Ste. Croix, "Voluntary Martyrdom," 153.

30. De Ste. Croix, "Voluntary Martyrdom," 154.

31. De Ste. Croix, "Voluntary Martyrdom," 169.

32. See the discussion of "Death and the Maiden" in chapter 1. De Ste. Croix's complicated taxonomy also includes "religious suicide," instances in which a young woman threatened with rape commits suicide rather than give up her chastity. For this terminology and conceptual category, De Ste. Croix draws upon Augustine's discussion of suicide in the *City of God* (1.16–28). There appears to be something of a tension, however, between this ambiguous category of "religious suicide" and the definition of the "quasi-voluntary martyr." Moreover, we should note that Augustine's writings on suicide in the fifth century mark a new direction in Christian perspectives on martyrdom and are, in part, generated by his encounter with the Donatists. See Dearn, "Voluntary Martyrdom."

33. Droge, "Crown," 155–67.

34. For the dating of this account and discussion of Quintus, see chapter 2.

35. For the view that Agathonike is Montanist, see Chapman, "Montanists," 10:523. For the view that she was merely influenced by Montanism, see Lietzmann, "Gestalt." For the view that Agathonike's death paralleled Montanism, see Frend, *Martyrdom,* 272. In all these cases her actions are related to Montanism although nothing other than the fact that she is viewed as a voluntary martyr would suggest this.

36. On the date of the Latin version of the account, see Barnes, "Pre-Decian *Acta,*" 514.

37. As Droge notes, "There was no agreed-upon definition of what constituted *martyria* (witness), nor was there a pejorative term (like *suicide*) to denote its negative counterpart" ("Crown," 166). Although I am deeply appreciative of Droge's insights, I disagree that we should search out positive and negative terms rather than merely categories that distinguish between different forms of martyrdom (be they positive or negative). Where Droge looks to invert a binary, I merely look for difference. Moreover, discourse rather than terminology is the target of my study.

38. For the importance of flight in Clement's position on martyrdom, see Droge, "Crown," 166; Droge and Tabor, *Noble Death,* 143–44; Ritter, "Clement of Alexandria"; and Boyarin, *Dying,* 63.

39. Markschies, *Valentinus Gnosticus?,* 146–49, observes that the phrase "race saved by nature" does not appear in Valentinus but was characteristic of another of Clement's sources, Theodotus (Clement, *Excerpts from Theodotus* 41.1–3). The Valentinian claim to be saved by nature goes back to Irenaeus, *Haer.* 1.6.1. For a survey of the problems in interpreting this passage as a window into Valentinus's views, see Dunderberg, *Beyond Gnosticism,* 35–37.

40. Holzhausen, "Valentinus," 1148.

41. See, for example, the comments of Attridge that the *Tripartite Tractate* 65:17–21 could refer to "fellow suffering" on the part of the Son in response to Pagels's paper in Layton, *Rediscovery,* 286; see also Tite, *Valentinian Ethics,* 162.

42. For the difficulties in reconstructing Gnosticism and the complicating role of Irenaeus, see Williams, *Rethinking "Gnosticism"*; King, *Gnosticism;* and Brakke, *Gnostics.*

43. Frend, "Gnostic Sects," 29. At least in attributing Gnostic reluctance to principle, Frend does not adopt the orthodox rhetoric that deems the Gnostics impious and cowardly.

44. Pagels, "Gnostic and Orthodox Views," 271, and see the fuller discussion in Pagels, *Gnostic Gospels,* 70–101.

45. According to Brakke, the *First Apocalypse of James* is not an example of Gnostic literature and is not included in his important work on the subject.

46. King, "Martyrdom."

47. On the importance of the forgiveness motif in early Christian depictions of martyrdom, see Matthews, *Perfect Martyr.*

48. I am grateful to Mikeal Haxby for allowing me to read both portions of his forthcoming dissertation and his paper "'I Have Not Suffered at All': Gender, Violence and Martyrdom in the *First Apocalypse of James.*" In both of these works Haxby distinguishes between the constructions of gender in *1 Apoc. Jas.* and in the *Passio* and *Lyons.*

49. Kasser, "Textes gnostiques," 79.

50. For Gnostic parallels, see *Letter of Peter to Philip* NHC 8.2; 134.6–135.1; TC 3.5–9. For non-Gnostic parallels, see "Imitatio Christi" in chapter 2. The use of the term "non-Gnostic" is an attempt to avoid rehearsing the orthodox/Gnostic binary.

51. On *1 Apoc. Jas* as revelation dialogue, see Hartenstein, *Die zweite Lehre;* and Petersen, *"Zerstört die Werke."*

52. The connection between ignorance and fear is more explicit in the Nag Hammadi version, in which Jesus encourages James, saying, "Fear not, James, you too will be arrested" (*1 Apoc. Jas.* NHC 25.13–14). This distinction is made by Haxby in his dissertation.

53. So Scholten, *Martyrium,* 68–80.

54. King, "Martyrdom," 31 n.39.

55. So King, "Martyrdom," 32. We might compare the task of *1 Apoc. Jas.* with that of 4 Macc, in which self-control also features prominently.

56. For this argument, see Pagels and King, *Reading Judas,* 59–75.

57. For the view that the account was composed during a period of persecution, see Iricinschi, Jenott, and Townsend, "Betrayer's Gospel"; and Pagels and King, *Reading Judas.*

58. Pagels and King, *Reading Judas.* See also a discussion of this perspective in Painchaud, "Polemical Aspects."

59. A number of scholars have seen the *Gospel of Judas* as anti-martyrdom. I here follow the reading of King, "Martyrdom," 34–38.

60. Pagels, "Gnostic and Orthodox Views," 262–83.

61. So Moss, *Other Christs,* 83–87.

Conclusion

1. Foxe, *Actes,* 34, 35, 139, for example. The interest in the witness to truth is not limited to Protestants in the early modern period. We might compare the contemporaneous statement by a Roman Catholic observer (likely Henry Walpole) that the death of Campion "confirms his doctrine is true" (Alfield, *True reporte,* sig.). On the interest in truth in Protestant and Catholic constructions of martyrdom in this period, see Monta, *Martyrdom,* 4; and Gregory, *Salvation,* 294.

2. Stevenson, *Reminiscences,* 6.

3. Sizgorich, *Violence.* Sizgorich borrows this terminology from Clifford Geertz, a point worth noting because it is precisely in those moments in which we seek to answer

the question "why martyrdom?" that our suppressed theoretical and philosophical commitments start to show. For a critique of the unexamined hegemony of social-scientific theories of religion in histories of Christianity, see Gregory, "Other Confessional History," 132.

4. This question was forcefully asked of Sizgorich by Frankfurter in his review of *Violence and Belief*. This question should be posed only if it would be asked of any and all ideologically weighty social practices.

5. On this point, see Drake, "Lambs into Lions"; and Gaddis, *No Crime,* 158–91.

6. I am drawing here on Coakley, ed., *Religion and the Body,* 1–14, in which she articulates the difficulty in pinning down precisely what the body is.

7. Douglas's famous statement that "just as it is true that everything symbolises the body, so it is equally true (and all the more so for that reason) that the body symbolises everything else" (*Purity,* 123) has some bearing on the relevance of ideologies of martyrdom for the bodies of actual Christians. See also the exemplary work of Gager, "Body Symbols."

Bibliography

Achtemeier, Paul J. *1 Peter: A Commentary on First Peter*. Edited by Eldon J. Epp. Hermeneia Commentary Series. Minneapolis, Minn.: Fortress, 1996.

Adinolfi, Marco. *Questioni Bibliche di Storia e Storiografia*. Esegesi Biblica 5. Brescia: Paideia, 1969.

Alexander, Loveday. "Mapping Early Christianity: Acts and the Shape of Early Christian History." *Interpretation* 57 (2003): 163–73.

Alfield, Thomas. *A true reporte of the death and martyrdome of M. Campion Iesuite and preiste, and M. Sherwin, and M. Bryan preistes, at Tiborne the first of December 1581*. London: Richard Verstegan, 1582.

Amat, Jacqueline. "L'Authenticité des songes de la Passion de Perpetué et de Felicité." *Augustinianum* 29 (1989): 177–91.

———. *Passion de Perpétue et de Félicité suivi des Actes: Introduction, texte critique, traduction, commentaire et index*. Sources chrétiennes 417. Paris: Cerf, 1996.

Ameling, Walter. "The Christian *lapsi* in Smyrna, 250 A.D. (*Martyrium Pionii* 12–14)." *VC* 62:2 (2008): 133–60.

———. "Pliny: The Piety of a Persecutor." Pages 271–99 in *Myths, Martyrs, and Modernity: Studies in the History of Religions in Honour of Jan N. Bremmer*. Edited by Jitse Dijkstra, Justin Kroesen, and Yme Kuiper. Leiden: Brill, 2010.

Ando, Clifford. *Imperial Ideology and Provincial Loyalty in the Roman Empire*. Berkeley: University of California Press, 2000.

Asad, Talal. *Formations of the Secular: Christianity, Islam, Modernity*. Stanford, Calif.: Stanford University Press, 2003.

Ascough, Richard S. *Paul's Macedonian Associations: The Social Context of Philippians and 1 Thessalonians*. WUNT 2:161. Tübingen: Mohr Siebeck, 2003.

Aune, David E. "The Apocalypse of John and the Problem of Genre." *Semeia* 36 (1986): 65–96.

———. "Mastery of the Passions: Philo, 4 Maccabees, and Early Christianity." Pages 125–58 in *Hellenization Revisited: Shaping a Christian Response within the Greco-Roman World*. Edited by W. E. Hellerman. Lanham, Md.: University Press of America, 1994.

Bagnall, Roger S. *Early Christian Books in Egypt*. Princeton, N.J.: Princeton University Press, 2009.

Bakhtin, Mikhail. *Speech Genres and Other Late Essays*. Translated by Vern W. McGee. Austin: University of Texas Press, 1986.

Balling, Jakob. "Martyrdom as Apocalypse." Pages 41–48 in *In the Last Days: On Jewish and Christian Apocalyptic and Its Period*. Edited by Knud Jeppesen, Kirsten Nielsen, and Bent Rosendal. Aarhus: Aarhus University Press, 1994.

Barnard, Leslie W. "In Defence of Pseudo-Pionius' Account of Saint Polycarp's Martyrdom." Pages 192–204 in *Kyriakon: Festschrift Johannes Quasten*. Edited by Patrick Granfield and Josef A. Jungmann. Münster: Aschendorff, 1970.

Barnes, Timothy D. "The Date of Ignatius." *Expository Times* 120 (2009): 119–30.

———. *Early Christian Hagiography and Roman History*. Tübingen: Mohr Siebeck, 2010.

———. "Eusebius and the Date of the Martyrdoms." Pages 137–43 in *Les Martyrs de Lyons (177)*. Edited by Jean Rougé and Robert Turcan. Paris: Cerf, 1978.

———. "Legislation Against the Christians." *JRS* 58 (1968): 32–50.

———. "A Note on Polycarp." *JTS* n.s. 18 (1967): 433–37.

———. "Pre-Decian *Acta Martyrum*." *JTS* n.s. 19 (1968): 509–31.

———. *Tertullian: A Historical and Literary Study*. Oxford: Clarendon, 1971.

Barton, Carlin A. "Savage Miracles: The Redemption of Lost Honour in Roman Society and the Sacrament of the Gladiator and the Martyr." *Representations* 45 (1994): 41–71.

———. "The Scandal of the Arena." *Representations* 27 (1989): 1–36.

———. *The Sorrows of the Ancient Romans: The Gladiator and the Monster*. Princeton, N.J.: Princeton University Press, 1993.

Bastiaensen, Antoon A. R., and Gioachini Chiarini. *Atti e Passioni dei Martiri*. 2d ed. Milan: A. Mondadori, 1990.

———. "Heeft Perpetua haar dagboek in het Latijn of in het Grieks geschreven?" Pages 130–35 in *De heiligenverering in de eerste eeuwen van het Christendom*. Edited by A. Hilhorst. Nijmegen: Dekker and Van de Vegt, 1988.

Bauer, Walter. *Orthodoxy and Heresy in Earliest Christianity*. Edited by Robert A. Kraft and Gerhard Krodel. 2d ed. Charlottesville, Va.: Sigler, 1996.

Baumeister, Theofried. *Die Anfänge der Theologie des Martyriums*. Münsterische Beiträge zur Theologie 45. Münster: Aschendorff, 1980.

Benko, Stephen. "Pagan Criticism of Christianity During the First Two Centuries A.D." *ANRW* 2.23.1 (1980): 1055–118.

Bergmann, Bettina, and Christine Kondoleon, eds. *The Art of Ancient Spectacle.* Studies in the History of Art 56. Center for Advanced Study in the Visual Arts Symposium Papers 34. New Haven, Conn.: Yale University Press, 1999.

Bihlmeyer, Karl. *Die Apostolischen Väter.* Tübingen: Mohr, 1924.

Billingsley, Nicholas. *Brachy-Martyrologia or, A Breviary of all the Greatest Persecutions which have befallen the Saints and People of God from the Creation to our Present Times.* London: Austin Rice, 1657.

Birley, Anthony R. "Persecutors and Martyrs in Tertullian's Africa." Pages 37–86 in *The Later Roman Empire Today: Papers Given in Honour of Professor John Mann 23 May 1992.* Edited by Dido Clark. London: Institute of Archaeology, 1993.

———. "Voluntary Martyrs in the Early Christian Church: Heroes or Heretics?" *Cristianesimo nella Storia* 27: 1 (2006): 99–127.

Birot, Pierre, and Jean Dresch. *La Méditerranée et le Moyen-Orient.* Paris: Presses Universitaires du France, 1956.

Bisbee, Gary A. "The Acts of Justin Martyr: A Form-Critical Study." *Second Century* 3:3 (1983): 129–57.

———. *Pre-Decian Acts of Martyrs and Commentarii.* Harvard Dissertations in Religion 22. Edited by Margaret R. Miles and Bernadette J. Brooten. Philadelphia: Fortress, 1988.

Bolgiani, Franco. "La polemica di Clemente Alessandrino contro gli gnostici libertini nel III libro degli Stromati." *Studi e materiali di storia delle religioni* 38 (1967): 86–136.

Bollandus, Jean et socii. *Acta Sanctorum.* 71 vols. Brussels: Société des Bollandistes, 1643–1940.

Bomgardner, D. L. *The Story of the Roman Amphitheatre.* London: Routledge, 2000.

Bonner, Gerald. "The Scillitan Saints and the Pauline Epistles." *Journal of Ecclesiastical History* 7 (1956): 141–46.

Bonwetsch, Nathaniel G. *Die Geschichte des Montanismus.* Erlangen: Deichert, 1881.

Bousset, Wilhelm, and Hugo Gressmann. *Die Religion des Judentums im Späthellenistischen Zeitalter.* Handbuch zum Neuen Testament 21. Tübingen: Mohr, 1966.

Bovon, François. "The Dossier on Stephen, the First Martyr." *HTR* 96:3 (2003): 279–315.

Bowersock, G. W. *Martyrdom and Rome.* Cambridge: Cambridge University Press, 1995.

Boyarin, Daniel. *Border Lines: The Partition of Judaeo-Christianity.* Philadelphia: University of Pennsylvania Press, 2004.

———. *Dying for God: Martyrdom and the Making of Christianity and Judaism.* Stanford, Calif.: Stanford University Press, 1999.

Bradley, Keith R. "The Social Role of the Nurse in the Roman World." Pages 13–36 in *Discovering the Roman Family: Studies in Roman Social History.* Edited by Keith R. Bradley. New York: Oxford University Press, 1991.

———. "Wet-Nursing at Rome: A Study in Social Relations." Pages 201–29 in *The Family in Ancient Rome: New Perspectives.* Edited by Beryl Rawson. Ithaca, N.Y.: Cornell University Press, 1986.

Brakke, David. *The Gnostics: Myth, Ritual, and Diversity in Early Christianity.* Cambridge, Mass.: Harvard University Press, 2011.

Brakke, David, Anders-Christian Jacobsen, and Jörg Ulrich, eds. *Beyond Reception: Mutual Influences Between Antique Religion, Judaism, and Early Christianity.* Early Christianity in the Context of Antiquity 1. Frankfurt: Peter Lang, 2006.

Bremmer, Jan N. *The Apocryphal Acts of Thomas.* Leuven: Peeters, 2001.

———. "Contextualizing Heaven in Third-Century North Africa." Pages 159–73 in *Heavenly Realms and Earthly Realities in Late Antique Religions.* Edited by Annette Yoshiko Reed and Ra'anan Boustan. Cambridge: Cambridge University Press, 2004.

———. "The Five Major Apocryphal Acts: Authors, Place, Time, Readership." Pages 149–70 in *The Apocryphal Acts of Thomas.* Edited by Jan N. Bremmer. Leuven: Peeters, 2001.

———. "Magic, Martyrdom, and Women's Liberation." Pages 36–59 in *The Apocryphal Acts of Paul and Thecla.* Edited by Jan N. Bremmer. Kampen: Kok Pharos, 1996.

———. "The Motivation of Martyrs: Perpetua and the Palestinians." Pages 535–54 in *Religion in Cultural Discourse.* Edited by B. Luchesi and K. von Stuckrad. Religionsgeschichtliche Versuche und Vorarbeiten 52. Berlin: De Gruyter, 2004.

———. "Myth and Ritual in Greek Human Sacrifice: Lykaon, Polyxena and the Case of the Rhodian Criminal." Pages 55–79 in *The Strange World of Human Sacrifice.* Edited by Jan N. Bremmer. Leuven: Peeters, 2007.

———. "Perpetua and Her Diary: Authenticity, Family and Visions." Pages 77–120 in *Märtyrer und Märtyrerakten.* Edited by Walter Ameling. Altertumswissenschaftliches Kolloquium 6. Stuttgart: Franz Steiner, 2002.

———. *The Rise of Christianity Through the Eyes of Gibbon, Harnack and Rodney Stark.* Groningen: Barkhuis, 2010.

———. "Sacrificing a Child in Ancient Greece: The Case of Iphigeneia." Pages 21–43 in *The Sacrifice of Isaac: The Aqedah (Gen 22) and Its Interpretations.* Edited by E. Noort and E. J. C. Tigchelaar. Leiden: Brill, 2001.

———. "Spartans and Jews: Abrahamic Cousins?" Pages 47–59 in *Abraham, the Nations, and the Hagarites.* Edited by Martin Goodman, George H. van Kooten, and Jacques van Ruiten. Leiden: Brill, 2010.

Bremmer, Jan N., and Marco Formisano. "Perpetua's Passions: A Brief Introduction." In *Perpetua's Passions.* Edited by Jan N. Bremmer and Marco Formisano. New York: Oxford University Press, forthcoming.

Brent, Allen. *Ignatius of Antioch: A Martyr Bishop and the Origin of Episcopacy.* New York: Continuum, 2007.

———. *The Imperial Cult and the Development of Church Order: Concepts and Images of Authority in Paganism and Early Christianity Before the Age of Cyprian.* VCSup 45. Leiden: Brill, 1999.

Brickhouse, Thomas C., and Nicholas D. Smith. *Plato's Socrates.* New York: Oxford University Press, 1994.

Bronfen, Elisabeth. *Over Her Dead Body: Death, Femininity and the Aesthetic.* Manchester: Manchester University Press, 1992.

Brown, Peter. *The Body and Society: Men, Women, and Sexual Renunciation in Early Christianity.* New York: Columbia University Press, 1988.

———. *The Cult of the Saints: Its Rise and Function in Late Antiquity.* Chicago: University of Chicago Press, 1981.

———. *The Making of Late Antiquity.* Cambridge, Mass.: Harvard University Press, 1978.

———. *The Rise of Western Christendom: Triumph and Diversity, A. D. 200–1000.* 2d ed. Oxford: Blackwell, 2003.

Brown, Shelby. "Death as Decoration: Scenes of the Arena on Roman Domestic Mosaics." Pages 180–211 in *Pornography and Representation in Greece and Rome.* Edited by A. Richlin. New York: Oxford University Press, 1992.

Brox, Norbert. *Zeuge und Märtyrer: Untersuchungen zur frühchristlichen Zeugnis-Terminologie.* Studien zum Alten und Neuen Testament 5. Munich: Kösel-Verlag, 1961.

Buell, Denise Kimber. *Making Christians: Clement of Alexandria and the Rhetoric of Legitimacy.* Princeton, N.J.: Princeton University Press, 1999.

Bultmann, Rudolf. "Ignatius and Paul." Pages 267–77 in *Existence and Faith: Shorter Writings of Rudolf Bultmann.* Translated by Schubert M. Ogden. New York: Meridian, 1960.

Burkitt, F. C. "The Oldest Manuscript of St. Justin's Martyrdom." *JTS* 11 (1910): 61–66.

Burris, Catherine, and Lucas Van Rompay. "Some Further Notes on Thecla in Syriac Christianity." *Hugoye: Journal of Syriac Studies* 6:2 (2003) http://syrcom.cua.edu /Hugoye/Vol6No2/HV6N2BurrisVanRompay.html.

———. "Thecla in Syriac Christianity: Preliminary Observations." *Hugoye: Journal of Syriac Studies* 5:2 (2002) http://syrcom.cua.edu/Hugoye/Vol5No2/HV5N2Burris VanRompay.html.

Burrus, Virginia. *Saving Shame: Martyrs, Saints, and Other Abject Objects.* Philadelphia: University of Pennsylvania Press, 2008.

———. "Torture and Travail: Producing the Christian Martyr." Pages 56–71 in vol. 12 of *A Feminist Companion to Patristic Literature.* Edited by Amy-Jill Levine and Maria Mayo Robbins. New York: T & T Clark, 2008.

Buschmann, Gerd. *Das Martyrium des Polycarp.* Göttingen: Vandenhoeck and Ruprecht, 1998.

———. *Martyrium Polycarpi: Eine formkritische Studie; Ein Beitrag zur Frage nach der Entstehung der Gattung Märtyrerakte.* Berlin and New York: De Gruyter, 1994.

Butler, Rex D. *The New Prophecy and "New Visions": Evidence of Montanism in the Passion of Perpetua and Felicitas.* Patristic Monograph Series 18. Washington, D.C.: Catholic University of America Press, 2006.

Butterweck, Christel. *"Martyriumssucht" in der Alten Kirche? Studien zur Darstellung und Deutung frühchristlicher Martyrien.* Beiträge zur historischen Theologie 87. Tübingen: J. C. B. Mohr (Paul Siebeck), 1995.

Bynum, Caroline Walker. "Women's Stories, Women's Symbols: A Critique of Victor Turner's Theory of Liminality." Pages 105–25 in *Anthropology and the Study of Religion.* Edited by Robert L. Moore and Frank E. Reynolds. Chicago: Center for the

Scientific Study of Religion, 1984; reprinted as pages 181–238 in *Fragmentation and Redemption: Essays on Gender and the Human Body in Medieval Religion.* Edited by Caroline Walker Bynum. New York: Zone, 1991.

Calder, William M. "The New Jerusalem of the Montanists." *Byzantion* 6 (1931): 421–25.

———. "Philadelphia and Montanism." *Bulletin of the John Rylands Library* 7 (1923): 309–53.

Cameron, Averil. *Christianity and the Rhetoric of Empire: The Development of Early Christian Discourse.* Berkeley: University of California Press, 1991.

Cancik, Hubert, and Jörg Rüpke, eds. *Römische Reichsreligion und Provinzialreligion.* Tübingen: Mohr Siebeck, 1997.

Carriker, Andrew James. *The Library of Eusebius of Caesarea.* VCSup 67. Leiden: Brill, 2003.

Cary, M., and H. H. Scullard. *A History of Rome: Down to the Reign of Constantine.* 3d ed. London: Macmillan, 1975.

Castelli, Elizabeth A. *Martyrdom and Memory: Early Christian Culture Making.* Gender, Theory, and Religion. New York: Columbia University Press, 2004.

Cave, Sydney. *The Doctrine of the Person of Christ.* London: Duckworth, 1925.

Champlin, E. J. *Fronto and Antonine Rome.* Cambridge, Mass.: Harvard University Press, 1980.

Chapman, John. "Montanists." Pages 521–24 in vol. 10 of *The Catholic Encyclopedia.* Edited by Charles G. Herbermann. 15 vols. New York: Robert Appleton, 1911.

Charles-Picard, Gilbert. *La civilization de l'Afrique romaine.* Paris: Études augustiniennes, 1990.

Charlesworth, Martin P. *Trade-Routes and Commerce of the Roman Empire.* Cambridge: Cambridge University Press, 1924.

Chevallier, Raymond. "Gallia Lugundunensis: Bilan de 25 ans de recherches historiques et archéologiques." *ANRW* 2.3 (1975): 860–1060.

Chiovaro, F. "Relics." Pages 250–56 of vol. 12 of *The New Catholic Encyclopedia.* 2d ed. Edited by F. Chiovaro. 15 vols. Detroit: Gale, 1967.

Chroust, Anton-Hermann. *Socrates, Man and Myth: The Two Socratic Apologies of Xenophon.* South Bend, Ind.: University of Notre Dame Press, 1957.

Clark, Elizabeth A. "The Lady Vanishes: Dilemmas of a Feminist Historian After the 'Linguistic Turn.'" *Church History* 67 (1998): 1–31.

———. "Women, Gender, and the Study of Christian History." *Church History* 70 (2001): 395–426.

Clark, Gillian. "Bodies and Blood: Late Antique Debate on Martyrdom, Virginity and Resurrection." Pages 99–115 in *Changing Bodies, Changing Meanings: Studies on the Human Body in Antiquity.* Edited by Dominic Montserrat. London: Routledge, 1998.

Clifford, Richard J. "The Roots of Apocalypticism in Near Eastern Myth." Pages 3–38 of vol. 1 of *The Encyclopedia of Apocalypticism: The Origins of Apocalypticism in Judaism and Christianity.* Edited by Bernard McGinn and John J. Collins. 3 vols. London: Continuum, 2000.

Coakley, Sarah, ed. *Religion and the Body.* Cambridge: Cambridge University Press, 1997.

Cobb, L. Stephanie. *Dying To Be Men: Gender and Language in Early Christian Martyr Texts*. Gender, Theory, and Religion. New York: Columbia University Press, 2008.

Cohn, Norman. *The Pursuit of the Millennium: Revolutionary Millenarians and the Mystical Anarchists of the Middle Ages*. 3d ed. New York: Oxford University Press, 1970.

Coleman, K. M. "Fatal Charades: Roman Executions Staged as Mythological Enactments." *JRS* 80 (1990): 44–73.

Coles, Revel A. *Reports of Proceedings in Papyri*. Papyrologica Bruxellenesis 4. Brussels: Fondation Egyptologique Reine Elisabeth, 1966.

Collins, Adela Yarbro. *Crisis and Catharsis: The Power of the Apocalypse*. Philadelphia: Westminster, 1984.

———. "From Noble Death to Crucified Messiah." *New Testament Studies* 40 (1994): 481–503.

———. "The Genre of the Passion Narrative." *Studia theologica* 47 (1993): 3–28.

Collins, John J. *Apocalyptic Imagination: An Introduction to Jewish Apocalyptic Literature*. 2d ed. Grand Rapids, Mich.: Eerdmans, 1998.

———. *Apocalypse: The Morphology of a Genre*. Semeia 14. Missoula, Mont.: Scholars Press, 1979.

———. *Daniel: A Commentary on the Book of Daniel*. Hermeneia—A Critical and Exegetical Commentary. Minneapolis, Minn.: Fortress, 1993.

Conzelmann, Hans. *Bemerkungen zum Martyrium Polykarps*. Göttingen: Vandenhoeck & Ruprecht, 1978.

Cook, John Granger. *Roman Attitudes Towards the Christians: From Claudius to Hadrian*. WUNT 1.261. Tübingen: Mohr Siebeck, 2010.

Cooper, Kate. "A Father, a Daughter and a Procurator: Authority and Resistance in the Prison Memoir of Perpetua of Carthage." *Gender and History* 23 (2011): 685–702.

———. "Closely Watched Households: Visibility, Exposure, and Private Power in the Roman *Domus*." *P&P* 197 (2007): 3–33.

———. *Fall of the Roman Household*. Cambridge: Cambridge University Press, 2007.

———. *The Virgin and the Bride: Idealized Womanhood in Late Antiquity*. Cambridge, Mass.: Harvard University Press, 1996.

———. "Voice of the Victim: Gender, Representation, and Early Christian Martyrdom." *Bulletin of the John Rylands Library* 80 (1998): 147–57.

Corbett, John H. "Relics." Pages 976–77 in *Encyclopedia of Early Christianity*. 2d ed. Edited by Everett Ferguson, Michael P. McHugh, and Frederick W. Norris. New York: Garland, 1998.

Crook, J. A. *Law and the Life of Rome, 90 B.C.–A.D. 212*. Ithaca, N.Y.: Cornell University Press, 1967.

Cureton, William. *Corpus Ignatianum: A Complete Collection of the Ignatian Epistles, Genuine, Interpolated, and Spurious: Together with Numerous Extracts from Them as Quoted by Ecclesiastical Writers Down to the Tenth Century in Syriac, Greek, and Latin: An English Translation of the Syriac Text, Copious Notes, and Introduction*. Berlin: Asher, 1849.

Davis, Stephen J. *The Cult of Saint Thecla: A Tradition of Women's Piety in Late Antiquity*. Oxford: Oxford University Press, 2001.

———. "Thecla." Pages 9101–2 in vol. 13 of *Encyclopedia of Religion*. 2d ed. Edited by Lindsay Jones. 15 vols. Detroit: Macmillan, 2005.

Dearn, Alan. "Voluntary Martyrdom and the Donatist Schism." *SP* 39 (2006): 27–32.

De' Cavalieri, Pio Franchi. "Gli Atti di S. Giustino." *Studi e Testi* 8 (1902): 33–6; 9 (1902): 73–75; 33 (1920): 5–17.

———. *Passio SS. Mariani et Iacobi*. Rome: Tipografia Vaticana, 1900.

———. *Scritti agiografici*. 2 vols. Rome: Tipografia Vaticana, 1962.

De Ste. Croix, G. E. M. "Voluntary Martyrdom in the Early Church." Pages 153–200 in *Christian Persecution, Martyrdom, and Orthodoxy*. Edited by G. E. M. De Ste. Croix, Michael Whitby, and Joseph Streeter. New York: Oxford University Press, 2006.

———. "Why Were the Early Christians Persecuted?" *P&P* 26 (1963): 6–38; reprinted as pages 105–52 in *Christian Persecution, Martyrdom, and Orthodoxy*. Edited by G. E. M. De Ste. Croix, Michael Whitby, and Joseph Streeter. New York: Oxford University Press, 2006.

———. "Why Were the Early Christians Persecuted?—A Rejoinder." *P&P* 27 (1964): 28–33.

Decret, François. *Early Christianity in North Africa*. Translated by Edward L. Smither. Eugene, Ore.: Cascade, 2009.

Decret, François, and Mohamed Fantar. *L'Afrique du nord dans l'Antiquité: Histoire et civilization—des origines au V siècle*. Paris: Payot, 1981.

Deferrari, Roy J. *Eusebius Pamphili—Ecclesiastical History, Books 1–5*. Edited by H. Dressler. The Fathers of the Church. Washington, D.C.: Catholic University of America Press, 1953.

Dehandschutter, Boudewijn. "A Community of Martyrs: Religious Identity and the Case of the Martyrs of Lyons and Vienne." Pages 3–22 in *The Discourse of Martyrdom and the Construction of Christian Identity in the History of Christianity*. Edited by Johan Leemans. Leuven: Peeters, 2005.

———. "Le Martyre de Polycarpe et la développement de la conception du martyre au deuxième siècle." *SP* 17 (1982): 659–68.

———. "The Martyrium Polycarpi: A Century of Research." Pages 485–522 in *ANRW* 2.27.1. Edited by Wolfgang Haase and Hildegard Temporini. Berlin: Walter de Gruyter, 1993.

———. *Martyrium Polycarpi: Een literair-krittisch studie*. Bibliotheca Ephemeridum Theologicarum Lovaniensium 52. Leuven: Peeters, 1979.

———. "The New Testament and the *Martyrdom of Polycarp*." Pages 395–406 in *Trajectories Through the New Testament and the Apostolic Fathers*. Edited by Andrew F. Gregory and Christopher M. Tuckett. Oxford: Oxford University Press, 2005.

Dehandschutter, Boudewijn, and Johan Leemans. *Polycarpiana: Studies on Martyrdom and Persecution in Early Christianity*. Leuven: Leuven University Press, 2007.

Delattre, Alfred L. *Gamart ou la nécropole juive de Carthage*. Lyons: Mougin Rusand, 1895.

Delehaye, Hippolyte. *Les legendes hagiographiques*. 3d ed. Subsidia Hagiographica 18. Brussels: Société des Bollandistes, 1927.

———. *Les passions des martyrs et les genres littéraires*. 2d rev. ed. Subsidia Hagiographica 13B. Brussels: Société des Bollandistes, 1966.

————. "Loca sanctorum." *Analecta Bollandiana* 48 (1930): 5–64.

————. *Sanctus. Essai sur le culte des saints dans l'antiquité.* Subsidia Hagiographica 17. Brussels: Société des Bollandistes, 1927.

Den Boeft, Jan, and Jan N. Bremmer, "Notiunculae Martyrologicae." *VC* 35 (1981): 43–56.

————. "Notiunculae Martyrologicae IV." *VC* 45 (1991): 105–22.

————. "Notiunculae Martyrologicae VI." Pages 47–63 in *Martyrdom and Persecution in Late Ancient Christianity: Festschrift Boudewijn Dehandschutter.* Edited by Johan Leemans. Leuven: Peeters, 2010.

Denzey, Nicola. "Facing the Beast: Justin, Christian Martyrdom, and Freedom of the Will." Pages 176–98 in *Stoicism in Early Christianity.* Edited by Tuomas Rasimus, Troels Engberg-Perdersen, and Ismo Dunderberg. Grand Rapids, Mich.: Baker Academic, 2010.

Derrida, Jacques. *The Post Card: From Socrates to Freud and Beyond.* Translated by Alan Bass. Chicago: University of Chicago Press, 1987.

Despois, Jean Jacques, and René Raynal. *Géographie de l'Afrique du Nord-Ouest.* Paris: Payot, 1975.

Dodds, E. R. *Pagans and Christians in an Age of Anxiety: Some Aspects of Religious Experience from Marcus Aurelius to Constantine.* Cambridge: Cambridge University Press, 1965.

Dolbeau, F. *Revue des Études Augustiniennes et Patristiques* 42 (1996): 312–13.

Dominik, William J. *Roman Eloquence: Rhetoric in Society and Literature.* New York: Routledge, 1997.

Döring, Klaus. *Exemplum Socratis: Studien zur Sokratesnachwirkung in der kynisch-stoischen Popularphilosophie der frühen Kaiserzeit und im frühen Christentum.* Wiesbaden: Franz Steiner, 1979.

Doty, W. G. "The Concept of Genre in Literary Analysis." Pages 413–48 in *Society of Biblical Literature Abstracts and Seminar Papers 1972.* Edited by L. McGaughy. Missoula, Mont.: Scholars Press, 1972.

Douglas, Mary. *Purity and Danger: An Analysis of the Concepts of Pollution and Taboo.* 2d ed. London: Routledge, 1978.

Drake, Hal A. "Lambs into Lions: Explaining Early Christian Intolerance." *P&P* 153 (1996): 3–36.

Drobner, Hubertus R. *Lehrbuch der Patrologie.* 2d ed. Frankfurt: Peter Lang, 2004.

Droge, Arthur J. "The Crown of Immortality: Toward a Redescription of Christian Martyrdom." Pages 155–70 in *Death, Ecstasy, and Other Worldly Journeys.* Edited by John J. Collins and Michael A. Fishbane. Albany, N.Y.: SUNY Press, 1995.

Droge, Arthur J., and James D. Tabor. *A Noble Death: Suicide and Martyrdom Among Christians and Jews in Antiquity.* San Francisco: Harper, 1992.

Dronke, Peter. *Women Writers of the Middle Ages.* Cambridge: Cambridge University Press, 1984.

DuBois, Page. *Torture and Truth.* New York: Routledge, 1991.

Duff, David. *Modern Genre Theory.* Harlow: Longman, 2000.

Dunderberg, Ismo. *Beyond Gnosticism: Myth, Lifestyle and Society in the School of Valentinus.* New York: Columbia University Press, 2008.

Dunn, James D. G. *The Parting of the Ways: Between Christianity and Judaism and Their Significance for the Character of Christianity.* 2d ed. London: SCM, 2006.

Eastman, David L. *Paul the Martyr: The Cult of the Apostle in the Latin West.* Writings from the Greco-Roman World Supplements Series. Leiden: Brill, 2011.

Ebbeler, Jennifer. "Letters." Pages 464–76 in *The Oxford Handbook of Roman Studies.* Edited by A. Barchesi and W. Schiedel. New York: Oxford University Press, 2010.

———. "Tradition, Innovation, and Epistolary Mores." Pages 270–84 in *The Blackwell Companion to Late Antiquity.* Edited by Philip Rousseau. Oxford: Blackwell, 2009.

Edmondson, J. C. "Dynamic Arenas: Gladiatorial Presentations in the City of Rome and the Construction of Roman Society in the Early Empire." Pages 69–112 in *Roman Theater and Society.* Edited by W. Slater. Ann Arbor: University of Michigan Press, 1996.

Edwards, Catharine. *Death in Ancient Rome.* New Haven, Conn.: Yale University Press, 2007.

Edwards, Mark J., Martin Goodman, Simon Price, and Christopher Rowland, eds. *Apologetics in the Roman Empire: Pagans, Jews, and Christians.* Oxford: Oxford University Press, 1999.

Egli, Emil. *Altchristliche Studien: Martyrien und Martyrologien ältester Zeit.* Zürich: Schulhess, 1887.

Ehrman, Bart D. *The Apostolic Fathers.* 2 vols. Loeb Classical Library. Cambridge, Mass.: Harvard University Press, 2003.

———. *The New Testament: A Historical Introduction to the Early Christian Writings.* 4th ed. New York: Oxford University Press, 2007.

Eigler, Ulrich. "Exitus illustrium virorum." *Der neue Pauly: Enzyklopädie der Antike* 4 (1998): 344–45.

Engberg-Pedersen, Troels. "Paul's Necessity: A Bourdieuesque Reading of the Pauline Project." Pages 69–88 in *Beyond Reception: Mutual Influences Between Antique Religion, Judaism, and Early Christianity.* Edited by David Brakke, Anders-Christian Jacobsen, and Jörg Ulrich. Early Christianity in the Context of Antiquity 1. Frankfurt: Peter Lang, 2006.

Ermoni, V. "La crise montaniste." *Revue des questions historiques* 72 (1902): 61–96.

Evans, Ernest. *Quinti Septimii Florentis Tertulliani de baptismo liber: Tertullian's Homily on Baptism; Text edited with an Introduction, Translation and Commentary.* London: SPCK, 1964.

Evans, Suzanne. "The Scent of a Martyr." *Numen* 49 (2002): 193–211.

Farell, Joseph, and Craig Williams. "The Passion of Saints Perpetua and Felicity." In *Perpetua's Passions.* Edited by Jan N. Bremmer and Marco Formisano. New York: Oxford University Press, forthcoming.

Farkasfalvy, Dennis M., and William R. Farmer. *The Formation of the New Testament Canon: An Ecumenical Approach.* Mahwah, N.J.: Paulist Press, 1983.

Farrer, Austin Marsden. *A Rebirth of Images: The Making of St. John's Apocalypse.* Albany, N.Y.: SUNY Press, 1986.

Février, Paul-Albert. *Approches du Maghreb romain: Pouvoirs, différences et conflits.* 2 vols. Aix-en-Provence: Edisud, 1989–90.

Fliche, Augustin. "A propos des origines chrétiennes de la Gaule." *Mélanges Lebreton RSR* 40 (1951–52): 158–67.

Foxe, John. *Actes and Monuments of these latter perilous days touching matters of the Churche* . . . . London: John Day, 1563.

Frankfurter, David. "Early Christian Apocalypticism: Literature and the Social World." Pages 425–53 in *The Origins of Apocalypticism in Judaism and Christianity*, vol. 1 of *The Encyclopedia of Apocalypticism*. Edited by Bernard McGinn and John J. Collins. New York: Continuum, 1998.

———. *Evil Incarnate: Rumors of Demonic Conspiracy and Ritual Abuse in History.* Princeton, N.J.: Princeton University Press, 2006.

———. "The Legacy of Jewish Apocalypses in Early Christianity: Regional Trajectories." Pages 129–200 in *The Jewish Apocalyptic Heritage in Early Christianity*. Edited by James C. VanderKam and William Adler. The Hague: Van Gorcum, 1996.

———. "Martyrology and the Prurient Gaze." *JECS* 17 (2009): 215–45.

———. *Religion in Roman Egypt: Assimilation and Resistance*. Princeton, N.J.: Princeton University Press, 1998.

———. Review of Thomas Sizgorich, *Violence and Belief in Late Antiquity: Militant Devotion in Christianity and Islam. JECS* 18 (2010): 148–50.

Frend, W. H. C. "The Gnostic Sects and the Roman Empire." *Journal of Ecclesiastical History* 5 (1954): 25–37.

———. *Martyrdom and Persecution in the Early Church*. Oxford: Blackwell, 1965.

———. Review of Hans von Campenhausen, "Bearbeitungen und Interpolationen des Polykarpmartyriums." *JTS* n.s. 9 (1958): 371.

Fridh, Åke. *Le problème de la* Passion des Saintes Perpétue et Félicité. Gothenburg: Acta Universitatis Gothenburgensis, 1968.

Frilingos, Christopher A. "Sexing the Lamb." Pages 297–318 in *New Testament Masculinities*. Edited by Stephen Moore and Janice Capel Anderson. Atlanta, Ga.: SBL, 2003.

———. *Spectacles of Empire: Monsters, Martyrs, and the Book of Revelation*. Philadelphia: University of Pennsylvania Press, 2004.

Futrell, A. *Blood in the Arena: The Spectacle of Roman Power*. Austin: University of Texas Press, 1997.

Gaddis, Michael. *There Is No Crime for Those Who Have Christ: Religious Violence in the Christian Roman Empire*. Berkeley: University of California Press, 2005.

Gager, John. "Body Symbols and Social Reality: Resurrection, Incarnation and Asceticism in Early Christianity." *Religion* 12:4 (1982): 345–64.

Gamble, Harry Y. *Books and Readers in the Early Church: A History of Early Christian Texts*. New Haven, Conn.: Yale University Press, 1995.

———. "The Pauline Corpus and the Early Christian Book." Pages 265–80 in *Paul and the Legacies of Paul*. Edited by William S. Babcock. Dallas, Tex.: Southern Methodist University Press, 1990.

Garnsey, Peter, and Richard Saller. *The Roman Empire: Economy, Society and Culture*. Berkeley: University of California Press, 1987.

Gebhardt, Oscar von. *Acta martyrum selecta: Ausgewählte Märtyreracten und andere Urkunden aus der Verfolgungszeit der christlichen Kirche*. Berlin: Duncker, 1902.

Geffcken, Johannes. "Die christlichen Martyrien." *Hermes* 45 (1910): 481–505.

———. *Zwei griechische Apologeten.* Leipzig: Teubner, 1907.

Gibbon, Edward. *The History of the Decline and Fall of the Roman Empire.* 6 vols. London: Strahan and Cadell, 1776–88.

Gilmore, David. *Manhood in the Making: Cultural Concepts of Masculinity.* New Haven, Conn.: Yale University Press, 1990.

Gleason, Maud W. *Making Men: Sophists and Self-Presentation in Ancient Rome.* Princeton, N.J.: Princeton University Press, 1995.

Goguel, Maurice. *L'Eucharistie des origines à Justin Martyr.* Paris: Fischbacher, 1910.

Grant, R. M. "Eusebius and the Martyrs of Gaul." Pages 129–36 in *Les Martyres de Lyon (177).* Edited by Jean Rougé and Robert Turcan. Paris: Cerf, 1978.

———. *Eusebius as Church Historian.* Oxford: Oxford University Press, 1980.

———. "A Woman of Rome: The Matron in Justin, 2 *Apology* 2.1–9." *Church History* 54 (1986): 461–72.

Grégoire, H., and P. Orgels, "La véritable date du Martyre de S. Polycarpe (23 février 177) et le Corpus Polycarpianum." *Analecta Bollandiana* 69 (1951): 1–38.

Gregory, Brad S. "The Other Confessional History: On Secular Bias in the Study of Religion." *History and Theory, Theme Issue* 45 (2006): 132–49.

———. *Salvation at Stake: Christian Martyrdom in Early Modern Europe.* Cambridge, Mass.: Harvard University Press, 1999.

Griffe, Élie. *La Gaule chrétienne à l'époque romaine.* 3 vols. Paris: Letouzey et Ané, 1947.

Grig, Lucy. *Making Martyrs in Late Antiquity.* London: Duckworth, 2004.

———. "Torture and Truth in Late Antique Martyrology." *Early Medieval Europe* 11 (2002): 321–36.

Grisé, Y. *Le suicide dans la Rome antique.* Montreal: Bellarmin, 1982.

Gruen, Erich S. "Greek Pistis and Roman Fides." *Athenaeum* 60 (1982): 50–68.

Guillaumin, M. L. "En marge du 'Martyre de Polycarpe': Le discernement des allusions scripturaires." Pages 462–69 in *Forma Futuri: Studi in onore del Cardinale Michele Pellegrino.* Turin: Bottega d'Erasmo, 1975.

Gunderson, Erik. "Catullus, Pliny, and Love Letters." *Transactions of the American Philological Association* 127 (1997): 201–31.

———. "The Flavian Amphitheatre: All the World as Stage." Pages 637–58 in *Flavian Rome: Culture, Image, Text.* Edited by A. J. Boyle and W. J. Dominik. Leiden: Brill, 2003.

———. "The Ideology of the Arena." *Classical Antiquity* 15 (1996): 113–51.

Hackett, Olwen. *Roman Gaul.* London: Bell, 1953.

Hackforth, Reginald. *Plato's Phaedo.* Cambridge: Cambridge University Press, 1955.

Hadot, Pierre. *What Is Ancient Philosophy?* Translated by Michael Chase. Cambridge, Mass.: Harvard University Press, 2002.

Haines-Eitzen, Kim. *Guardians of Letters: Literacy, Power, and the Transmitters of Early Christian Literature.* New York: Oxford University Press, 2000.

Harland, Philip A. "Connections with Elites in the World of the Early Christians." Pages 385–408 in *The Handbook of Early Christianity: Social Science Approaches.* Edited by Anthony J. Blasi, Paul-André Turcotte, and Jean Duhaime. Walnut Creek, Calif.: AltaMira, 2002.

Harrill, J. Albert. "Cannibalistic Language in the Fourth Gospel and Greco-Roman Polemics of Factionalism (John 6:52–66)." *JBL* 127:1 (2008): 133–58.

———. "The Domestic Enemy: A Moral Polarity of Household Slaves in Early Christian Apologies and Martyrdoms." Pages 231–54 in *Early Christian Families in Context: An Interdisciplinary Dialogue.* Edited by David Balch and Carolyn Osiek. Grand Rapids, Mich.: Eerdmans, 2003.

———. "Paul and Empire: Studying Roman Identity After the Cultural Turn." *Early Christianity* 2 (2011): 281–311.

———. "Servile Functionaries or Priestly Leaders? Roman Domestic Religion, Narrative Intertextuality, and Pliny's Reference to Slave Christian *Ministrae* (Ep. 10,96,8)." *ZNW* 97 (2006): 111–30.

———. *Slaves in the New Testament: Literary, Social, and Moral Dimensions.* Minneapolis, Minn.: Fortress, 2006.

———. "Stoic Conflagration Physics and the Eschatological Destruction of the 'Ignorant and Unstable' in 2 Peter." Pages 115–40 in *Stoicism in Early Christianity.* Edited by Tuomas Rasimus, Troels Engberg-Pedersen, and Ismo Dunderberg. Grand Rapids, Mich.: Baker Academic, 2010.

Harris, William V. *Restraining Rage: The Ideology of Anger Control in Classical Antiquity.* Cambridge, Mass.: Harvard University Press, 2001.

———. "Why Did the Codex Supplant the Book-Roll?" Pages 71–85 in *Renaissance Society and Culture: Essays in Honor of Eugene F. Rice Jr.* Edited by John Monfasani and Ronald G. Musto. New York: Italica, 1991.

Hartenstein, Judith. *Die zweite Lehre: Erscheinungen des Auferstandenen als Rahmenerzählungen frühchristlicher Dialog.* Berlin: Akademie, 2000.

Hartog, Paul. *Polycarp and the New Testament: The Occasion, Rhetoric, Theme and Unity of the Epistle to the Philippians and Its Allusions to New Testament Literature.* WUNT 2.134. Tübingen: Mohr Siebeck, 2002.

Harvey, Susan Ashbrook. *Scenting Salvation: Ancient Christianity and the Olfactory Imagination.* Transformation of the Classical Heritage 42. Berkeley: University of California Press, 2006.

Haxby, Mikeal. "'I Have Not Suffered at All': Gender, Violence and Martyrdom in the *First Apocalypse of James.*" Paper presented at the Annual Meeting of the Society of Biblical Literature. Atlanta, Ga., November 20, 2010.

Heffernan, Thomas J. "Philology and Authorship in the Passio Sanctarum Perpetuae et Felicitatis." *Traditio* 50 (1995): 315–25.

Helbig, Jörg. *Intertextualität und Markierung: Untersuchungen zur Systematik und Funktion der Signalisierung von Intertextualität.* Beiträge zur neueren Literaturgeschichte 3.141. Heidelberg: Winter, 1996.

Hellholm, David. "The Problem of Apocalyptic Genre and the Apocalypse of John." *Semeia* 36 (1986): 13–64.

Heyman, George W. *The Power of Sacrifice: Roman and Christian Discourses in Conflict.* Washington, D.C.: Catholic University of America Press, 2007.

Hilhorst, A. "Christian Martyrs Outside the Catholic Church." *Journal of Eastern Christian Studies* 60 (2008): 23–36.

———. "Tertullian on the Acts of Paul." Pages 150–63 in *The Apocryphal Acts of Paul and Thecla*. Edited by Jan N. Bremmer. Kampen: Kok Pharos, 1996.

Hiltbrunner, Otto. *Latina Graeca. Semasiologische Studien über lateinische Wörter im Hinblick auf ihr Verhältnis zu griechischen Vorbildern*. Bern: Francke, 1958.

Hirzel, R. "Der Selbstmord." *Archiv für Religionswissenschaft* 11 (1908): 75–104, 243–84, 417–76.

Holloway, Paul A. *Coping with Prejudice: 1 Peter in Social-Psychological Perspective*. WUNT 1.244. Tübingen: Mohr Siebeck, 2009.

Holmes, Michael W. *The Apostolic Fathers: Greek Texts and English Translations*. 3d ed. Grand Rapids, Mich.: Baker Academic, 2007.

———. "The Martyrdom of Polycarp and the New Testament Passion Narratives." Pages 407–32 in *Trajectories Through the New Testament and the Apostolic Fathers*. Edited by Andrew F. Gregory and C. Tuckett. Oxford: Oxford University Press, 2005.

Holtzmann, H. J. "Das Verhältnis des Johannes zu Ignatius und Polykarp." *ZWT* 20 (1877): 187–214.

Holzhausen, Jens. "Valentinus and Valentinians." Pages 1144–57 in vol. 2 of *Dictionary of Gnosis and Western Esotericism*. Edited by Wouter J. Hanegraaff, et al. 2 vols. Leiden: Brill, 2005.

Hopkins, Keith. *Death and Renewal*. Sociological Studies in Roman History 2. Cambridge: Cambridge University Press, 1983.

Horner, Timothy. *"Listening to Trypho": Justin Martyr's Dialogue Reconsidered*. Leuven: Peeters, 2001.

Hübner, R. M. "Überlegung zur ursprünglichen Bedeutung des Ausdrucks 'katholische Kirche' (katholikè ekklèsia) bei den frühen Kirchenvätern." Pages 31–80 in *Väter der Kirche: Ekklesiales Denken von den Anfängen bis in die Neuzeit*. Edited by J. Arnold. Paderborn: Schöningh, 2004.

Iricinschi, Eduard, Lance Jenott, and Philippa Townsend. "The Betrayer's Gospel." *New York Review of Books* 53:10 (2006): 32–37.

Janssen, L. F. "Die Bedeutungsentwicklung von Superstitio/superstes." *Mnemosyne* 28 (1975): 135–89.

———. "'Superstitio' and the Persecution of the Christians." *VC* 33 (1979): 131–59; reprinted as pages 79–107 in *Church and State in the Early Church*. Edited by Everett Ferguson. New York: Garland, 1993.

Johanny, Raymond. "Ignatius of Antioch." Pages 48–70 in *The Eucharist of the Early Christians*. Edited by Willy Rordorf, et al. Translated by Matthew J. O'Connell. Collegeville, Minn.: Liturgical Press, 1980.

Johnston, Sarah Iles. "A New Web for Arachne." Pages 1–22 in *Antike Mythen: Medien, Transformationen und Konstruktionen*. Edited by Christine Walder and Ueli Dill. Berlin: De Gruyter, 2009.

Joly, Robert. *Le dossier d'Ignace d'Antioche*. Brussels: Éditions de l'Université de Bruxelles, 1979.

Joshel, Sandra R. "Nurturing the Master's Child: Slavery and the Roman Child-Nurse." *Signs* 12 (1986): 3–22.

Joslyn-Siemiatkoski, Daniel. *Christian Memories of the Maccabean Martyrs.* New York: Palgrave, 2009.

Julien, Charles-Andre. *Histoire de l'Afrique du Nord: Des origins à 1830.* Paris: Payot, 1994.

Kaizer, T. *The Religious Life of Palmyra: A Study of the Social Patterns of Worship in the Roman Period.* Oriens et Occidens 4. Stuttgart: Franz Steiner, 2002.

Kasser, Rodolphe. "Textes gnostiques: Nouvelle remarques à propos des apocalypses de Paul, Jacques et Adam." *Muséon* 78 (1965): 71–98.

Keim, Theodor. *Aus dem Urchristentum: Geschichtliche Untersuchungen in zwangloser Folge.* Zurich: Orell, Füssli, 1878.

Kelley, Nicole. "Philosophy as Training for Death: Reading the Ancient Christian Martyr Acts as Spiritual Exercises." *Church History* 75:4 (2006): 723–47.

Keresztes, Paul. "Marcus Aurelius a Persecutor?" *HTR* 16 (1968): 321–41.

———. "The Massacre at Lugdunum in 177 A.D." *Historia* 16 (1967): 75–86.

King, Karen L. "Martyrdom and Its Discontents in the Tchacos Codex." Pages 23–42 in *Codex Judas Papers: Proceedings of the International Congress on the Tchacos Codex Held at Rice University, Houston, Texas, March 13–16, 2008.* Edited by April D. DeConick. Nag Hammadi and Manichean Studies 71. Leiden: Brill, 2009.

———. *What Is Gnosticism?* Cambridge, Mass.: Harvard University Press, 2003.

Klauck, Hans-Josef. *The Apocryphal Acts of the Apostles: An Introduction.* Translated by Brian McNeil. Waco, Tex.: Baylor University Press, 2008.

Knopf, Rudolf. *Ausgewählte Märtyrerakten* (Tübingen: Mohr, 1901)

Knox, Ronald A. *Enthusiasm: A Chapter in the History of Religion, with Special Reference to the XVII and XVIII Centuries.* Oxford: Oxford University Press, 1950.

Knust, Jennifer Wright. "Latin Versions of the New Testament." In *Encyclopedia of Ancient History.* Edited by Roger Bagnall, Kai Broderson, Craig Champion, Andrew Erskine, and Sabine Huebner. London: Blackwell, forthcoming.

Koester, Helmut. *History and Literature of Early Christianity.* Vol. 2 of *Introduction to the New Testament.* New York: De Gruyter, 2000.

Köhne, Eckart, and Cornelia Ewigleben, eds. *Gladiators and Caesars: The Power of Spectacle in Ancient Rome.* Los Angeles: UCLA Press, 2000.

Kraft, H. "Die altkirchliche Prophetie und die Entstehung des Montanismus." *Theologische Zeitschrift* 11 (1955): 249–71.

Kunkel, Wolfgang. *An Introduction to Roman Legal and Constitutional History.* 2d ed. New York: Oxford University Press, 1973.

Kyle, Donald. *Spectacles of Death in Ancient Rome.* New York: Routledge, 1998.

Labriolle, Pierre de. *La crise montaniste.* Paris: Leroux, 1913.

Lake, Kirsopp. *The Apostolic Fathers.* 2 vols. Loeb Classical Library. Cambridge, Mass.: Harvard University Press, 1977.

Lallemand, Annick. "Le parfum des martyrs dans les Actes des martyrs de Lyon et le Martyre de Polycarpe." *SP* 16:2 (1985): 189–92.

Lampe, Peter. *From Paul to Valentinus: Christians at Rome in the First Two Centuries.* Edited by Marshall D. Johnson. Translated by Michael Steinhauser. Minneapolis, Minn.: Fortress, 2003.

Lane Fox, Robin. *Pagans and Christians.* New York: Knopf, 1987.

Layton, Bentley, ed. *The Rediscovery of Gnosticism. Proceedings of the Conference at Yale March 1978*. Vol 1: *The School of Valentinus*. Leiden: Brill, 1980.

Lazzati, Giuseppe. "Gli Atti di S. Giustino Martire." *Aevum* 27:6 (1953): 473–97.

———. *Gli sviluppi della letteratura sui martiri nei primi quarto secoli*. Torino: Società editrice Internazionale, 1956.

Le Blant, Edmond. "Polyeucte et le zèle térméraire." In *Mémoires de l'Institut Nationale de France*. Académie des Inscriptions et Belles-Lettres 28 (1876): 335–52.

Lechner, Thomas. *Ignatius adversus Valentinianos?: Chronologische und theologiegeschichtliche Studien zu den Briefen des Ignatius von Antiochien*. VCSup 47. Leiden: Brill, 1999.

Leclercq, Henri. "Lyon." *Dictionnaire d'archéologue chrétienne et de liturgie* 10:74.

Leemans, Johan. *More Than a Memory: The Discourse of Martyrdom and the Construction of Christian Identity*. Leuven: Peeters, 2005.

Le Goff, Jacques. *La naissance du Purgatoire*. Paris: Gallimard, 1981.

Lietzmann, Hans. "Die älteste Gestalt der Passio SS. Carpi, Papylae et Agathonices." Pages 239–50 in *Kleine Schriften I: Studien zur spätantiken Religionsgeschichte*. Texte und Untersuchungen, NS 67. Berlin: Akademie-Verlag, 1958.

Lieu, Judith M. "Constructing Judaism/Constructing Heresy in the Second Century." Paper presented at the sixty-fifth general meeting of the Studiorum Novi Testamenti Societas. Berlin, July 27–31, 2010.

———. *Image and Reality: The Jews in the World of the Christians in the Second Century*. Edinburgh: T & T Clark, 1996.

———. *Neither Jew nor Greek? Constructing Early Christianity*. London: T & T Clark, 2002.

Lightfoot, Joseph Barber. *The Apostolic Fathers*. 4 vols. London: Macmillan, 1889.

Lintott, A. *Imperium Romanum: Politics and Administration*. London: Routledge, 1993.

Lipsius, R. A. *Die apokryphen Apostelegeschichten und Apostellegenden*. 2 vols. Braunschweig: C. A. Schwetschke, 1883–1890.

———. "Der Märtyertod Polykarps." *ZWT* 17 (1874): 188–214.

Löhr, Winrich A. "Der Brief der Gemeinden von Lyon und Vienne (Eusebius *h.e.* V, 1–2 (4))." Pages 135–49 in *Oecumenica et Patristica: Festschrift für Wilhelm Schneemelcher*. Edited by Damaskinos Papandreou, Wolfgang A. Bienert, and Knut Schäferdiek. Stuttgart: Kohlhammer, 1989.

Loraux, Nicole. *Tragic Ways of Killing a Woman*. Cambridge, Mass.: Harvard University Press, 1987.

Lorde, Audre. "Eye to Eye: Black Women, Hatred and Anger." Pages 145–75 in *Sister Outsider*. Crossing Press Feminist Series. Freedom, Calif.: Crossing, 1984.

Louth, Andrew. "Hagiography." Pages 358–61 in *The Cambridge History of Early Christian Literature*. Edited by Frances M. Young, Lewis Ayres, and Andrew Louth. Cambridge: Cambridge University Press, 2004.

Lüdemann, Gerd. *Heretics: The Other Side of Early Christianity*. Louisville, Ky.: Westminster John Knox, 1996.

Ludolph, Matthias. *Epistolographie und Selbstdarstellung: Untersuchungen zu den 'Parade-briefen' Plinius des Jüngeren*. Tübingen: Gunter Narr, 1997.

MacMullen, Ramsay. *Christianizing the Roman Empire*. New Haven, Conn.: Yale University Press, 1984.

———. "Judicial Savagery in the Roman Empire." *Chiron* 16 (1986): 147–66.

Mahé, J. P. *Le Témoignage Véritable (NH IX, 3): Gnose et Martyre*. Bibliothèque copte de Nag Hammadi section "Textes" 23. Leuven: Peeters, 1996.

Mair, A. W. "Suicide (Greek and Roman)." Pages 26–30 in vol. 12 of *Encyclopaedia of Religion and Ethics*. Edited by J. Hastings. 12 vols. Edinburgh: T & T Clark, 1921.

Malbon, Elizabeth Struthers. *The Iconography of the Sarcophagus of Junius Bassus*. Princeton, N.J.: Princeton University Press, 1990.

Maraval, Pierre. *Lieux saints et pèlerinages d'Orient: Histoire et géographie des origines à la conquête arabe*. Paris: Cerf, 1985.

———. *Les persecutions des chrétiens durant les quatre premiers siècles*. Bibliothèque d'histoire du christianisme 30. Paris: Desclée/Mame, 1992.

Marchesi, Ilaria. *The Art of Pliny's Letters: A Poetics of Allusion in the Private Correspondence*. Cambridge: Cambridge University Press, 2008.

Markschies, Christoph. *Valentinus Gnosticus?: Untersuchungen zur valentinianischen Gnosis; mit einem Kommentar zu den Fragmenten Valentins*. WUNT 1.65. Tübingen: Mohr Siebeck, 1992.

Marrou, H. I. "La date du Martyre de Saint Polycarpe." *Analecta Bollandiana* 71 (1953): 5–20.

Martin, Dale B. *Inventing Superstition*. Cambridge, Mass.: Harvard University Press, 2004.

Marx, F. A. "Tacitus und die Literatur der exitus illustrium virorum." *Philologus* 92 (1937): 83–103.

Matthews, Shelly. *Perfect Martyr: The Stoning of Stephen and the Construction of Christian Identity*. New York: Oxford University Press, 2010.

Mazzaferri, Frederick David. *The Genre of the Book of Revelation from a Source-Critical Perspective*. Beiheft zur Zeitschrift für die neutestamentliche Wissenschaft und die Kunde der älteren Kirche 54. Berlin and New York: De Gruyter, 1989.

McGowan, Andrew. "Eating People: Accusations of Cannibalism Against Christians in the Second Century." *JECS* 2 (1994): 413–42.

Merz, Annette. "The Fictitious Self-Exposition of Paul." Pages 113–32 in *The Intertextuality of the Epistles: Explorations of Theory and Practice*. Edited by Thomas L. Brodie, Dennis R. MacDonald, and Stanley E. Porter. Sheffield: Sheffield Phoenix, 2006.

Metzger, Bruce. *The Canon of the New Testament: Its Origin, Development, and Significance*. Oxford: Clarendon, 1997.

Middleton, Conyers. *A Free Inquiry into the Miraculous Powers which Are Supposed to have Subsisted in the Christian Church*. London: R. Manby and H. S. Cox, 1749.

Middleton, Paul. *Radical Martyrdom and Cosmic Conflict in Early Christianity*. London: T & T Clark, 2006.

Miles, Margaret R. *Image as Insight: Visual Understanding in Western Christianity and Secular Culture*. Boston: Beacon, 1985.

Millar, Fergus. *The Emperor in the Roman World*. Ithaca, N.Y.: Cornell University Press, 1977.

Miller, Patricia Cox. *Dreams in Late Antiquity*. Princeton, N.J.: Princeton University Press, 1994.

Milner, Joseph, and Isaac Milner. *The History of the Church of Christ*. 7 vols. Rev. ed. London: Longman, 1847.

Minns, Dennis, and Paul Parvis. *Justin: Philosopher and Martyr*. Oxford Early Christian Texts. Oxford: Oxford University Press, 2009.

Mitchell, Stephen. *Anatolia: Land, Men, and Gods in Asia Minor*. Vol. 2: *The Rise of the Church*. Oxford: Clarendon, 1993.

Mommsen, Theodor. *Römisches Strafrecht*. Leipzig: Duncker and Humblot, 1899.

Monceaux, Paul. "Les colonies juives dans l'Afrique Romaine." *Revue des études juives* 44 (1904): 1–28.

Monta, Susannah Brietz. *Martyrdom and Literature in Early Modern England*. Cambridge: Cambridge University Press, 2005.

Montuori, Mario. *Socrates: Physiology of a Myth*. Amsterdam: Gieben, 1981.

Moore, Stephen D., and Janice Capel Anderson. "Taking It Like a Man: Masculinity in 4 Maccabees." *JBL* 117 (1998): 249–73.

Morford, Mark P. O. "Tacitus' Historical Methods in the Neronian Books of the 'Annals.'" *ANRW* 2.33.2 (1990): 1582–627.

Moss, Candida R. "Blood Ties: Martyrdom, Motherhood, and Family in the *Passion of Perpetua and Felicitas*." Pages 183–202 in *Women and Gender in Ancient Religions: Interdisciplinary Approaches*. Edited by Stephen P. Ahearne-Kroll, James A. Kelhoffer, and Paul A. Holloway. WUNT 1.263. Tübingen: Mohr Siebeck, 2010.

———. "The Discourse of Voluntary Martyrdom: Ancient and Modern." *Church History*, forthcoming.

———. "On the Dating of Polycarp: Rethinking the Place of the *Martyrdom of Polycarp* in the History of Christianity." *Early Christianity* 1:4 (2010): 539–74.

———. *The Other Christs: Imitating Jesus in Ancient Christian Ideologies of Martyrdom*. New York: Oxford University Press, 2010.

———. "Polycarphilia and the Origins of Martyrdom." In *The Rise and Expansion of Christianity in the First Three Centuries C.E.* Edited by Jens Schröter and Clare K. Rothschild. WUNT. Tübingen: Mohr Siebeck, forthcoming.

Mossman, Judith. *Wild Justice: A Study of Euripides' Hecuba*. London: Bristol Classical, 1995.

Münter, F. *Religion der Karthager*. Copenhagen: J. H. Schubothe, 1816.

Musurillo, Herbert. *The Acts of the Christian Martyrs*. Oxford: Clarendon, 1972.

———. *Méthode d'Olympe: Le Banquet*. Sources Chrétiennes 95. Paris: Cerf, 1963.

Nancy, Claire. "Φάρμακον σωτηρίας: Le mécanisme du sacrifice humain chez Euripide." Pages 17–30 in *Théâtre et spectacles dans l'antiquité: Actes du Colloque de Strasbourg 5–7 novembre 1981*. Edited by Hubert Zehnacker. Leiden: Brill, 1983.

Nautin, Pierre. *Lettres et écrivains chrétiens des IIe et IIIe siècles*. Paris: Cerf, 1961.

Navia, Luis E. *Socrates: The Man and His Philosophy*. New York: University Press of America, 1985.

Newman, John Henry. *Callista: A Sketch of the Third Century*. London: Burns and Lambert, 1856.

Neyrey, Jerome H. "The 'Noble Shepherd' in John 10: Cultural and Rhetorical Background." *JBL* 120 (2001): 267–91.

The Nicene and Post-Nicene Fathers. Series 2. Edited by Phillip Schaff. 14 vols. Repr. Peabody, Mass.: Hendrickson, 1994.

Nock, Arthur Darby. *Conversion: The Old and New Religion from Alexander the Great to Augustine of Hippo*. Oxford: Clarendon, 1933.

Nongbri, Brent. "The Motivations of the Maccabees and Judean Rhetoric of Ancestral Tradition." Pages 85–112 in *Ancient Judaism in Its Hellenistic Context*. Edited by Carol Bakhos. Leiden: Brill, 2005.

Noreña, Carlos F. "The Social Economy of Pliny's Correspondence with Trajan." *American Journal of Philology* 128:2 (2007): 239–77.

Novum Testamentum Graece. Edited by Kurt and Barbara Aland. 27th ed. Stuttgart: Deutsche Bibelgesellschaft, 1993.

Oliver, J. H., and R. E. A. Palmer. "Minutes of an Act from the Roman Senate." *Hesperia* 24 (1955): 320–49.

Pagels, Elaine. "Gnostic and Orthodox Views of Christ's Passion: Paradigms for the Christian's Response to Persecution?" Pages 262–88 in vol. 1 of *The Rediscovery of Gnosticism: Proceedings of the Conference on Gnosticism at Yale, New Haven, Connecticut, March 28–31, 1978*. 2 vols. Edited by Bentley Layton. Leiden: Brill, 1980.

———. *The Gnostic Gospels*. New York: Random House, 1979.

Pagels, Elaine, and Karen L. King. *Reading Judas: The Gospel of Judas and the Shaping of Christianity*. New York: Viking, 2007.

Painchaud, Louis. "Polemical Aspects of the *Gospel of Judas*." Pages 171–86 in *The Gospel of Judas in Context: Proceedings of the First International Conference on the Gospel of Judas*. Edited by Madeleine Scopello. Leiden: Brill, 2008.

Parvis, Paul. "Justin, Philosopher and Martyr: The Posthumous Creation of the Second Apology." Pages 22–37 in *Justin Martyr and His Worlds*. Edited by Sara Parvis and Paul Foster. Minneapolis, Minn.: Fortress, 2007.

Parvis, Sara. "Justin Martyr and the Apologetic Tradition." Pages 115–27 in *Justin Martyr and His Worlds*. Edited by Sara Parvis and Paul Foster. Minneapolis, Minn.: Fortress, 2007.

Parvis, Sara, and Paul Foster, eds. *Justin Martyr and His Worlds*. Minneapolis, Minn.: Fortress, 2007.

Penn, Michael Phillip. *Kissing Christians: Ritual and Community in the Late Ancient Church*. Divinations: Rereading Late Ancient Religion. Philadelphia: University of Pennsylvania Press, 2005.

Peppard, Michael. *The Christian Son of God in the Roman World*. New York: Oxford University Press, 2011.

Pergola, Philippe. *Le catacombe romane: Storia e topografia*. Rome: Carocci, 1998.

Perkins, Judith. "The Rhetoric of the Maternal Body in the *Passion of Perpetua*." Pages 313–32 in *Mapping Gender in Ancient Religious Discourses*. Edited by Todd Penner and Caroline Vander Stichele. Leiden: Brill, 2007.

———. *The Suffering Self: Pain and Narrative Representation in the Early Christian Era*. London: Routledge, 1995.

Perler, Othmar. "Das vierte Makkabäerbuch, Ignatius von Antiochien und die ältesten Martyrerberichte." *Rivista di archeologia Cristiana* 25 (1949): 47–72.

Pervo, Richard. "Early Christian Fiction." Pages 239–54 in *Greek Fiction: The Greek Novel in Context*. Edited by J. R. Morgan and Richard Stoneman. London: Routledge, 1994.

Petersen, Silke. *"Zerstört die Werke der Weiblichkeit!" Maria Magdalena, Salome, und andere Jüngerinnen Jesu in christlich-gnostischen Schriften*. Nag Hammadi and Manichean Studies 48. Leiden: Brill, 1999.

Petersen, William L. "Patristic Biblical Quotations and Method: Four Changes to Lightfoot's Edition of Second Clement." *VC* 60 (2006): 389–419.

———. "Textual Traditions Examined: What the Text of the Apostolic Fathers Tells Us About the Text of the New Testament in the Second Century." Pages 29–46 in *The Reception of the New Testament in the Apostolic Fathers*. Edited by A. Gregory and C. Tuckett. Oxford: Oxford University Press, 2005.

Pfitzner, Victor C. *Paul and the Agon Motif: Traditional Athletic Imagery in the Pauline Literature*. Leiden: Brill, 1967.

Phipps, Charles B. "Persecution Under Marcus Aurelius: An Historical Hypothesis." *Hermathena* 47 (1932): 167–201.

Pietri, Charles. "Les origines de la mission Lyonnaise: Remarques critiques." Pages 211–31 in *Les Martyrs de Lyon (177): Lyon 20–23 septembre, 1977*. Colloques internationaux du Centre national de la recherche scientifique 575. Edited by Jean Rougé and Robert Turcan. Paris: Cerf, 1978.

Plass, Paul. *The Game of Death in Ancient Rome: Arena Sport and Political Suicide*. Madison: University of Wisconsin Press, 1995.

Potter, David. "Martyrdom as Spectacle." Pages 53–88 in *Theater and Society in the Classical World*. Edited by R. Schoedel. Ann Arbor: University of Michigan Press, 1993.

Potter, David, and D. J. Mattingly, eds. *Life, Death, and Entertainment in the Roman Empire*. Ann Arbor: University of Michigan Press, 1999.

Rajak, Tessa. "Dying for the Law: The Martyr's Portrait in Jewish-Greek Literature." Pages 36–67 in *Portraits: Biographical Representation in the Greek and Latin Literature of the Roman Empire*. Edited by M. J. Edwards and Simon Swain. Oxford: Clarendon, 1997.

Ramsay, W. M. "The Cities and Bishoprics of Phrygia." *Journal of Hellenic Studies* 4:43 (1883): 434–35.

Raven, Susan. *Rome in Africa*. 3d ed. London: Routledge, 1993.

Reardon, B. P. *Collected Ancient Greek Novels*. Berkeley: University of California Press, 1989.

Resnick, Irven M. "The Codex in Early Jewish and Christian Communities." *Journal of Religious History* 17 (1992): 1–17.

Réville, J. *De anno dieque quibus Polycarpus Smyrnae martyrium tulit*. Geneva: Shuchardt, 1880.

Rhee, Helen. *Early Christian Literature: Christ and Culture in the Second and Third Centuries*. London: Routledge, 2005.

Rice, Stuart A. "Statistical Opportunities and Responsibilities." *Journal of the American Statistical Association* 29:185 (1934): 1–4.

Richardson, J. *Roman Provincial Administration 227 BC to AD 117.* Basingstoke: Macmillan, 1976.

Ritter, A. M. "Clement of Alexandria and the Problem of Christian Norms." *SP* 18 (1989): 421–39.

Rius-Camps, Josep. *The Four Authentic Letters of Ignatius the Martyr.* Rome: Pontificium Institutum Orientalium Studiorum, 1980.

Rives, James B. "Accusations of Human Sacrifice Among Pagans and Christians." *JRS* 85 (1995): 65–85.

———. "The Decree of Decius and the Religion of the Empire." *JRS* 89 (1999): 135–54.

———. "Piety of a Persecutor." *JECS* 4:1 (1996): 1–25.

———. *Religion and Authority in Roman Carthage: From Augustus to Constantine.* Oxford: Clarendon, 1995.

Robert, Louis. "Une visione Perpétue martyre à Carthage en 203." Pages 228–76 in *Comptes rendus de l'Académie des Inscriptions et Belles-Lettres* (1982); reprinted as pages 791–839 in vol. 5 of *Opera minora selecta.* Edited by Louis Robert. Amsterdam: Hakkert, 1989.

Roberts, C. H., and T. C. Skeat. *The Birth of the Codex.* Oxford: Oxford University Press, 1983.

Robinson, J. Armitage. *The Passion of S. Perpetua.* Texts and Studies 1. Cambridge: Cambridge University Press, 1891.

Romanelli, Pietro. *Storia delle Province romane dell'Africa.* Rome: Istituto Italiano per la Storia Antica, 1959.

Ronchey, Silvia. *Indagine sul martirio di San Policarpo: Critica storica e fortuna di un caso giudiziario in Asia Minore.* Nuovi Studi Storici 6. Rome: Istituto Italiano per il Medio Evo, 1990.

Ronconi, Alessandro. "Exitus illustrium virorum." *Studi Italiani di Filologia Classica* 17 (1940): 3–32.

Ronsse, Erin. "Rhetoric of Martyrs: Listening to Saints Perpetua and Felicitas." *JECS* 14 (2006): 283–327.

Rordorf, Willy. *Liturgie, foi et vie des premiers Chrétiens.* Paris: Beauchesne, 1986.

———. "Tertullien et les Actes de Paul (à propos de bapt. 17,5)." Pages 475–85 in *Lex orandi, lex credendi: Gesammelte Aufsätze zum 60. Geburtstag.* Edited by Willy Rordorf. Freiburg: Universitätsverlag, 1993.

Roskam, Geert. "The Figure of Socrates in the Early Christian *Acta Martyrum.*" Pages 241–56 in *Martyrdom and Persecution in Late Ancient Christianity: Festschrift Boudewijn Dehandschutter.* Edited by Johan Leemans. Leuven: Peeters, 2010.

Rosweyde, Heribert. *Fasti sanctorum quorum Vitae in Belgicis bibliothecis manuscriptae.* Antwerp: Ex Officina Plantiniana, 1607.

Rousseau, A. *Irénée de Lyon contre les Hérésies. Livre IV.* 5 vols. Paris: Cerf, 1965.

Roussel, P. "Le thème du sacrifice volontaire dans la tragédie d'Euripide." *Revue belge de philologie et d'histoire* (1922): 225–40.

Ruinart, Thierry. *Acta primorum martyrum sincera et selecta.* Paris: Muguet, 1689.

Ruysschaert, José. "Les 'martyrs' et les 'confesseurs' de la lettre des églises de Lyon et de Vienne." Pages 155–66 in *Les Martyrs de Lyon (177): Lyon 20–23 septembre, 1977*. Colloques internationaux du Centre national de la recherche scientifique 575. Edited by Jean Rougé and Robert Turcan. Paris: Cerf, 1978.

Salisbury, Joyce E. *The Blood of the Martyrs: Unintended Consequences of Ancient Violence*. New York: Routledge, 2004.

———. *Perpetua's Passion: The Death and Memory of a Young Roman Woman*. 3d ed. London: Routledge, 1997.

Saxer, Victor. "L'Authenticité du Martyre de Polycarpe: Bilan de 25 ans de critique." *Mélanges de l'Ecole française de Rome* 94 (1982): 979–1001.

———. *Bible et hagiographie: Textes et thèmes bibliques dans les Actes des Martyrs authentiques des premiers siècles*. Bern: Lang, 1986.

Scarry, Elaine. *The Body in Pain: The Making and Unmaking of the World*. New York: Oxford, 1985.

Schaff, Philip. *History of the Christian Church*. Vol. 2: *Ante-Nicene Christianity*. A.D. 100–325. 8th ed. New York: Scribner, 1901.

Schmidt, Victor. "Reaktionen auf das Christentum in den *Metamorphosen* des Apuleius." *VC* 51 (1997): 51–71.

Schoedel, William S. "Are the Letters of Ignatius of Antioch Authentic?" *Religious Studies Review* 6 (1980): 196–201.

———. *Ignatius of Antioch: A Commentary on the Letters of Ignatius of Antioch*. Hermeneia. Philadelphia: Fortress, 1985.

Scholten, Clemens. *Martyrium und Sophiamythos im Gnostizismus nach den Texten von Nag Hammadi*. Münster: Aschendorff, 1987.

Schwartz, Daniel R. *2 Maccabees*. Berlin: De Gruyter, 2008.

Schwegler, F. C. Albert. *Der Montanismus und die christliche Kirche des zweiten Jahrhunderts*. Tübingen: Fues, 1841.

Seeley, David. *The Noble Death: Graeco-Roman Martyrology and Paul's Concept of Salvation*. Journal for the Study of the New Testament Supplement Series 28. Sheffield: JSOT, 1990.

Seesengood, Robert. *Competing Identities: The Athlete and the Gladiator in Early Christian Literature*. New York: T & T Clark, 2007.

Segal, Alan F. *Life After Death: A History of the Afterlife in Western Religion*. New York: Doubleday, 2004.

Segal, J. B. *Edessa, 'The Blessed City.'* Piscataway, N.J.: Gorgias, 1970.

Setzer, Claudia. *Resurrection of the Body in Early Judaism and Early Christianity*. Leiden: Brill, 2004.

Shaw, Brent D. "Body/Power/Identity: Passions of the Martyrs." *JECS* 4 (1996): 269–312.

———. "The Passion of Perpetua: A Christian Woman Martyred at Carthage in A.D. 203." *P&P* 139 (1993): 3–45; reprinted with a postscript as pages 286–325 in *Studies in Ancient Greek and Roman Society*. Edited by Robin Osborne. Cambridge: Cambridge University Press, 2004.

Sherwin-White, A. N. "Why Were the Early Christians Persecuted?—An Amendment." *P&P* 27 (1964): 23–27.

Simonetti, Manlio. "Alcune osservazioni sul martirio de S. Polycarpo." *Giornale italiano di filologia* 9 (1956): 328–44.

Simpson, William. *An Epitome of the History of the Christian Church during the First Three Centuries; and of the reformation in England: with Examination Questions.* 2d ed. Cambridge: Macmillan, 1851.

Sizgorich, Thomas. *Violence and Belief in Late Antiquity: Militant Devotion in Christianity and Islam.* Philadelphia: University of Pennsylvania Press, 2008.

Slusser, Michael. "Justin Scholarship: Trends and Trajectories." Pages 13–21 in *Justin and His Worlds.* Edited by Sara Parvis and Paul Foster. Minneapolis, Minn.: Fortress, 2007.

Smith, Lacey Baldwin. *Fools, Martyrs, Traitors: The Story of Martyrdom in the Western World.* Chicago: Northwestern University Press, 1999.

Snyder, Glenn E. "Remembering the *Acts of Paul.*" Ph.D. diss., Harvard University, 2010.

Stager, L. E., and S. R. Wolff. "Child Sacrifice at Carthage: Religious Rite or Population Control?" *Biblical Archaeology Review* 10:1 (1984): 30–52.

Steenberg, M. C. *Irenaeus on Creation: The Cosmic Christ and the Saga of Redemption.* VCSup 91. Leiden: Brill, 2008.

Steinhauser, Kenneth B. "Augustine's Reading of the *Passio sanctarum Perpetuae et Felicitatis.*" *SP* 33 (1997): 244–49.

Steitz, G. E. "Der Charakter der kleinasiatischen Kirche und Festsitte um die Mitte des zweiten Jahrhunderts." *Jahrbuch für deutsche Theologie* 6 (1861): 102–41.

Sterling, Gregory E. "*Mors philosophi:* The Death of Jesus in Luke." *HTR* 94:4 (2001): 383–402.

Stevenson, Edward. *Reminiscences of Joseph, the Prophet.* Salt Lake City: Stevenson, 1893.

Stevenson, J. *The Catacombs: Rediscovered Monuments of Early Christianity.* London: Thames and Hudson, 1978.

Stone, I. F. *The Trial of Socrates.* New York: Anchor, 1989.

Strathmann, H. "Martus, etc." Pages 477–520 in vol. 4 of *Theological Dictionary of the New Testament.* Edited by Gerhard Kittel. 10 vols. Stuttgart: Kohlhammer, 1939.

Straw, Carole. "'A Very Special Death': Christian Martyrdom in Its Classical Context." Pages 39–57 in *Sacrificing the Self: Perspectives on Martyrdom and Religion.* Edited by Margaret Cormack. Oxford: Oxford University Press, 2002.

Streete, Gail Corrington. *Redeemed Bodies: Women Martyrs in Early Christianity.* Louisville, Ky.: Westminster John Knox, 2009.

Tabbernee, William. "Christian Inscriptions from Phrygia." Pages 128–39 in vol. 3 of *New Documents Illustrating Early Christianity.* Edited by G. H. R. Horsley and S. R. Llewellyn. Grand Rapids, Mich.: Eerdmans, 1978.

———. "Early Montanism and Voluntary Martyrdom." *Colloquium* 17 (1985): 33–44.

———. *Fake Prophecy and Polluted Sacraments.* VCSup 84. Leiden: Brill, 2007.

———. *Montanist Inscriptions and Testimonia: Epigraphic Sources Illustrating the History of Montanism.* Macon, Ga.: Mercer University Press, 1997.

Tajra, Harry W. *The Martyrdom of St. Paul.* WUNT 2.67. Tübingen: Mohr Siebeck, 1994.

Tanner, Kathryn. *Theories of Culture: A New Agenda for Theology.* Minneapolis, Minn.: Fortress, 1997.

Tanner, R. G. "Martyrdom in Saint Ignatius of Antioch and the Stoic View of Suicide." *SP* 16 (1985): 201–5.

Telfer, W. "The Date of the *Martyrdom of Polycarp.*" *JTS* n.s. 3 (1952): 79–83.

Terry, Jennifer. *An American Obsession: Science, Medicine, and Homosexuality in Modern Society.* Chicago: University of Chicago Press, 1999.

Tertulliani Opera Pars I: Opera Catholica. Edited by J. G. Ph. Borleffs. Corpus Christianorum Series Latina 1. Turnhout: Brepols, 1954.

Thompson, James Westfall. "The Alleged Persecution of the Christians at Lyons in 177." *American Journal of Theology* 16:3 (1912): 359–84.

Tite, Philip J. *Valentinian Ethics and Paraenetic Discourse: Determining the Social Function of Moral Exhortation in Valentinian Christianity.* Nag Hammadi and Manichean Studies 67. Leiden: Brill, 2009.

Trevett, Christine. *Montanism: Gender, Authority and the New Prophecy.* Cambridge: Cambridge University Press, 1996.

Trout, Dennis E. Review of Silvia Ronchey, *Indagine sul martirio di San Policarpo: Critica storica e fortuna agiografica di un caso giudiziario in Asia Minore. Speculum* 68 (1993): 251–53.

Trumbower, Jeffrey A. *Rescue for the Dead: The Posthumous Salvation of Non-Christians in Early Christianity.* New York: Oxford University Press, 2001.

Turcan, Robert. *Les religions de l'Asie dans la vallée du Rhône.* Études préliminaires aux religions orientales dans l'Empire romain 30. Leiden: Brill, 1972.

Turner, Victor. "Death and the Dead in the Pilgrimage Process." Pages 24–39 in *Religious Encounters with Death: Insights from the History and Anthropology of Religions.* Edited by Frank Reynolds and Earle Waugh. University Park: Pennsylvania State University Press, 1977.

Ussher, James. *Polycarpi et Ignatii epistolae.* Oxford: Lichfield, 1644.

Van Beek, C. J. M. J. *Passio sanctarum Perpetuae et Felicitatis.* Vol. 1. Nijmegen: Van de Vegt, 1936.

Van Dam, Raymond. *Families and Friends in Late Roman Cappadocia.* Philadelphia: University of Pennsylvania Press, 2003.

Van den Hoek, Annewies. "Clement of Alexandria on Martyrdom." *SP* 26 (1993): 324–41.

Van den Hoek, Annewies, and John J. Herrmann, Jr. "Thecla the Beast Fighter: A Female Emblem of Deliverance in Early Christian Popular Art." *Studia Philonica Annual* 13 (2001): 212–49.

Van Henten, Jan Willem. *The Maccabean Martyrs as Saviours of the Jewish People: A Study of 2 and 4 Maccabees.* Supplements to the Journal for the Study of Judaism 57. Leiden: Brill, 1997.

Van Henten, Jan Willem, and Friedrich Avemarie. *Martyrdom and Noble Death: Selected Texts from Graeco-Roman, Jewish and Christian Antiquity.* London and New York: Routledge, 2002.

Van Hoof, Anton. "From Voluntary Death to Self-Murder: The Dialogue on Self-Killing Between Antiquity and Christian Europe." Pages 269–90 in *Alma Parens Originalis?:*

The Receptions of Classical Literature and Thought. Edited by John Hilton and Anne Gosling. Bern: Peter Lang, 2007.

Versnel, H. S. "Self-Sacrifice, Compensation and the Anonymous Gods." *Entretiens sur l'Antiquité Classique* 27 (1981): 135–94.

———. "Two Types of Roman *devotio*." *Mnemosyne* 29 (1976): 365–410.

Ville, G. *La gladiature en Occident des origines à la mort de Domitien.* Rome: École française de Rome, 1981.

Voisin, Jean-Louis. "Prosopographie des morts volontaires chrétiens (en particulier chez Eusèbe de Césarée)." Pages 351–62 in *Prosopographie et histoire religieuse: Actes du colloque tenu en l'Université Paris XII-Val de Marne les 27 & 28 octobre 2000.* Edited by Marie-Françoise Baslez and Françoise Prévot. Paris: De Boccard, 2005.

Völker, Walter. *Quellen zur Geschichte der Gnosis.* Tübingen: Mohr, 1932.

Von Campenhausen, Hans. "Bearbeitungen und Interpolationen des Polykarpmartyrium." Pages 253–301 in *Aus der Frühzeit des Christentums: Studien zur Kirchengeschichte des ersten und zweiten Jahrhunderts.* Tübingen: Mohr Siebeck, 1963.

———. *Die Idee des Martyriums in der alten Kirche.* Göttingen: Vandenhoeck und Ruprecht, 1936.

Von Harnack, Adolf. *Analecta zur ältesten Geschichte des Christentums in Rom.* Appended to *Beiträge zur Textkritik von Origines' Johannescommentar,* by Paul Koetschau. Texte und Untersuchungen 28.2. Leipzig: J. C. Hinrichs, 1905.

———. *Die Chronologie der altchristlichen Literatur bis Eusebius.* Vol. 2. Leipzig: Hinrichs, 1904.

———. *The Mission and Expansion of Christianity in the First Three Centuries.* Translated by James Moffat. 2 vols. 2d ed. London: Williams and Norgate, 1908.

———. "Über das Alter der Bezeichnung 'Die Bücher' ('Die Bibel') für die heiligen Schriften in der Kirche." *Zentralblatt für Bibliothekswesen* 45 (1928): 337–42.

———. "Das ursprüngliche Motiv der Abfassung von Märtyrer- und Heilungsakten in der Kirche." SPAW 7 (1910): 106–25.

Von Winterfeld, P. "Revelatio sancti Stephani." ZNW 3 (1902): 358.

Voss, Isaac. *Epistolae genuinae S. Ignatii martyris; quae nunc primum lucem vident ex bibliotheca Florentina.* Amsterdam: Blaev, 1646.

Wagemakers, Bart. "Incest, Infanticide, and Cannibalism: Anti-Christian Imputations in the Roman Empire." *Greece and Rome* 57 (2010): 337–54.

Waterfield, Robin. *Why Socrates Died: Dispelling the Myths.* New York: Norton, 2009.

Weijenborg, Reinoud. *Les lettres d'Ignace d'Antioche: Étude de critique littéraire et de théologie.* Leiden: Brill, 1969.

Welch, Katherine E. *The Roman Amphitheatre from Its Origins to the Colosseum.* Cambridge: Cambridge University Press, 2007.

White, L. Michael, ed. *Social Networks in the Early Christian Environment: Issues and Methods for Social History.* Semeia 56. Atlanta, Ga.: Scholars Press, 1992.

Wickham, Chris. *The Inheritance of Rome: A History of Europe from 400–1000.* New York: Viking, 2009.

Wilcken, Ulrich. *Zum alexandrinischen Antisemitismus.* Leipzig: Teubner, 1909.

Wilhite, David. *Tertullian the African: An Anthropological Reading of Tertullian's Context.* Berlin: De Gruyter, 2007.

Wilken, Robert L. *The Christians as the Romans Saw Them.* 2d ed. New Haven, Conn.: Yale University Press, 2003.

Williams, Craig. *Roman Homosexuality: Ideologies of Masculinity in Classical Antiquity.* 2d ed. New York: Oxford University Press, 2010.

Williams, Michael A. *Rethinking "Gnosticism": An Argument for Dismantling a Dubious Category.* Princeton, N.J.: Princeton University Press, 1996.

Wilson, Emily R. *The Death of Socrates.* London: Profile, 2007.

Wuilleumier, Pierre. *Lyon: Métropole des Gaules.* Paris: Belles lettres, 1953.

Wypustek, Andrzej. "Magic, Montanism, Perpetua, and the Severan Persecution." *VC* 51:3 (1997): 276–97.

Young, Robin Darling. "4 Maccabees." Pages 317–32 in *The Women's Bible Commentary.* Edited by Carol Ann Newsom and Sharon H. Ringe. Louisville, Ky.: Westminster John Knox, 1998.

———. *In Procession Before the World: Martyrdom as Public Liturgy in Early Christianity.* Milwaukee, Wis.: Marquette University Press, 2001.

———. "'The Woman with the Soul of Abraham': Traditions About the Mother of the Maccabean Martyrs." Pages 67–81 in *"Women Like This": New Perspectives on Jewish Women in the Greco-Roman World.* Edited by Amy-Jill Levine. Atlanta, Ga.: Scholars Press, 1991.

Zerubavel, Yael. *Recovered Roots: Collective Memory and the Making of Israeli National Tradition.* Chicago: University of Chicago Press, 1995.

Ziadé, Raphaëlle. *Les martyrs Maccabées: de l'histoire juive au culte chrétien: Les homélies de Grégoire de Nazianze et de Jean Chrysostome.* VCSup 80. Leiden: Brill, 2007.

General Index

Index of Modern Authors

Index of Ancient Sources

See the General Index for general discussion of these works. Page numbers are given in italics.